Inheriting the Past

Inheriting the Past
The Making of Arthur C. Parker and Indigenous Archaeology

Chip Colwell-Chanthaphonh

With a Foreword by Tracey L. Pierre

The University of Arizona Press   Tucson

The University of Arizona Press
© 2009 The Arizona Board of Regents
All rights reserved

www.uapress.arizona.edu

Library of Congress Cataloging-in-Publication Data
Colwell-Chanthaphonh, Chip (John Stephen), 1975–
   Inheriting the past : the making of Arthur C. Parker and indigenous archaeology /
Chip Colwell-Chanthaphonh ; with a foreword by Tracey L. Pierre.
      p. cm.
   Includes bibliographical references and index.
   ISBN 978-0-8165-2655-0 (hard cover : alk. paper)—ISBN 978-0-8165-2656-7
(pbk. : alk. paper)
   1. Parker, Arthur Caswell, 1881–1955.   2. Archaeologists—United States—
Biography.   3. Seneca Indians—Biography.   4. Anthropologists—United
States—Biography.   5. Scholars—United States—Biography.   6. Indians of North
America—Antiquities.   7. Human remains (Archaeology)—Repatriation—United
States.   8. Cultural property—Repatriation—United States.   9. Ethnoarchaeology—
United States.   10. Archaeology—Moral and ethical aspects—United States.   I. Title.
   E76.45.P36C656   2009
   974.7004′9755—dc22
   [B]   2009024819

Publication of this book is made possible in part by the proceeds
of a permanent endowment created with the assistance of a
Challenge Grant from the National Endowment for the
Humanities, a federal agency.

Manufactured in the United States of America on acid-free,
archival-quality paper containing a minimum of 30%
post-consumer waste and processed chlorine free.

14 13 12 11 10 09   6 5 4 3 2 1

To those who inspire and sustain our work,
Arthur's Beulah and Anne,
my own Soumontha

> I do not have an Indian name.
> The wind never spoke to my mother
> when I was born. My heart was hidden
> beneath the shells of walnuts switched
> back and forth.

—*from Sherman Alexie, "What the Orphan Inherits"*

Contents

List of Figures xi
Foreword, by Tracey L. Pierre xiii
Preface xix

Part I   Introduction

1 The Moral Predicaments of Archaeology   3

Part II   The Roots of Ambition

2 At Heart I Am   29
3 Then Let Us Spare, at Least, Their Graves   44

Part III   The Summer of 1903

4 Vast Unexplored Treasure Fields   65
5 You Boys Have Dreamed   91

Part IV   The Archaeologist Gáwasowaneh

6 It Is Knowledge, Solely, That We Are Seeking   115
7 We Can't Get Away from History   140

Part V   Conclusion

8 The Promise of Indigenous Archaeologies   179

Notes   201
Bibliography   233
Index   261

Figures

Arthur C. Parker, 1918   17
Nicholson Parker in his later years   31
Configuration of the Iroquois land base after major land losses   37
Portraits of Levi Parker and Caroline Parker Mountpleasant   46
Arthur C. Parker and M. Raymond Harrington   67
View of the Silverheels Site   70
Walls and ditch of the Double Walled Site   73
Parker excavating a trench, 1903   92
Map of the Silverheels Site   97
Peabody Museum storage area   106
Bertha Parker, ca. 1930   170
Arthur C. Parker, ca. 1945   175

Foreword

While studying archaeology as an undergraduate at the University of Washington, my tribe, the Colville Confederated Tribes of Washington State, became involved in a lawsuit over the repatriation of the Ancient One, also known as Kennewick Man; the controversial skeleton dating to 9,300 years ago discovered on the banks of the lower Columbia River in 1996. At the time, I was conducting research at the archaeology department of the Burke Museum, where his remains are housed. During one of the regular examinations by the Army Corps of Engineers, I was left alone with only a door separating me from the Ancient One. While standing there, I contemplated the circumstances surrounding the ongoing litigation, my association as a tribal member, and my desire to be an archaeologist. Meanwhile, the decision was pending whether to conduct DNA analysis in an effort to determine cultural affiliation, despite opposition from the five tribes involved (Colville, Umatilla, Yakama, Wannapum, and Nez Perce) to the destructive testing of human remains. Perplexed, I questioned how to balance my Native and professional identity.

Paradoxically, that experience inspired me to specialize in molecular genetics while pursuing a doctorate in biological anthropology. One might say that in parallel to Arthur C. Parker, as an Indigenous person I am a pioneer in the field of molecular anthropology. Yet inasmuch as my theoretical approach and methodology differ from the archaeology Parker practiced, they are considered to be nonetheless invasive. Strong opposition from the Native American community has resulted in many tribes' placing a moratorium on genetic research. In addition, some tribes have demanded the repatriation of DNA samples, and others are pursuing lawsuits over the uninformed consent for the use of DNA samples in medical research. What continues to motivate me against these odds? The dichotomy between being an Indigenous person and a scientist is a double-edged sword. I am challenged to find equilibrium.

My determination is essentially rooted in the conviction that Indigenous peoples must be able to represent their interests by exercising self-determination; this includes gaining command over a science that impacts their biological resources and knowledge systems. In this respect, I am neither alone nor the first. For decades, Indigenous archaeologists have overcome many obstacles in order to mitigate the intellectual biases patterned by the scientism typical of Parker's time. Through their efforts, as illustrated by Chip Colwell-Chanthaphonh in this book, significant progress has been made within the discipline to "decolonize archaeology" and challenge the prevailing views of race. Like my predecessors, I seek to remedy the distorted version of the past through a science responsible for undermining it.

DNA analysis is a relatively novel tool for examining population dynamics in anthropology. It is revolutionizing the way Indigenous peoples are studied and interpreted. By default, the discipline's relationship with descendant communities is changing dramatically. A growing concern over the misappropriation and exploitation of Indigenous biological resources has fueled suspicion and distrust toward anthropologists. Scientists have often failed to consult with Native communities throughout the planning process, and a significant amount of genetic research has been conducted without their knowledge, consent, or participation. Wide-scale endeavors intent on creating public databases, such as the Human Genome Diversity Project and the Genographic Project, threaten to expose Indigenous populations worldwide to discrimination, biocolonialism, and biopiracy. Scientific findings and Eurocentric theories are challenging traditional cultural identities and belief systems as well as autochthonous rights to territories and resources. The very concept of self-determination is in effect jeopardized because non-Indigenous scientists have conducted most genetic research involving Indigenous populations. As this book illustrates, the four moral predicaments—privilege, ownership, authorship, and participation—that have dominated archaeology for more than a century are still today unresolved issues that have not been adequately addressed.

This debate over the legal, ethical, and social ramifications of genetic research is further complicated by the issue of race. DNA analysis has demonstrated not only the similarities shared by all humans but also the genetic variation between them. Most of these differences occur within rather than between populations. Thus, race is an invalid taxonomic construct; it is social, not biological. The majority of ancestry-informative markers used to identify Native American haplogroups are not Native American specific, but rather occur in higher frequencies in the Americas. However, Native American–specific polymorphisms, "derived haplotypes," and rare but informative "tribal-specific polymorphisms" are found only in the Americas. This creates the illusion that Indigenous Americans are biologically unique in comparison to other populations and thus implies that race is biological by association. In this sense, genetic research has revived an ethnocentric, racialist perspective through the subjective assumption of race based on scientifically founded claims.

This epistemological viewpoint of race inherent in anthropology today is not dissimilar to the scientific racism of Parker's day, which propagated a colonialist belief and a racial ideology through anthropometric studies that not only do races exist but there are also significant biological differences between them. The social Darwinism dominating mainstream America during this time is reflected in Parker's many excavations of human remains and in his steadfast adherence to social evolutionist theories. Archaeologists today reject these pseudoscientific practices, yet racism and discrimination subtly linger.

The real question about the biology of race is political. In retrospect, experience now tells me that although DNA analysis of the Ancient One was inconclusive, it is improbable that this individual is any different from other pre-Columbian human remains tested successfully thus far. Throughout the Americas, all ancient DNA (aDNA) studies conducted to date have yielded results synonymous with the five major mitochondrial DNA (mtDNA) haplogroups present among modern Indigenous populations. Hence, these peoples today are the direct descendants of the original inhabitants, America's founding population. Furthermore, Y chromosome and autosomal DNA analyses support these findings. In spite of this evidence, the U.S. Court of Appeals for the Ninth Circuit ruled that a cultural affiliation between the Ancient One and claimant tribes could not be determined. On these grounds, the Ancient One was not subject to repatriation under the Native American Graves Protection and Repatriation Act (NAGPRA), even though pre-Columbian human remains are by definition "Native American."

Ancient DNA analysis of culturally unidentified human remains is problematic by virtue of its nature. Age, preservation, degradation, and contamination all determine whether DNA can be successfully extracted and sequenced. For these reasons, mtDNA is often easier to extract simply due to the greater number of mitochondrion copies per cell.

The technical problem herein lies in the ability to amplify an adequate amount of DNA from ancient remains that will enable the identification of Native American–specific markers. Furthermore, cultural affiliation with a descendant tribe is virtually impossible because of the degree of separation between generations, or "genetic drift," which involves the random changes of genetic frequencies compounded over time and space. Notwithstanding these caveats, the potential value of aDNA analysis increases exponentially with younger human remains, and an exact match with a living relative or tribe can be possible even if several generations separate the two.

Although the techniques for studying Native American populations have become remarkably more sophisticated since Arthur C. Parker's day in the early twentieth century, the questions addressed and the challenges faced by archaeologists and anthropologists are essentially the same. Genetics has greatly improved our current understanding of the underlying evolutionary processes that have influenced past demographic events. It is also refining our ability to assess genetic affinities and estimate divergence times among and between populations back hundreds of generations across vast geographical regions. But how can scientific data be translated into a meaningful dialogue with Indigenous communities?

This burning question reverberates throughout Native America today. The United Nations Convention on Biological Diversity describes the concept of "access and benefit sharing" of Indigenous genetic resources as the "equitable sharing of the benefits arising from their use," which includes the "protection of traditional knowledge." Indigenous communities, however, do not consider scientific research to be beneficial when their traditional values and belief systems are compromised. This is a fundamental rationalization for Indigenous opposition to genetic research. As a result, non-Indigenous scientists carry out the majority of DNA studies, and Indigenous peoples are underrepresented in scientific communities. There is a price to pay for this status quo. Future repercussions may far outweigh those that Native American tribes now experience for the past events that led up to repatriation and NAGPRA.

Ironically, this is an opportunity for developing stewardship roles to confront these new challenges facing Indigenous communities. Protocols for ethical and moral codes of conduct and practice need to be established for scientific studies involving genetic research, as well as legislation for the protection of Indigenous biological resources. Indigenous scientists can provide consultation and technical services to those tribes involved in genetic research and monitor studies conducted by institutions and governments. Indigenous archaeologists and anthropologists can address questions related to prehistory and oral histories. Indigenous geneticists can study chronic illnesses and infectious diseases afflicting Indigenous populations in the context of biomedical research. Indigenous lawyers can study treaty rights in association with genetic findings in order to corroborate land and natural-resource claims. By understanding the implications, risks, and benefits of DNA analysis, Indigenous peoples will be better able to represent their own interests.

Not surprisingly, Arthur C. Parker never publicly acknowledged the fact that a Native American became the first president of the Society for American Archaeology. In fact, he was never quite "at home" in either the scientific community or the Indigenous community. This fear of being stigmatized is familiar to many Indigenous archaeologists still today. How can we give up the premises of race without sacrificing our Native and cultural identities? The polarization of science and tradition is not what defines us as Indigenous archaeologists. For these reasons, it is important to reflect on Parker's life. Being Native American during an era of extreme political and social oppression as well as economic unrest must have had a profound influence on Parker's professional and Native identities. His legacy serves as a lesson not only to Indigenous archaeologists, but to the entire discipline about how the past can be reconciled with the future.

—Tracey L. Pierre
University of Cambridge

Preface

As I stood at the threshold of Nelson Mandela's prison cell, the epiphany at last came, after months of doubt and disbelief, and I abruptly realized that my anthropology degree was perhaps not worthless after all. I knew that if the dream of peace and unity could come from such a barren, hopeless room, I would do better to confront the problems of archaeology as best I could rather than run away from them.

In the autumn of 1996, I had begun traveling abroad several months after receiving a bachelor's degree in anthropology from the University of Arizona because I did not know what else to do. For years, I had wanted nothing more than to be an archaeologist. But this desire, so long a part of me that I didn't know what else I could replace it with, faded as I became ever more enmeshed in the field. This crisis occurred only a few years after the passage of the Native American Graves Protection and Repatriation Act, and the relations between many Indigenous communities and professional archaeologists were a tapestry worn thin and frayed. As I went out on digs, sat hunched over laboratory tables, and wandered the halls of museums, I grew increasingly disheartened to see and hear archaeologists habitually dismiss the concerns and beliefs that living Native Americans held about their ancestors. A quiet grumble was the background noise to my training—a hushed, steady complaint about Indians being just political, just getting it wrong, or just being a pain.

I couldn't make sense of the contradiction. How could people spend their lives attempting to understand past Native Americans, but seem to care so little about living ones? How could archaeologists honestly profess to care about past religious beliefs, burial practices, and ceremonial rites, but systematically ignore these Native traditions as they persist in the present? No good answer came to me. Dispirited, I decided I could not be part of a profession so callous to the very people it professed to be so concerned about. Without direction, I traveled. And so I had been wandering for some months when I ended up in South Africa, made the trip to Robben Island, and came across Mandela's dank cell. Standing in the bleakness of the prison, contemplating Mandela's courage, his sacrifice and dedication, was for me like sticking scissors in an electrical outlet. With a jolt, I knew I would return home to try to help break down the wall that separated professional archaeologists from Native communities.

In the years since, I have sought to work collaboratively with a range of Native American communities in an array of capacities. In a sense, I have learned how easy it can be to tear down the wall by finding projects that are mutually beneficial and carried out with genuine respect. Through this work, I have come to see that some walls prove illusory, often as much in our minds as something real to tear down or climb over.

When I first learned the outline of Arthur C. Parker's life, he struck me as a tremendously important historical figure—a scholar who embodied the notion that there doesn't have to be a wall separating archaeologists and Native Americans as he sought to use science to preserve the historical memory of his people. A man of proud Seneca ancestry who pursued archaeology for nearly six decades, Parker at first seemed to me a perfect illustration of the balance between Native interests and scientific curiosity, of how more than a century ago Native Americans could and did become archaeologists. I knew he came from a distinguished line of Seneca-Iroquois leaders, and he seemingly thrived as an archaeologist, publishing some 450 works and even becoming the first president of the Society for American Archaeology, today's preeminent archaeological organization.[1] However, after learning more about Parker, I came to see that whereas some walls separate human lives, others are erected within the self, brick by brick. I came to understand how Parker wrestled for years to reconcile his ambiguous identities.

The contemporary archaeological community only slightly remembers Arthur C. Parker, his struggles and successes. I think this neglect is in part due to the fact that although there have been writings on Parker's contributions to the Society of American Indians, Iroquois ethnography, and museology as well as a general biography of him, there are no major works examining his life in archaeology.[2] With this book, I don't merely want to fill a gap in Parker's official life history. Rather, I think his experiences have something more to teach us about archaeology's historical development, the making of the discipline's moral community, and its current ethical predicaments. Parker's path was not easy, and he made choices that some may judge harshly, but understanding the circumstances in which he made these choices can help us understand Parker as well as the social and political contexts in which archaeology was forged. Through his life, we can learn as much about archaeology's problems as about the discipline's promise and unfulfilled potential—the long, tangled, and still evolving relationship between archaeology and Native America.

"Writing is like driving at night in the fog," the novelist E. L. Doctorow once claimed. "You can only see as far as your headlights, but you can make the whole trip that way." Certainly, this book project began somewhat vaguely. In the autumn of 2005, I had just started a year-long postdoctoral fellowship at the American Academy of Arts & Sciences in Cambridge, Massachusetts, when one afternoon I stopped by the Peabody Museum of Archaeology and Ethnology. I was warmly met by curators Patricia Capone and Diana Loren, and in the course of our conversation they mentioned to me Arthur C. Parker's archived papers stored at the museum. Several days later I returned to look at the files. Within minutes of reading Parker's looping handwriting, I was hooked.

Thus, my research and writing on Parker began and continued over the next year and then into my tenure as project director for Anthropological Research, LLC, in Santa Fe, New Mexico. The generous support of a 2007 National Endowment for the Humanities summer stipend allowed me to focus my energy on completing a draft for peer review. Finally, at the Denver Museum of Nature & Science, which strongly encourages its curators to pursue research in conjunction with public outreach and collections care, I have had the time and support to bring this work to print. I am tremendously grateful to all these institutions and the individuals who enable them for helping this book project to proceed despite, as Doctorow might observe, the vaporous twists and turns of research, writing, and editing, and to arrive at last at this destination.

I am especially indebted to Adel Derosa, Marilyn Kim, Kim Walters, Minnie Murray, Patricia Kervick, Eleanor Brown, Dan Brown, Lea Kemp, Malcolm Stevenson, Stephen M. Rowland, David L. Browman, Sarah Song, Diana Loren, Patricia Capone, David Hurst Thomas, Allyson Carter, John R. Welch, Robert W. Preucel, Stephen E. Nash, Kirk Johnson, T. J. Ferguson, Soumontha Chanthaphonh, copyeditor Annie Barva, and the anonymous reviewers who commented on this work.

The royalties from publication of this book have been donated to the Society for American Archaeology Native American Scholarships Fund, which finances the Arthur C. Parker Scholarship. I hope other writers consider donating their royalties to this worthy grant program for aspiring Indigenous scholars.

Part I
Introduction

I
THE MORAL PREDICAMENTS OF ARCHAEOLOGY

The Myth of Kennewick

Anthropologists, it might be said, are fond of myths. So let us begin with a story that was born of true events but has now taken on mythical proportions.

One summer day in 1996 two college students attending a boat race stumbled across a human skull at the water's edge of the Columbia River, near Kennewick, Washington.[1] They dutifully reported the bones to the authorities, and a forensic archaeologist was called in to examine the remains. In a short time, the body came to be the center of a fiery controversy. The man had been buried for more than nine thousand years—for some Native American groups a most ancient ancestor, but for some archaeologists an individual too old to be affiliated with any living Indian community and a uniquely important set of remains to help us understand the first peoples to walk North America. American Indian tribes, scientists, and even a white pride organization laid claims to the remains, which became known as the Kennewick Man or, alternately, the Ancient One. The U.S. Army Corps of Engineers took possession of the remains and sought to abide by the Native American Graves Protection and Repatriation Act (NAGPRA) of 1990—a federal law that in part directs how newly discovered American Indian remains should be handled—but a group of eight scientists challenged its actions in federal court.

Two years after the remains were first found and excavated, the U.S. Department of the Interior became involved, and for the next two years more than eighteen scientists conducted a range of analyses, including sedimentary, taphonomic, DNA, radiocarbon, and lithic studies. Amidst proposed bills by the U.S. Congress, responses from U.S. presidents, FBI investigations, a passel of media reports and commentaries, the case slowly moved through the court system. In 2002, Judge John Jelderks ruled in favor of the scientists, finding, among other things, that the remains did not fit the legal definition of "Native American." The U.S. Court of Appeals Ninth Circuit frustrated the appeals of five tribes and the U.S. government, and the government decided not to take the case to the Supreme Court. In 2005, a handful of scientists began intensively studying the human remains.

This story is now mythical in the sense that it has become a symbol of the troubled relationship between archaeologists and Native Americans as well as in the sense that it serves to explain fundamental worldviews in American society. The moral to the Kennewick saga, as portrayed in the popular press and academic circles, is that Native Americans derive their beliefs about the past from religion, whereas archaeologists adhere only to an objective science. So the story becomes one of Us versus Them and Good versus Bad, a biblical tale of diametrically opposed forces. As the story is so often related, it presumes such a neat and clear divide. As the promotional materials in the recent documentary *Kennewick Man: An Epic Drama of the West* aver, "These events pitted science against religion and scientists against Native Americans."[2] Although such dichotomies fuel the flames of myths, is it true that Native religion and Western science are always opposed? Are Native Americans and archaeologists truly divided by a wall of irreconcilable beliefs? Are Indigenous peoples and non-Indigenous scholars living in two worlds that can never meet?

Such binary language is problematic for many reasons, but most tellingly because it overlooks the fact that there are individuals who are both religious believer and scientific practitioner—and some who are both Indian and archaeologist. Joe Watkins, Dorothy Lippert, and Eldon Yellowhorn are just a few of the Native Americans who are practicing professional archaeologists today. They are part of a growing minority that has written about the challenges and potential of a discipline fused with Indigenous perspectives, values, and practices.[3] There is also an unknown though not small number of Native American archaeologists at present in programs run by tribes, "hidden archaeologists" they might be called, who quietly work both to preserve their communities' cultural and historical heritage and to ensure that housing, roads, and other projects proceed without delay.[4] This said, Native American archaeologists constitute only a fraction of the profession. As Dorothy Lippert has recently written, by 2005, out of the thousands of living archaeologists who had a Ph.D., only thirteen asserted "Native American" as their primary identity.[5] It is in part this fact that propels a handful of scholarship funds to encourage and support Native American students interested in pursuing archaeology. Perhaps among the most prominent is the Society for American Archaeology's Arthur C. Parker Scholarship.

"Who was Arthur C. Parker, anyway?" David Hurst Thomas asks this question in a brief but eloquent epilogue to the edited volume *Working Together*. Perhaps there is a simple answer and a complex one. The simple answer is that Parker was the first Native American to be a professional archaeologist. The more complex one is that he was a Seneca Indian with an Anglo matrilineage, an intransigent scientist who treasured his clan traditions, an advocate for American Indian empowerment who embraced eugenics, and a writer who penned scores of technical reports but also novels, comics, and children's books. Arthur Parker was a complex human being who illustrates how even from the beginning there has been no simple dichotomy between Indian and archaeologist.

As scholars seek to dispatch historical tensions and heal the breaches that have arisen from the colonialist agenda of anthropological inquiry, it is timely and appropriate to think about the complex answer to this question—to delve into and reflect on what Parker's life and legacy evince about archaeology's historical formation and contemporary context. For too long, too little has been said about Parker's extraordinary life in archaeology: how more than a century ago, when it wasn't clear what it meant to be an archaeologist or an Indian, when most American Indians weren't even American citizens, a young man raised on the Cattaraugus Reservation befriended John Wesley Powell, Franz Boas, and Fredric Ward Putnam and came to be the first state archaeologist of New York, the director of the Rochester Museum of Arts and Sciences, a member of the National Academy of Sciences, vice president of the American Association of Museums, and the first president of the Society for American Archaeology.

As the Myth of Kennewick lives on, passed on to the next generation of archaeologists and Native activists, the time is ripe to rethink the historical relationship between the archaeological and the Native American communities, to respond to the unanswered questions of Parker's life: What exactly were the experiences of the first Native archaeologist? How did Parker find his way along this career path, and why didn't more Native Americans immediately follow in his footsteps? What did Parker say, and why has it taken so long for Native peoples to find a voice in archaeology?

Four Moral Predicaments

The Myth of Kennewick is perhaps in recent times the most well-known story depicting the contentious relationship between archaeologists and Native Americans, but this single controversy represents many kinds of conflicts, including the recent debates over repatriation and reburial as well as the centuries of dispute over American Indians' rights to govern their ancestral lands, represent their cultures and histories, and determine the course of their future. To understand the current relationship and the contemporary moral predicaments facing archaeology, we must delve into the past of both the discipline itself and the historic battles over Indian sovereignty. We must look at the history of archaeological science and the history of Native Americans as entwined, together forming the bricks and mortar of archaeology's intellectual architecture.

More than five hundred years ago, when Europeans first arrived on the shores of what they believed to be the outer edge of India, they came with unbridled dreams of staggering wealth. The European voyagers believed themselves to have an inherent right to the "new" world and to everything and everyone within it, claimed in the names of kings and queens, and consecrated by the hand of God.[6] The plunder began at once, from the conquest of the Aztecs to the conquest of the Incas and every nation in between and beyond.[7] The sympathetic priest Bartolomé de las Casas estimated in 1552 that in the first forty years of European colonization, some twelve to fifteen million Indians perished through "unjust, cruel, bloody and tyrannical war" and the murder of "anyone and everyone who has shown the slightest sign of resistance." Casas coolly explained that "the reason the Christians have murdered on such a vast scale and killed anyone and everyone in their way is purely and simply greed."[8] Although focused on the riches of minerals, spices, and slaves, later explorers also made clear their belief that even the Indian dead and their last belongings were for the taking. As early as 1620, just days after the Pilgrims arrived in New England, they excavated the graves of an Indian man and child, and spirited away the burial goods.[9]

As the newest Americans spread the boundaries of their mushrooming empires, the presumption persisted that both the land and the dead entombed within it were ripe for harvesting. Perhaps the first quasi-formal excavations of burials for the purpose of understanding American Indian history were undertaken by Thomas Jefferson, who explored a Virginia burial mound in 1784.[10] However, it was not until the publication of *Ancient Mounds of the Mississippi Valley* in 1848—a carefully systematic and analytical study of the "mound builder theory" demonstrating that the mysterious earthworks were the result of Indian ingenuity and labor—that the field began to take shape, as Bruce Trigger has written, now purged of its speculative tendencies and steeped in the inductive Baconian tradition.[11] Even as nineteenth-century archaeologists sought a more rigorous scientific pursuit, their endeavors in North America, frequently sponsored by government agencies, complemented the corporeal devastation wrought on Indigenous communities. Just as the Indian Wars served to confiscate land and resources in the name of the nation, archaeology served to arrest the detritus of Indian history in the name of science.

With the surrender of Geronimo and his Apache confreres in 1886 and the massacre at Wounded Knee in 1890, the Indian Wars of the United States drew to a melancholy close. By the turn of the century, the country's American Indian population reached its nadir of some 237,000 tribal members.[12] U.S. government policies vacillated between recognizing and eliminating the autonomy and rights of Native Americans.[13] The General Allotment Act of 1887 severed many tribes from their traditional homelands, but the Indian Reorganization Act of 1934 empowered tribes to form constitutions and governments. Then, in another reversal, the U.S. Congress implemented the Indian Termination Policy of the 1950s and 1960s to assimilate Native Americans into mainstream Euro-American society. In the late 1960s, however, Native America underwent a profound political resurgence, a reempowering of Indian nationhood, and an embrace of pan-Indian solidarity and activism.[14]

Incongruously, as Native Americans were vociferously reasserting their rights to land and heritage, archaeology's paradigm was radically shifting from a cultural historical approach to the New Archaeology, or processualism, a novel embrace of "intersubjective verifiability" in an attempt to explain cultural behavior scientifically—like ethnology among living cultures—through the lens of material remains.[15] This disjuncture between Native American and scientific interests only served to further alienate the two communities, already in strained relations after more than a century of archaeological disregard for Indian welfare.

The American Indian Religious Freedom Act of 1978 codified the U.S. government's rekindled concern for the survival of Indian culture and the preservation of traditional religions. In this same period, the government increased protection of Native American archaeological resources through legislation such as the National Historic Preservation Act of 1966 and the Archaeological Resources Protection Act of 1979.[16] Notably, however, because professional archaeologists were the ones given the authority to oversee archaeological management and conservation, Native Americans had to continue to protest the archaeological appropriation of their ancestors, history, and heritage into the 1980s. Human remains and objects of cultural patrimony, such as Iroquois wampum belts and Zuni War Gods, became the center of a heated exchange about the future of countless museum holdings and the ethics of archaeology and anthropology.[17] Despite these controversies, by the mid-1980s, archaeological theories were again shifting, now to a postprocessual mode that enabled a closer alignment of archaeological and Native interests.[18] At the same time, a handful of tribes had developed their own cultural resource management programs, illustrating that archaeological science could be put into the service of Indian communities.[19]

A turning point came with the passage of the National Museum of the American Indian Act of 1989, which in part established a new museum on the National Mall in Washington, D.C., and was the first major federal legislation to mandate the repatriation of human remains and other important objects. On its heels came NAGPRA in 1990, an expansive law that compelled museums that had received federal funding to inventory their collections of human remains, funerary objects, sacred objects, and objects of cultural patrimony, and to allow for the remains and objects to be returned to culturally affiliated tribes. NAGPRA also gave federally recognized tribes a central role in determining the disposition of newly discovered Native American remains. Only two years later, in 1992, Congress amended the National Historic Preservation Act to allow tribes to establish their own Tribal Historic Preservation Offices (THPOs) to parallel those offices run by state governments; the revision also made traditional cultural properties eligible for the National Register of Historic Places and thus gave an immense level of protection to those places tribes consider especially sacred. Within just three years, three pieces of legislation signaled a sea change in power structures between Indians and the archaeologists who had for so long been the nearly exclusive legal stewards of the nation's Native American heritage.

Archaeologists were now compelled by law to work with Native American communities. Although in fact a small cadre of them had already been doing so voluntarily throughout the 1980s, and other archaeologists quickly embraced the new shift toward inclusiveness,[20] in the years following the passage of NAGPRA a stark divide continued to separate many scholars and Native communities.[21]

With time and brave new partnerships, however, many Native Americans and archaeologists have transformed the legislated consultation process into mutually beneficial collaborations. Across North America, Australia, Africa, and Asia, collaboration with descendant communities is now perceived to be a vital means of overcoming past inequities and making archaeological research relevant, accurate, and ethical.[22] Increasing numbers of Native Americans are becoming professional archaeologists; more tribes are creating their own THPOs.[23] These new engagements have led us to the cusp of another paradigm shift—the exciting possibility of forming an Indigenous archaeology, a methodological and theoretical approach that seeks to decolonize the discipline by engaging with the difficult past, but not being burdened by it.[24]

The conflicts represented in this long and tangled history as well as the recent shift toward more inclusive and democratic approaches extend far beyond Native America. In recent years, archaeology's colonial legacy and the values of heritage now expressed by disparate publics have provoked the ostensibly unanswerable question: "Who owns the past?"[25] Just as archaeologists in North American have come to realize that Indigenous peoples have a certain and definable stake in the archaeological past, scholars elsewhere have come to doubt that archaeologists alone should be the beneficiaries of research or, for that matter, that archaeologists are always and necessarily doing good. In just the past two decades, scholars have explored a diverse array of controversies involving the discipline: the Nazi regime's use of archaeology to underpin its genocidal agenda;[26] the ways in which archaeology has often been distorted in the service of the state;[27] the riots at Stonehenge in the 1980s between New Agers who wanted to reclaim the stones for religious purposes and English authorities who sought to preserve the site as a pristine national symbol;[28] England's dispute with Greece over the repatriation of the Elgin Marbles;[29] a host of national treasures, from Icelandic manuscripts to Maori wooden Taranaki panels to Schliemann's Treasure of Troy, at the center of repatriation disputes;[30] the scores of treaties, conventions, and lawsuits spurred by the international market in looted antiquities;[31] development projects that have irreparably destroyed precious sites;[32] terrorist attacks that have systematically targeted heritage sites;[33] the destruction of archaeological sites as a part of ethnic cleansing;[34] the looting of Iraq;[35] the Taliban's obliteration of the

Bamiyan Buddhas.[36] In essence, scores of examples now illustrate that politics pervades archaeology, that suspect ethics have underpinned much research and heritage preservation both within the precincts of North America and far beyond it.

Four key moral predicaments dominate contemporary archaeology. First is the predicament of *privilege*. As Joe Watkins points out, it has been assumed over the years that scientific archaeologists have the first right to ancient sites and objects, a kind of droit de seigneur over Indian history. "Archaeologists, based on their credentials as scientists, have consistently considered themselves to be the authorities when it comes to decisions concerning the archaeological record," he writes. "Their training in the scientific method, generally accepted as the basis for scientific research, requires that they consider information objectively. Additionally, because of society's emphasis on formal education and the role of scientists within the society of which they are a part, archaeologists are generally seen to possess knowledge that is somehow beyond the understanding of nonscientists; they are the keepers of that knowledge."[37] As myriad stakeholders and descendant communities challenge archaeologists' exclusive right to control and interpret the past, the question of who has the "right" to study Native Americans and their material history remains unresolved.

Second is the predicament of *ownership*. This predicament points to questions not so much about who de facto does control sites, artifacts, and human remains, but who, if anyone, *ought* to control them. For years, scholars debated whether heritage should be controlled by the nation or should be considered open to all of humanity.[38] Some writers have recently begun to suggest that the nationalist versus internationalist view misses entirely the stance of the intra-nationalists, or smaller groups within the nation that also have a right to control their communities' pasts.[39] Indeed, who gets to decide who can legitimately own what? As recently as 1965, a U.S. court ruled in favor of a student who removed the skull of a Seminole Indian who had died just two years earlier, in essence because Seminole burial places and practices did not meet the legal definition of "cemeteries."[40] And what are the consequences of "owning" the past, of turning antiquities into commodities? Many archaeologists have argued that the past should not be reduced to objects to be bought and sold, and have written of the dire consequences of the antiquities market for archaeological sites, but many collectors and dealers have passionately defended what they consider to be their own right to enjoy the aesthetic and historical values embedded in antiquities.[41] Some writers have observed that archaeologists do not have the high moral ground because they have used Indian history as a means to achieve their own material ends: grants, books, and tenure. "Like medieval alchemists," Dorothy Lippert has caustically observed, "archaeologists have taken base material, the everyday relics of individual lives, and transformed it into a scholarly commodity."[42] Is the past a property that can be owned? Copyrighting culture is no straightforward task.[43] In a polemic, John Carman argues against the very idea of heritage as property, a concept "so blithely accepted by the archaeological community."[44]

Third is the predicament of *authorship*. More than twenty years ago, cultural anthropologists began exploring how the act of writing constituted the means by which power and authority were asserted.[45] The "crisis of representation" led to new modes of writing: if the classic single-authored ethnography of a single place stuck in the "ethnographic present" was problematic, then it could be undermined by creating texts that were coauthored with "informants," that tacked back and forth between multiple locales, and that investigated culture as a richly historical phenomenon.[46] Archaeologists, however, have been slower to grapple with questions about who gets to write the past, how the past is written, and the ways in which archaeological texts construct particular kinds of historical representations.[47] Whose historical voices are heard in academic research and the public sphere? In recent years, Native American academics have given voice to the need for more texts about Indian history to come directly from Indian peoples, urging a new ethic of respect and inclusiveness to underpin the writing process.[48] Although a few archaeologists have sought to transform the critique into a practical reality,[49] flipping through any current issue of *American Antiquity* or the *Journal of Field Archaeology* indicates well enough the continued scholarly resistance to including multiple voices and interpretations of the past.

Fourth is the predicament of *participation*. Who does and should participate in the study of the past? Which public or publics should archaeologists serve? Who is a stakeholder in the study, management, and interpretation of the past? What role ought stakeholders have in academic research and public programs, as well as in defining heritage for their own uses and ends? These thorny questions have been explicitly asked only in recent years, though they have suffused archaeological research since its beginnings. The archaeological community never expressly stated that its discipline was intended for archaeologists alone, but engaging the public and sharing the results of research were neither expected nor widely appreciated. However, with the rise of cultural resource management, the first formulations of "public archaeology" and the ethical quandaries it raised were articulated.[50] As the public were increasingly supporting archaeological research through taxes, scholars began to emphasize that the public should benefit from these endeavors, and, if nothing else, it was simply smart politics to show them what they were paying for. By the beginning of the 1990s, archaeologists recognized that they serve not one public, but many publics with multiple (and sometimes conflicting) interests.[51] Engaging these publics is now a common feature of many projects.[52] Nevertheless, like the predicament of authorship, there is nothing akin to consensus on how participation can and should unfold.

These predicaments are moral because ultimately they involve *ought* questions—how archaeologists *should* behave. The answers to these dilemmas are not self-evident. Rather, they come unevenly through professional dialogues, private conversations, public controversies, popular movies, television documentaries, Internet blogs, and newspaper articles and editorials. As the archaeological community shapes and responds to these forces, it is important to recognize that the creation of solutions also creates communities. That is, the responses to these predicaments make moral communities. When archaeologists group together and decide that unscientific excavations are unethical, they are building figurative moral walls that inevitably include some people and exclude others; scientific excavators become moral insiders, but looters and collectors become moral outsiders. Significantly, these responses have shifted through the decades, as have the definitions of archaeology's moral community. More than a century ago private collectors and dealers were held in high esteem, working hand in hand with researchers; in recent years, however, private collectors and dealers have been widely reviled. The ways in which archaeologists respond to these predicaments become the means of establishing the archaeological community's moral identity.

The Relevance of Race

In his afterword to the volume *Working Together*, David Hurst Thomas writes, "To be sure, Parker deserves to be memorialized in the SAA's Native American Scholarship Fund. But does Arthur C. Parker—Indian intellectual turned archaeologist—have any relevance to American archaeology in the twenty-first century?"⁵³ Undoubtedly, Parker's life has much to teach us about archaeology's past, present, and future. Through a close look at his trials and tribulations, we can come to understand the ways in which archaeology's predicaments of privilege, ownership, authorship, and participation have been with the discipline for more than a century, lingering and unresolved. Parker's experiences are a lens to view more closely the development of archaeology's moral community in the first half of the twentieth century and the sweeping net of politics, economics, and social institutions in which both archaeology and Native America were caught. A central part of Parker's story is his racial identity as an American Indian.

Race is important in archaeology: archaeologists have explored the historical dynamics of race and racism through the material record; and archaeological theories themselves have also at times buttressed racist agendas.⁵⁴ However, few scholars have openly addressed how race and racism, particularly in relation to Native Americans, have shaped the development of the discipline itself.⁵⁵ Parker's complex life illustrates that issues of race have been inescapable in the field.

Ironically, perhaps no academic discipline has done more than anthropology to promote and engender racism, and yet none has also done more than anthropology to combat it. The birth of scientific anthropology in the mid-1800s legitimized the race concept, but then only half a century later many anthropologists began working to discredit this concept that their academic forefathers had shepherded into the popular imagination. As happened so often in Parker's life, he was caught in between at this transformational moment: he lived through the shift of power in anthropology from the museum to the academy and from mentorship to academic credentials; he was raised in a time when racialist thinking was flourishing in America, only to mature into the field as the biological foundations of race were proven to be but a chimera.

Although most anthropologists today recognize that biology shapes the human experience, they "insist that racial categories are nevertheless biologically incoherent and heuristically misleading," that races are neither geographically nor phenotypically distinct.⁵⁶ In 1998, the American Anthropological Association even went so far as to issue a "statement on race" to make a case that race is not a natural phenomenon, but rather a social and political construct cultivated through centuries of colonialist propaganda, an "ideology of inequality devised to rationalize European attitudes and treatment of the conquered and enslaved peoples."[57] The statement acknowledges, as many books and articles on the subject attest, that anthropology itself was and is a protagonist in the unfolding drama of race. Early anthropology is intimately tied to the construction of races because it focused intensely on building typologies and classifying human subspecies; such categorizations, combined with Darwin-inspired tenets of evolution and nineteenth-century global imperialism, led to a quasi-scientific ordering of races into hierarchies, an imagined progression of human development that only served to justify the sociopolitical order and legitimize the exploitation of the powerless.[58] The research of early ethnologists such as Lewis Henry Morgan worked in concert with that of physical anthropologists to categorize human groups along a path of unilinear evolution from savagery to civilization, tracking mental, intellectual, and moral development, which was believed to carry the seeds of cultural advancement.[59]

At the turn of the twentieth century, Franz Boas, his students, and a few like-minded colleagues took up the project of fighting racism and challenging the race concept.[60] By the 1940s, particularly after the fall of Nazism, anthropological arguments about the biological fallacy of race were well in place, and anthropology helped underpin aspirations to a "color-blind society."[61] Yet even Boas often equated race with a diaphanous concept of "blood" as a "biological essence" and argued that race, though limited, had some scientific utility.[62] Indeed, notions of "blood" interlinked with Indian authenticity and identity have suffused Indian country since at least the late 1800s. Blood quantum continues to be used for tribal memberships throughout North America, and the language of blood ("full blood," "half-blood") as proof of belonging continues to pervade public and scientific discourse.[63]

The continued prevalence of the race concept in North America and beyond it points to anthropology's inability to undermine not just *racist* thinking, but also *racialist* thinking. The two terms are not synonymous.[64] As historian Roger Echo-Hawk and archaeologist Larry Zimmerman write, racialism "is the cultural idea that humankind is composed of racial groups that are biologically distinct." They argue that this idea is a "faith-based belief" because it is founded on perceived though scientifically false understandings of superficial physical differences such as skin color and hair types. "Thus, if one believes in and accepts race and racial groupings, one is a *racialist*," they conclude. "When a journal like *American Indian Quarterly* employs the term 'American Indian' as a matter of institutional self-definition, it deliberately practices and perpetuates racialism. When universities create 'Indian studies' programs, they have consciously chosen to engage in racialism. . . . The vast majority of Americans are racialists. Being so is almost impossible to avoid." In contrast, racism, they explain, "exists as a natural and common extension of racialism. When a person or group converts their racial categories from belief to action by preferentially ranking the groups, one is a *racist*. Thus, when museums deliberately segregate and exclude items by racial categories on a preferential basis, they reflect the systematic ranking of racism."[65]

Like most Americans of his time, Parker was an unabashed racialist and an occasional racist. He lived in an age when the halls of science resounded with the debate between those who argued for polygeny, the idea that humans were made up of distinct species, and those who argued for monogeny, the idea that all humans were descended from one individual or kind; when between 1880 and 1924 more than two million eastern Europeans immigrated to the United States, stoking the fires of racial discord; when the four centuries of the Indian Wars ended and the "extinction" of the Indian was thought inexorable; when Americans read *The Passing of the Great Race*, which blamed recent immigrants for America's woes, and watched the film *Birth of a Nation* vilifying black Americans; when the Eugenics Record Office was established, and the U.S. Congress and state legislatures passed a flood of racial segregation and miscegenation laws.[66] These were the politics and the social milieu that surrounded Parker, so it is not surprising that he understood race as a biological fact, equivalent to the terms we today might use to describe animals: *stock*, *lineage*, and *breed*. As George Stocking Jr. has noted, in the late 1800s "[the term] 'blood'—and by extension 'race'—included numerous elements that we would today call cultural; there was not a clear line between cultural and physical elements or between social and biological heredity. The characteristic qualities of civilizations were carried from one generation to another both *in* and *with* the blood of their citizens."[67]

Parker's writings fit neatly with popular conceptions of race at the time. *Webster's International Dictionary*, first published in 1900 and revised in 1913, actually defined the term *race* by summarizing then current anthropological thinking:

> Naturalists and ethnographers divide mankind into several distinct varieties, or races. Cuvier refers them all to three, Pritchard enumerates

seven, Agassiz eight, Pickering describes eleven. One of the common classifications is that of Blumenbach, who makes five races: the Caucasian, or white race, to which belong the greater part of the European nations and those of Western Asia; the Mongolian, or yellow race, occupying Tartary, China, Japan, etc.; the Ethiopian, or negro race, occupying most of Africa (except the north), Australia, Papua, and other Pacific Islands; the American, or red race, comprising the Indians of North and South America; and the Malayan, or brown race, which occupies the islands of the Indian Archipelago, etc. Many recent writers classify the Malay and American races as branches of the Mongolian.[68]

This confused portrait of humanity was precisely the picture Parker held in his mind when he spoke (in racialist terms) about a pan-Indian identity and when he suggested (in racist terms) the superiority of American Indians over American blacks.

For most of his life, Parker paradoxically sought to shed his race even as he clung to it. He wanted to be judged above all as an individual, yet he recognized how his Indian heritage could help shape a career in anthropology. As a neophyte in archaeology, he made frequent mention of his Seneca family; his dedication to preserve the "memory of my people" was key in helping him to land his first full-time employment in the field. But Parker, as either a "mixed-blood," as he would refer to himself, or a "half-breed," as others would refer to him, was ambivalent about his identity. For the first twenty-two years of his life, until he was adopted into a clan, some Senecas saw him as an outsider because his mother was Anglo, but at the same time whites perceived him to be an Indian because his father was Seneca. The dark-skinned man in the elegant suits perhaps epitomized this incongruity. Yet, in a way, this ambivalence was to Parker's advantage because it enabled him to play at times the role of outsider and at other times the role of insider. Like a specter, he floated between worlds, silently traveling through cultural boundaries to live among his dissimilar kindred. At the beginning of his career, he frequently self-identified as a Seneca man, but then as he aged and became established as a scholar and archaeologist, he rarely mentioned his Native roots in connection to his profession. By the time he was elderly, we see for the first time in his life a palpable comfort with his mixed background as he frequently signed his name "Arthur C. Parker, Gáwasowaneh."

The Moral Predicaments of Archaeology 17

Arthur C. Parker in 1918. (Adapted from Parker, *The Life of General Ely S. Parker*, Buffalo Historical Society, 201)

Some might label Parker a "cultural broker," an intermediary that moves across cultural frontiers.[69] The term may suggest a semblance of balance, but as John L. Kessell has noted, "because cultural exchange was so dynamic, rarely, it seems, did anyone maintain that balance for long. . . . Brokers went too far and became part of the other, drew back disillusioned into their own culture, or found themselves ostracized by both."[70]

Parker often struggled to be a part of both the archaeological community and the Native American community at a time when they were acutely at odds, and so he risked acceptance by neither and contempt from both. But what should perhaps be of most interest to us today is not merely Parker's desire to find a balance, but the struggle itself, which illuminates when and why archaeologists and American Indians could not meet on common ground.

For nearly all of the twentieth century, the American Indian archaeological past was studied and written by non-Indians. The intellectual biases that resulted from racial prejudices are now clear enough, from inaccurate portraits of ancient peoples to the spiritual indifference showed to sacred objects and human remains. As the first professional Native American archaeologist, Parker in some ways indicated the first possibility of an Indigenous archaeology; for example, his writing style was often at once profoundly humanistic yet intensely scientific, drawing on oral traditions as well as systematic observations. In other ways, however, Parker adopted mainstream approaches and values—for example, in his lifelong apathy to Native American concerns about the disturbance and exhumation of human burials. He did not seek to integrate a "traditional" Native viewpoint into archaeology because he himself was fully committed to the belief that science was a fundamental moral good and because he was committed to a politics of assimilation, believing that Indians should let go of much of their traditional ways and beliefs. (Consider that Parker's life was almost perfectly bracketed by the Dawes Act and the Termination Policy.) So although Parker's career in archaeology points to the origins of an Indigenous archaeology— an archaeology informed by Native values and carried out by, for, and with Native peoples—it is an uneasy beginning to be sure.

Was Parker's indifference to many of his community's concerns, particularly in respect to human remains, inevitable? Could it have been any other way? American Indians clearly expressed to him their displeasure in his diggings, and Parker, the first Native American professional, should have been sensitive to their concerns. Instead, he reinforced the mainstream values of archaeology and remained indifferent to pleas to protect the graves of his own ancestors. Kirin Narayan suggests that as more anthropologists from minority backgrounds have become professionals, the field's ethnocentric foundations have been ruptured.[71] Delos J. Jones, however, counters that "the ideas presented by Third World and minority anthropologists are often more oppositional than transformative and actually embrace the same perspective as those found in mainstream anthropology."[72] The latter case was certainly true for Parker, who did little to undermine mainstream norms, but instead by virtue of his background helped legitimize the ethics of the time. It is not hard to imagine hearing from across the century Parker's non-Indian colleagues saying, "If an Indian can dig graves, then surely so can we." Changing the norms of his time would realistically have been a professionally suicidal task for Parker, however. He was an outsider and had few alternate choices. If he wanted to be an archaeologist, he had to dig graves. At the turn of the twentieth century, no white scientist doubted the merits of studying Indian human remains; the calls for respectful partnerships were still decades away. There simply wasn't any other paradigm for Parker to invoke.

Why have so few Native Americans become archaeologists, even though the first Native American archaeologist found success almost one hundred years ago? Parker's experiences demonstrate that changing the dynamics of race in archaeology was not and is not merely about the introduction of Indian peoples into the profession; it is also about creating the necessary frameworks for new kinds of relationships to be formed. Certainly, as more Native Americans join the field, the paradigm will continue to shift, but unless the methods, theories, and ethics shift concurrently, few Native peoples will likely join.[73] Furthermore, Parker was largely, if not entirely, successful by dint of his formidable intelligence, amazing perseverance, and capacity for constant work. As we shall see in the pages that follow, he faced tremendous hurdles throughout his life and undertook an endless stream of projects; he worked day and night for years on end. Parker was a unique man who overcame the institutionalized racism of his age by his personal determination, but also by cultivating an exclusive set of family connections to well-placed (and well-heeled) Anglos such as Harriet Maxwell Converse and John Wesley Powell. He was thus uniquely situated and gifted to find a path in archaeology.

Today, Native American archaeologists continue to feel caught between two worlds. "Native archaeologists exist in a sort of heterotopia ourselves," Lippert explains, "in that our work within archaeology is viewed by some Natives as an act of treason and by others as an act of revolution."[74] Nevertheless, it appears that increasing numbers of Native scholars are pursuing the field, aspiring, as Davina Two Bears has written, to publish more culturally appropriate textbooks for Native youth and the wider public, to serve as professors and role models, to devise culture- and language-preservation programs, and to work with NAGPRA and care for sacred and ceremonial objects.[75] Tribal archaeology programs are seemingly on the rise, providing solid archaeological study and reports while reinforcing tribal sovereignty by removing "state officials from the decision-making process managing heritage resources."[76] As Watkins reminds us, however, we have a long way to go before Parker's legacy can be fully realized and Native peoples and values are truly embedded in the archaeological endeavor:

> American Indians and Canadian First Nations have made advances regarding the way that their perspectives have influenced the practice of archaeology in North America, but few aspects of those perspectives have been truly integrated into the discipline. Because of the nature of North America society, cultural resources/heritage management laws recognize scientific values as transcending Indigenous cultural values when it comes to heritage issues, deferring to Indigenous wishes primarily when legal restrictions require such deference. Until archaeologists more fully involve Indigenous populations in collaborative research and are able to represent more fully Indigenous issues, American Indians and Canadian First Nations will continue to be second-class citizens in the cultural resources world of North America, and will continue to feel they are outsiders in a system supposedly designed to protect their heritage.[77]

Echo-Hawk and Zimmerman rhetorically ask in their dialogue about race, "Is it possible to employ racialism in a manner that serves a useful social purpose and does not do violence to human biology? Is it possible, for example, to divorce race from its origins as pseudo-biology and employ it strictly to classify cultural identity or ethnicity?" They answer with skepticism, arguing that racialism at heart "involves a circular logic that invariably returns to the assumption that racial categories somehow reflect human biology," and thus it is in the end untenable. Nevertheless, they recognize that to recalibrate archaeology so that it is open to all people, in particular descendant communities that have long been excluded, the field must in the near term use "conjoint racism" to fight the discipline's long legacy of "unilateral racism." Native American scholarship programs can thus serve the short-term need to level the playing field, but because "race is inherently dehumanizing . . . we have an obligation to ultimately disempower its presence in our shared world."[78]

Even while expressing excitement about the possibilities of an Indigenous archaeology to transform the discipline, Echo-Hawk and Zimmerman are keen to emphasize that the movement draws on racialist assumptions.[79] How, then, can we talk about race without using the language and concepts of race? How can we talk about how Indians think about Indianness and whites about whiteness without using the terms *Indian* and *white*? How can we explore Parker's experiences, but not acknowledge his role as the first "Indian" archaeologist? If anthropologists deny the validity of race, then some will say that the scientists are denying the history of racism and the lived experiences embodied in ideas of race, but if anthropologists give in and speak in racialist terms, then they are complicit in perpetuating a destructive fallacy. This quagmire has no easy exit.[80] This book does not offer any easy answer either. However, by critically reflecting on Parker's life, we can seek to understand better the role of race in archaeology's development, what race meant to the first "Indian" archaeologist, and what this history might mean for the discipline's future trajectory so that it is fully engaged with all people who have an interest and stake in the past.

An Anthropological Microhistory

Studies in the history and philosophy of science are a way to peel back the layers of scientific research, to understand how science is above all a *practice*, a social endeavor fashioned by the tides of politics, economics, and cultures. Histories of archaeology have been written since at least the 1940s, but as Thomas C. Patterson has written, most narratives until the 1980s focused on the "adventure of men and ideas."[81] Patterson posits that archaeological histories are often linked to paradigm shifts: with the rethinking of theories and methods comes a rethinking of the discipline's past. Indeed, we have seen how in the 1980s a new history focused on class and power relations accompanied the rise of Marxist-oriented archaeology and how new histories focused on gender and nation came with the postprocessual turn.[82]

Although a few profoundly important papers about the historical relationship between archaeology and Native America appeared in the years before and just after the passage of NAGPRA, only recently have scholars provided book-length treatment of these issues—most notably David Hurst Thomas's *Skull Wars: Kennewick Man, Archaeology, and the Battle for Native American Identity*, published in 2000, a history that evocatively reorients how we view the discipline's difficult birth and trying adolescence.[83] Underlying such histories is the truism that to understand the present, we must understand the past. Thus, to reconceptualize our present predicaments of privilege, ownership, authorship, and participation, we must critically reconceptualize the events and personalities that led us to this present moment. As Sonya Atalay has persuasively written,

> If we are to take serious the effort of moving beyond the colonial past toward further positive growth and more ethical and just practices in fields such as archaeology, it is necessary that contemporary practitioners of the discipline not ignore the effect of past practices by placing the acts in a historical context that works to excuse them. Rather, archaeologists might take a more reflexive approach and contextualize the present situation by tracing archaeologists' . . . current position of power to both colonization and the historical reality of the egregious acts that led to the collections held by museums, universities, and historical societies internationally.[84]

Not ignoring archaeology's past is perhaps particularly important for archaeologists concerned about the field's relations with Native American communities because, although archaeologists may have largely forgotten about the field's lasting impact on Native communities, the memory of injustice runs deep across Indian country. In the native tongue of the Stó:lo Nation, for instance, the word used today for "archaeologist" literally translates as "thief," a linguistic remembrance of the first archaeologists in the Stó:lo homeland.[85]

To remember Parker is to remember the precarious balance between the establishment of archaeology and the colonial experience of Native American communities more than a century ago. Hence, this book aims to be more than a biography, but also, in Jill Lepore's terms, a story that forms a microhistory. Whereas biography has long "had its roots in the Romantic view of the artist as Hero and in the Great Man theory of history," writers of microhistories "have particular non-biographical goals in mind: even when they study a single person's life, they are keen to evoke a period, a *mentalité*, a problem: the origins of religious beliefs, the power of popular culture, the clash of Western and non-Western peoples." Lepore shares Ronald Hoffman's view that this trend is a recent one in historiography, developed, she says, as "a number of historians [began] to approach these questions from a biographical perspective informed by anthropology, psychology, literary analysis, and material culture. A common purpose seemed to mark their investigations—an endeavor to discern through the lives of individuals or families the broader contours of the social and cultural landscape."[86]

Thus, in order to illuminate both Parker's personal story and the emergence of the discipline, this book explores the intersection of people, things, and institutions; it is part biography, part intellectual history, part ethnohistory. It draws exclusively from the archival, ethnological, and archaeological records at ten institutions, though mainly from the Cornell University Library, Harvard University Archives, New York State Library, Peabody Museum of Archaeology and Ethnology, and University of Rochester. Although patently interdisciplinary in spirit and historical in practice, it is intended to be deeply anthropological, a study of how one man's life shaped and was shaped by his social world.

A superabundance of documents record Parker's life—it would be only a slight overstatement to say that we know where Parker was and what he was doing on just about any day of his adult life—but I have attempted to highlight what other writers have left out. Hence, I omit a long discussion about Parker's work for the Society of American Indians and his ethnographic research, and instead shine a light in the darkened recesses of his life: his start in archaeology, his relationships with other archaeologists, and how his personal identity affected his professional career. In turn, I also explore the ways in which Parker's experiences reflect how the discipline of archaeology was, like Frankenstein's monster, brought to life from the bits and pieces of nineteenth-century antiquarianism, social evolutionism, curiosity cabinets, territorial expansion, and governmental purpose.

Part II explores the ways in which Parker's genealogy manifestly shaped his sense of self, his worldview, and his commitments to politics and anthropology. And so this section begins by exploring the influence of family—in particular his grandfather Nicholson, his famous granduncle Ely S. Parker, and his "fictive kin" Lewis H. Morgan. It also explores Seneca history, the Cattaraugus Indian Reservation's development, and the long exploitation of its resources, including its archaeological past. Parker's personal story is interwoven with these histories—his early years on the Cattaraugus Reservation, then his life in New York City beginning in 1892, where he eventually met Fredric Ward Putnam and began his mentorship in anthropology.

Time slows in Part III to focus on Parker's expedition to the Cattaraugus Reservation in the summer of 1903, a personal and professional turning point for the ambitious student. Although he was planning to become a minister, the expedition pulled him to an archaeology career. This part focuses exclusively on the Silverheels expedition, illustrating how nearly all the predicaments Parker had to deal with that summer (and there were many) are predicaments still being dealt with by archaeologists today.

Part IV begins with how Parker became the New York State archaeologist in 1906, a job that made him a bona fide archaeologist. It explores his early years as an archaeologist, focusing on his different expeditions, his singular mode of writing cultural histories, and how he represented in his research both Native Americans and himself as an Indigenous scholar. Parker's troubled first marriage to an Abenaki woman and his second marriage to an Anglo woman also provide insight into his sense of identity; moreover, his love of archaeology inspired one of his daughters, Bertha, to pursue a life in anthropology. In 1935, Parker was elected the first president of the Society for American Archaeology and thereafter received numerous prizes and honors. As he grew older and became more established as a professional, he emphasized his Seneca identity less and less. By the time he retired in 1945—as he was flooded with awards and honorary degrees—he was first and foremost "a man of science."

The conclusion examines what it has meant in the past and what it means today to be a Native American archaeologist. Addressing this point helps us understand that the ethical quandaries scholars face today were born from the unresolved conflicts of previous generations. Parker came of age as an American Indian and as a professional archaeologist precisely at a time when both of these identities in America were uncertain. As Fredrik Barth argues, identities are formed by boundaries,[87] and these dueling identities certainly shaped Parker's life. I argue that as Parker's choices in moments of ethical crisis were both configured and guided by issues of identity, so too the ethical dilemmas archaeologists face today are not always or simply about moral responsibility. In the end, this book elucidates how questions of identity infuse our moral choices and how these choices build communities. The "moral community" of archaeologists thus refers to the ways in which notions of good and bad, right and wrong, cultivate a sense of shared purpose and identity.

Inheriting the Past

In his famous compilation of essays *The Interpretation of Cultures*, Clifford Geertz writes, "If you want to understand what a science is, you should look in the first instance not at its theories or its findings, and certainly not at what its apologists say about it; you should look at what the practitioners of it do."[88] Ethnographers, he suggests, mainly write, and so to understand them we must look closely at their writings. What archaeologists have long done is dig things up and put them in museums. Even more fundamentally, North American archaeologists have transformed Indian history and heritage into objects of wonder and scientific inquiry.

So this book is not about understanding Parker only, but rather about understanding the relationship between archaeologists and Native peoples. As a bridge between these worlds, Parker's life is an important and fascinating way to disentangle the messy nature of archaeological study. This book, the first to address directly Parker's work as an archaeologist, is biographical only insofar as it is a vehicle to explore the intersection of archaeologists, the material worlds they explore and create, and the institutions that enable their endeavors. Weaving a story from archival documents, ethnographic data, and material remains thus becomes an interdisciplinary engagement in the humanities.

In this way, the book seeks to move beyond traditional disciplinary boundaries to rethink how archaeologists have written the past, how we represent the discipline today, and how effective collaborations can be crafted in the future. It is therefore an anthropological study of archaeology's historical formation and its future potential. It explores the ways in which people—whether Parker or contemporary scholars—inherit the past, how the moral predicaments with which researchers grapple today are the progeny of the unresolved conflicts that were born in archaeology's beginning.

Part II
The Roots of Ambition

2

At Heart I Am

A White Man as Well as an Indian

To begin to understand Arthur Parker's personal and academic history, we must begin with his family history. Although we all are biological and social products of our family lineage to some degree, Parker's genealogy manifestly shaped his sense of self, his worldview, and his commitments to politics and anthropology. It is difficult not to interpret much of Parker's life as a wordless conversation with his family's past.

Arthur Caswell Parker was born on April 5, 1881, in the house adjoining the United Presbyterian Mission Church on the Cattaraugus Indian Reservation in western New York, some forty miles south of Buffalo and just east of the waters of Lake Erie.[1] His mother was Geneva Hortense Griswold Parker, for a time a teacher on the reservation. She was originally from Connecticut, and her family was of English and Scotch ancestry. In 1879, Geneva married twenty-two-year-old Frederick Ely Parker. Having graduated from the Fredonia Normal School, near his childhood home on the Cattaraugus Reservation, Frederick had become a teacher, too. In addition to Arthur, the couple had two more children, Dorothy and Edna. Seneca traditions dictated that family lines and tribal membership be traced through the mother, so because Arthur and his siblings had an Anglo mother, they could only later be adopted into a clan.[2] At the same time, the U.S. government traced American citizenship through the father, so the Parker children were not automatically American citizens because authorities considered Frederick a Seneca and citizenship was not extended to all Indians until 1924. From the very beginning of Arthur's life, his identity was uncertain.

This ambiguity of race, ethnicity, and nationality also befell Arthur's father, Frederick, whose own parents were from disparate backgrounds. Arthur's paternal grandmother was Martha Hoyt, whose family had long settled in Massachusetts. She was the niece of Laura Sheldon Wright, a missionary who with her husband helped develop and spread a written form of the Seneca language with their local newspaper *The Mental Elevator*; the couple also vigorously defended Seneca land rights.[3] While Nicholson Henry Parker, Gaiewagowa (Great Message), whose father and uncle, William and Samuel, had been members of a Baptist mission church since the 1820s,[4] was assisting the Wrights in translating the Bible into Seneca, he met Martha, and they soon married.[5] The couple did not work on Sunday and did not allow alcohol in their home. Arthur's grandfather, by all accounts, was a highly intelligent and dynamic man, graduating from a teacher's college, the Albany Normal School, in 1854, and serving as the Seneca Nation's chief clerk for several decades.[6] He also had a career as a civil engineer. As accomplished as Nicholson was, his brother was even more prominent, obtaining positions as powerful as any an Indian might hope for in the mid-1800s.

Ely Samuel Parker—Arthur's granduncle—was Lewis Henry Morgan's close friend and his key informant for the publication of Morgan's first major anthropological tract, *League of the Ho-de-no-sau-nee, or Iroquois*. At the age of twenty-three, Ely was given the honored name and title "Donehogawa" (Keeper of the Western Door) among the Seneca. It was said that when Ely's mother, Elizabeth, was carrying him in 1828, she had a dream that her son would be "a white man as well as an Indian."[7] As a youth, Ely attended various schools in western New York, which lay the foundation for a life spent with each foot planted in a different world. Although he studied law and engaged in a legal defense of Seneca lands, his legal career was cut short by the Supreme Court, which ruled that lawyers had to be (male) American citizens and could not be, like Ely, only a "natural born"; he instead, like his brother Nicholson, became an engineer.[8]

With the start of the Civil War, Ely joined the Union army, eventually becoming Ulysses S. Grant's military secretary and obtaining the rank of brigadier general. On April 9, 1865, Ely recorded the terms of surrender to end the war. Pictures of Grant from this period quite often include Ely near his side; Ely is always wearing an impeccable uniform or suit and a serious expression. In his late thirties in the photos, he has a round fleshy face with eyebrows perpetually narrowed. His dark skin and long, thin goatee make him stand out. He always seems to be somewhat apart from Grant and any others in the photos.

In 1867, Ely married Minnie Sackett, an eighteen-year-old New York socialite. "Some people thought I married the General because he was an Indian," she once proclaimed. "Now I don't care for Indians—I married the General because I loved him."[9] In 1869, Grant, then president,

Nicholson Parker, Arthur's grandfather, in his later years. (Adapted from Parker, *The Life of General Ely S. Parker*, Buffalo Historical Society, 189)

nominated Ely for the position of commissioner of Indian affairs, and he thus became the first Native person to hold the office overseeing Indians in the country. Ely worked in this position for little more than two years, but his tenure was tainted by the corruption scandals that spread throughout the Grant administration.[10] After Ely's resignation, he became a clerk for the New York Police Department, a position he held until his death in 1895. In his later years, he began a platonic friendship with Harriet Maxwell Converse, an Anglo New Yorker with a strong interest in the Seneca.[11] Although neither would know it at the time, Converse would be central in helping Arthur launch a career in anthropology.

Ely and Nicholson's mother was Elizabeth Johnson Parker, an industrious and tough woman who usually carried "an ax and was a very good shot with either a gun or a bow. She always had both with her and would shoot rabbits, coons, big birds and other game."[12] Elizabeth was purportedly descended from the Seneca prophet Handsome Lake and the Seneca leader Red Jacket. She was married to William Parker, Jonoacádoewah (Dragonfly), who himself purportedly fought with Red Jacket in the War of 1812. William later set up a mill on the Tonawanda Reservation near Buffalo, where he and Elizabeth raised their seven children in a two-story log cabin. It was said, probably mistakenly, that still further back Arthur was descended from "Jigonsaseh, the Peace Queen of the Neuter Indians, who together with Hiawatha and Dekanawida around 1550 was a founder of the League of the Iroquois."[13]

Some scholars have written that Arthur Parker was a man "at home on either side of the buckskin curtain"—that is, in both the world of Anglo Americans and the world of American Indians.[14] Arthur undoubtedly lived his life in the interstice of two parallel societies, but his family history begins to explain why and how he was able to negotiate a seemingly divided identity. Arthur's father, grandfather, and granduncle were Seneca men educated in American missionary schools. All of them held prominent positions in both their Native community and mainstream American society. All three men were throughout their lives in essence cultural interpreters, translating back and forth between Anglo and Indian communities.

This dual role left the men at times alienated, never feeling quite at home in either world. "Like his brother Ely," Arthur wrote in 1919 of Nicholson, "he never could completely accept civilization's teachings or wholly neglect the philosophy of his fathers. Seeing true virtue in each, according to his mood he argued for each. Many Indians have this same characteristic and often appear vacillating and uncertain in judgment when in reality the quality is merely the involuntary mental struggle between hereditary impressions and proclivities and those acquired." Such statements from Arthur's pen, it has been suggested, are as much about Arthur as about his elders. The strain of feeling divided, which Arthur himself must have experienced often, is indicated in his solution:

either wholesale cultural transformation or a reinvigoration of Indian identity. "Until civilization crushes out all the old instincts, or wisdom brings with it a strongly balanced judgment," Arthur believed, "Indians will ever be at moral sea."[15]

It was no secret that Arthur's mother, grandmother, and even his beloved granduncle's wife were of European ancestry. A few writers have intimated that Parker was bitter toward these women, in particular his own mother, because their race precluded the possibility of his being a full member of the Seneca tribe.[16] Being among the "outside people" "limited his political and social role on the reservation and excluded him from birthright membership in clan and tribe," Joy Porter points out. His "status within the Seneca Iroquois Nation was therefore circumscribed and ambiguous."[17] Even though Parker was ceremonially adopted into a Seneca clan in the summer of 1903, he indeed railed against matrilineal descent. "Legalists point out that only animals, slaves, and some Indians, among them the Iroquois of New York, take their descent from the female line," he once said.[18] His prose was occasionally callous to "halfbreeds," an attitude that further belied his own discomfort with being of mixed heritages. Once when asked about his Indian background, Arthur nearly apologized for it, writing, "At heart I am very much an Indian though in reality I am but a 'quarter blood.'"[19]

And yet, as we will see, Arthur Parker in the end did not accept a self divided by a buckskin curtain, but built an identity as a human being who could genuinely be both Indian and "American." In a speech in 1911, he stated, "Good Indian blood and good white blood have produced some of the finest Americans who ever lived. . . . It is the manhood, the character, the usefulness of men that counts. It is his environment that determines his conservatism or progress, and not his racial blood."[20] Arthur's struggle for self-determination was the struggle of all the Parker patriarchs—Frederick, Nicholson, and Ely—a struggle that perhaps none of them fully resolved. But Arthur believed his destiny flowed from his genealogy: in anthropology, he would see his chance to be an interpreter like those before him, a translator between two people whose futures, he believed, were not separate but shared.

Cattaraugus

"In the distant past, all the earth was covered by deep water, and the only living things there were water animals," begins an Iroquois origin myth.

"There was no sun, moon, or stars, and the watery earth was in darkness." To begin the story of human life amidst water and in darkness recalls how all of us begin life in the womb of our mothers. It is a rich and multilayered metaphor that says the origin of the Iroquois extends beyond consciousness, beyond time itself. Anthropologist Dean R. Snow points out that there are dozens of recorded Iroquois origin stories like this one and that they relate moral precepts as much as historicity; researchers are only starting to get a clear picture of the Iroquoian ancestors who lived through the millennia in what is now New York.[21]

Whatever their more distant origins, Seneca groups were living along the eastern shore of Lake Erie by the time of European contact.[22] The Seneca were one of the five tribes that joined an alliance known as the League of the Haudenosaunee (Iroquois), which may have been founded as early as A.D. 1142, the year of a spectacular solar eclipse, but was firmly in place certainly by the early 1500s.[23] The league is conceived of as a long house stretching across the Northeast. As the community farthest west, the Onontowaka (Seneca) are the Keepers of the Western Door; eastward are the Kayohkhono (Cayugas), the Onontakeka (Onondagas), the Oneyoteaka (Oneida), and the Kanyenkehaka (Mohawk).[24] In the early 1700s, a sixth nation, the Tuscarora, was admitted into the confederacy when pushed from its homelands in North Carolina. The early years of colonial relations between the Iroquois and the Dutch, British, and French were tremendously complex, but the ever-shifting alliances between the various Native groups and the Europeans revolved around trading, land use, sovereignty, raiding, and warfare.

The beginning of the American Revolution split the league as the Oneidas became allied with the rebel Americans, and the Senecas and Mohawks joined the British in the late 1770s.[25] When peace came in 1783 with the Treaty of Paris, no provisions were made for the Native allies and enemies. Each group was forced to negotiate its own terms. Flush with victory, the new U.S. government aspired to gain as much as possible from the Indians while sacrificing as little as possible. Washington's secretary of war, General Henry Knox, "wanted to develop a policy that would gradually obtain Indian land, would be as cheap as possible, would avoid war, would redound to the honor of the United States, and would benefit the Indian as well as the advancing frontiersmen."[26] In short, Knox imagined a suite of goals that would be impossible to obtain.

With the close of the 1700s, the steady demise of the Seneca land base began. In 1786, both New York and Massachusetts claimed what is now western New York, and as part of the agreement between the states, Massachusetts sold a large tract of land, which was resold yet again. The area along Cattaraugus Creek, however, was reserved for around four hundred Senecas living there, first with the 1794 Canandaigua Treaty.[27] The subsequent 1797 Treaty of Big Tree involved the sale of nearly all Seneca lands for one hundred thousand dollars, to be invested on behalf of the tribe. From this agreement, the Seneca Nation was to retain 310 square miles, including forty-two square miles at Cattaraugus.[28] In 1810, the Holland Land Company, the putative owner of much of western New York, sold nearly 200,000 acres to David A. Ogden for fifty cents an acre.[29] A subsequent 1826 "treaty," recognized both then and now as illegitimate, further reduced Seneca lands by 86,887 acres, including 5,120 acres at Cattaraugus.[30] The loss of land had broad consequences. As Snow recounts the tragedy of the late eighteenth century,

> the reservations slid into deplorable wilderness slums. Iroquois men no longer ruled the world beyond the edge of the woods, abroad for months on end to deal with hunting, diplomacy, and warfare. Rather, they found themselves confined to a woman's world of farming and village affairs. Hunting was restricted and villages could not relocate easily when soils declined.... Fueled by alcoholism, families fragmented, the mechanism of reciprocal condolences came apart, and Indian society fell into a darkness of mutual suspicion and rumors of witchcraft.... Families that had previously been parts of extended matrilineal households had to survive on their own at the very moment at which stress on traditionally weak marriage links reached its maximum. The traditional ceremonies, with their emphasis on thanksgiving, solidarity, and catharsis, did little to relieve the general hostility. By the end of the [eighteenth] century, Iroquois culture was near death.[31]

By this time, non-Indians were flocking westward, and the U.S. government's policy was focused on the advancement of its civilization. The appropriation of Indian lands for industrial and agricultural production was only part of this strategy, which also depended on schools and missions to convert the Indians to the ways of whites.[32] The complementary forces of colonialism—land threats, Christian missionaries, and American schools—combined to imperil the social and political bonds of Seneca society. In 1838, the afflicted Iroquois communities were faced with yet another crisis when the Treaty of Buffalo was completed, an accord that crushed what might have been left of Knox's hope to establish honorable covenants. As Lawrence M. Hauptman has recounted, the Treaty of Buffalo was "one of the major frauds in American Indian history."[33] It permanently affected every Iroquois citizen for years to come. Plying Indians with alcohol and relying on the old standards of bribery and forgery, the Ogden Land Company swayed the Senecas to cede *all* of their remaining lands with the exception of the Oil Spring Reservation, a postage stamp of one square mile. The treaty's most direct legacies included a forced migration accompanied by disease and starvation, internal strife among Senecas, and a land battle the Senecas had to wage for five decades, which sapped the tribe's moral energy and limited resources. Also as a direct result, Senecas incensed with the traditional leadership overthrew it, establishing a constitution and elected government.[34]

With the assistance of Quakers, the U.S. Senate ratified the Supplementary Treaty of 1842, and the Senecas regained control over the Allegany and Cattaraugus reserves. The land around what is now Buffalo was not recovered, although the Tonawanda band was "allowed" to buy back some lots northwest of Buffalo in 1856.[35] Even more than forty years after the Treaty of Buffalo, the status of the land was a major concern to the Senecas. As one Indian agent wrote in 1882, the Ogden "claim is a source of great uneasiness to the Indians, and every attempt made, either by the state or the United States, to make them citizens, or to change the manner of their lands, excites in them the greatest apprehensions lest they lose their lands altogether. They have frequently been put to great expense and inconvenience in sending delegations to Washington and Albany to oppose legislation affecting their title to their lands in the most serious manner."[36] The Ogden Land Company even today purportedly has legal "first right" to purchase the Allegany and Cattaraugus reservations should the Senecas ever elect to sell them.[37]

When Congress passed the Dawes General Allotment Act of 1887, which allotted tribal lands to individual tribal members in order to integrate them into American society, Senecas made clear their disapproval of the plan. "The Indians," as an agent wrote in 1886, "especially the Senecas on the Cattaraugus and Allegany reservations have been very much excited over the bill presented in Congress at the last session . . . to divide the land in severalty. In their present situation they are strongly opposed to any division of their land."[38] The Senecas were one of a dozen tribes excluded from the Dawes Act, although even into the 1890s

The configuration of the Iroquois land base after the major land losses of the 1800s.

the government was still actively trying to compel them to join in the spirit if not the letter of the new law.[39]

And so as Arthur Parker was growing up on the Cattaraugus Reservation in the 1880s, the U.S. government was still seeking to diminish the Seneca land base while also "converting the Indian into a farmer and stock raiser capable of blending with the general population."[40] These goals of assimilation can clearly be seen in the annual reports of the commissioner of Indian Affairs, which until the early 1900s kept yearly statistics of the reservations spread across the country. These statistics naturally focus on population and land tenure, but also on various markers of civilization as defined by the U.S. government. In them, we see numbers for those Senecas "who undertake manual labor in civilized pursuits," those who learned to read during the year, and those in boarding school and day school. The numbers recorded for the Cattaraugus Reservation for 1881 are a fascinating list that gives a definite impression of the world into which Arthur was born, even if that impression comes through the eyes of government agents:[41]

Population on Cattaraugus Reservation	1,711
Acres in Reservation	21,680
Indian families engaged in agriculture	232
Male Indians who undertake manual labor in civilized pursuits	450

Indian apprentices	15
Houses occupied by Indians	277
Houses built during the year	5
Children in boarding school	100
Children in day school	530
Boarding school	1
Day schools	9
Amount expended for education during year by government	$11,242
Indians who can read	789
Indians who learned to read during the year	20
Missionaries	4
Church buildings	3
Births	47
Deaths	62
Whites unlawfully on Reservation	50
Acres occupied by White intruders	410
Acres cultivated during year by school children	50
Acres cultivated during year by Indians	8,725
Acres broken during the year by Indians	4,135
Allotments in severalty	0
Bushels of wheat	3,842
Bushels of corn	22,000
Bushels of oats and barley	42,000
Bushels of vegetables	21,000
Feet of lumber sawed	1,790
Rods of fencing made	650
Horses and mules	334
Cattle	576
Swine	919
Percent[age] of subsistence obtained by Indians	100

These raw numbers say something about the mixed community of Arthur's youth, but also something about his own sense of self-worth and self-sufficiency. Although we know the residents of Cattaraugus in the 1880s were facing tremendous pressures, their labor provided 100 percent of the community's subsistence needs. There was a house for about every six residents. Nearly half of the community members could read. This community was thus not living in desperation, even though their struggles were certainly at times desperate and their future still uncertain. It is easy to imagine Arthur growing up here alongside Cattaraugus Creek, well fed and content in the company of men and women who through their hard work were able to care for themselves and one another.

The Policy of the Office

The genesis of archaeology in western New York must be seen within its social and political context. Sociologist Stephen Cornell argues that the U.S. government's "Indian problem" of the past several centuries essentially was three interlinked problems for elites and government agents.[42] The first problem was economic, how to control Indian land and resources. The second problem was cultural, how to make Indians live like whites. The third problem was political, how to subvert Indian political will. The core issue, from government officials' viewpoint, revolved around the "incorporation" of Native peoples into the web of white American political, cultural, and economic institutions. Cornell's theory also explains in part the emergence of archaeological authority in the late 1800s. Just as the government sought to incorporate living Native peoples, so too they sought to incorporate the history of Native peoples.[43]

Thus, the mechanisms of control we see exerted at Cattaraugus over land and sociopolitical organization were tied to the attempt to control archaeological "resources," an endeavor that Arthur Parker himself would later become part of. As we shall see, when Parker began to argue for the preservation of archaeological objects and sites, his reasoning was based on the right of government and the profit of science. He badly wanted to save sites from destruction not for the benefit of the Senecas, the prospective heirs of these ancient sites, but for the benefit of science, which, he assumed, benefits all humankind.

When the Antiquities Act of 1906 was passed—the first major federal legislation to protect archaeological sites on federal lands, including Indian reservations—the commissioner of the Office of Indian Affairs made clear that his agency had long sought to protect ancient sites and that the only legitimate authority to work these places were government archaeologists and scholars associated with prestigious museums. "After a long and only partly successful struggle to stem the tide of vandalism, which was gradually destroying the most interesting relics of ancient art and architecture in this country, effective Federal legislation has been procured," Commissioner Francis E. Leupp wrote in 1906. "Before the passage of the act the Office had kept up an earnest effort to prevent, by such means as lay within its reach, the despoliation of relics on Indian reservations.... It has been the policy of the Office to refuse other than Government scientists and persons connected with recognized scientific institutions for permits to enter reservations for the examination of ruins, the excavation of archaeological sites, and the collection of objects of antiquities, and scientists not connected with the Government have obtained permission only under certain conditions."[44]

Legal scholar and anthropologist Robert H. McLaughlin has written from today's vantage point that this law is notable for "the absence of Native American voice in the language of the Act and [for] the Act's emphasis on the scientific value of the archaeological record to the exclusion of alternative or competing systems of valuation, culturally specific systems with religious, spiritual, and historic dimensions of their own."[45] The Antiquities Act did not address how ancient Indian sites were related to Indians' identity, their histories in ancestral places, or their social affinities to sacred landscapes. Yet these connections were not unknown by researchers and policymakers at the time; they were simply ignored—they didn't matter because archaeological sites needed to be incorporated into the American mainstream. Connections to ancestral places would have to go away, perhaps to the same purgatory as traditional Indian languages, religious practices, and subsistence practices. The museums and government scientists given the "right" to explore ruins in the late 1800s and early 1900s did not concern themselves with the Indians living on reservations. Their constituencies were the urban denizens of Chicago, Washington, D.C., New York City, and Boston.[46]

In This Home

In 1881, Helen Hunt published *A Century of Dishonor*, which gained national attention for openly discussing the long history of the maltreatment of Indians at the hands of American frontiersmen, soldiers, and government agents. The book truly was, as H. B. Whipple wrote in the preface, a "sad revelation of broken faith, of violated treaties, and of inhuman deeds of violence."[47]

Reframing the "Indian problem" as a problem born from government myopia, Hunt's work challenged readers to rethink the education, civilization, and citizenship of Native Americans. It somewhat ironically arrived when the Indian Wars were nearly over—when vast tracts of Indians lands had already been subsumed by the wave of American westward migration. Nonetheless, it at last opened a sweeping public dialogue about the historical mistreatment of Native peoples. Even then, though, the book's answer was not autonomy but assimilation. Hunt herself was not so explicit, but in an introductory remark to the book, Julius H. Seelye argued that the conclusion to be drawn from the century of dishonor was the urgent need for radical assimilation. "When the Indian, through wise and Christian treatment, becomes invested with all the rights and duties of citizenship, his special tribal relations will become extinct," he wrote, and "all our policy should be shaped toward the gradual loosening of the tribal bond, and the gradual absorption of the Indian families among the masses of our people."[48] The solution to the Indian problem, according to a growing contingent, was the dissolution of the reservation system, Indian lands, and the Indian way of life. These advocates were not insincere, but we can now recognize the injustice of this remedy to the crimes of colonial subjugation.

This was the age into which Arthur Parker was born, although as a child on the rural Cattaraugus Reservation, he was somewhat removed from the controversies that reverberated across Indian country. His formative years were contented if not joyous, a halcyon childhood he largely spent out of doors, playing with friends, fishing in a brook behind his grandparents' house, and collecting bird eggs, a hobby he had developed by age nine.[49] His first job was shoveling snow, and his boyhood ambition was to be mailman because he enjoyed putting letters in their boxes.[50] With an Anglo mother, Arthur's first language was English, but he picked up enough Seneca from his friends and family to communicate in the native vernacular.[51] Grandparents Nicholson and Martha were an important influence during these years. In Arthur's memory, their farm at Cattaraugus was a veritable Eden with an apple orchard, open pasture, and crystal stream.[52] Before Arthur reached age ten, Nicholson had read to him *Paradise Lost*, *King Lear*, and *A Midsummer Night's Dream*, while Martha read to him more "sensible" fare, such as *Common Things We Should Know*, *The Book of Why*, and *The Primer of the Stars*. Nicholson taught Arthur some algebra and read with him from Isaiah and Proverbs, and Martha would recite Psalms from memory.

His grandfather would also impart their common Seneca heritage, recounting folktales and legends, and pulling from his bedroom old, tattered documents that detailed the family history. When Ely visited the homestead, as he did once or twice a year, all the prominent Senecas in the area came to catch up and reminisce of bygone days. Many prominent Anglos would visit as well, writers such as Minnie Myrtle and Harriet S. Caswell, and some of the era's key figures in anthropology, including Henry Schoolcraft, John Wesley Powell, and Lewis H. Morgan.[53] The mix of Anglo and Seneca culture in the household was silently expressed by the decorations hanging above the mantle, which these guests must have seen: beaded sashes, tomahawks, old flintlocks, family photos, and an illustration of scenes from *The Pilgrim's Progress*. In Martha's kitchen were her "curio shelves" packed with autumn maple and oak leaves, minerals, fossils, horseshoes, coins, silver ornaments, arrow and spearheads, stone axes, polished stones, pottery sherds, pipes, and fragments of human crania—all picked up from the farm. "It was to this farm that many distinguished men and women of a generation ago came—writers, scientists, missionaries, newspaper men, tourists, philanthropists," Arthur later wrote. "In this home and the mission across the fence—in this family, of the grandfather generation—grew and were nursed the forces that did most to bring civilization to the Senecas of New York and to save their lands from the spoiler's cunning."[54]

In 1892, Arthur's life suddenly changed when his father's job with New York Central Railroad required the family to move to White Plains, a suburb north of New York City.[55] Moving from the rural setting of Cattaraugus and leaving his friends and extended family must have been unsettling for the eleven-year-old Arthur, but the move would ultimately introduce him to the great anthropologists who would shape his life and career. He was perhaps willing enough to trade for a while the woods of Cattaraugus for the corridors of museums. At this time, museums were undergoing dramatic changes as anthropology in America shifted from a diversion to a bona fide science and academic pursuit. Just one year after the Parker family moved to White Plains, Chicago hosted the now famous World's Columbian Exposition. It is unlikely that Arthur visited the show, but if he had, he, like so many other Americans, surely would been transfixed by the thousands of artifacts of natural and man-made wonder seemingly culled from every corner of the earth—the replicated Javanese village, the sixty-five-foot Pueblo cliff dwelling, and racy belly dancers of the Orient.[56] The exposition brought anthropology into public view; perhaps just as significantly, it helped launch the career of a young German American anthropologist named Franz Boas and secured the prominence of a kindly professor named Frederic Ward Putnam.

Had Arthur visited the exposition, he might have heard a historian named Frederick Jackson Turner present a paper entitled "The Significance of the Frontier in American History." Turner sought to explain what the closing of the frontier three years earlier would mean to the social fabric and collective psyche of the American people. America's relation to the frontier and its original inhabitants was indeed shifting. With the 1890 census, the American Indian population in the United States was nearing its sad nadir of less than 250,000 individuals, waning from more than five million when Columbus landed on what he believed to be the outer edges of India.[57] The outrageous massacre at Wounded Knee in 1890 brought the Indian Wars to a close; the martial violence of the U.S. government's Indian policy was soon transmuted to a subtle though sure political and social hostility. The Dawes Act of 1887, which allowed for the parsing of Indian lands, was already taking effect. Within a half-century, more than 150,000 square miles would be lost to the Indians.[58] Although scholars continue to debate the merits of Turner's thesis, he was right about a marked change for America and American Indians at the close of the nineteenth century. "And now, four centuries from the discovery of America, at the end of a hundred years of life under the Constitution," he famously claimed, "the frontier has gone, and with its going has closed the first period of American history."[59]

3

THEN LET US SPARE, AT LEAST, THEIR GRAVES

Fictive Kin

Not many months after Arthur Parker was born, Lewis Henry Morgan died at the age of sixty-three. Morgan was among the most prominent nineteenth-century anthropologists, whose research focused on Iroquois ethnography and material culture, kinship systems, and social evolution. His work introduced Iroquois culture and history into the public imagination; and his more technical work influenced such grand thinkers as W. H. R. Rivers, A. R. Radcliffe-Brown, Claude Lévi-Strauss, and even Friedrich Engels and Karl Marx, who were attracted to his evolutionary schema and the scientific evidence that Iroquois "communism in living" had preceded bourgeois designs on property and family.[1] Morgan, as a friend and a scholar, was intimately linked to the Parker family. He would have a profound effect on Arthur even though their actual lives barely intersected.

In a chance encounter at an Albany bookstore, Morgan had met Ely Parker, and the two soon became fast friends.[2] At the time, they both were young, ambitious men who shared a common interest: the Iroquois. Morgan, a native New Yorker and lawyer by profession, by then had started a society to "play Indian," the Grand Order of the Iroquois, and he was eager to learn more about Iroquois customs.[3] In 1845, Ely took Morgan to meet his family living at Tonawanda. After long conversations with Ely's parents, Elizabeth and William Parker, Morgan became increasingly interested in Seneca kinship and tribal history as topics worthy of serious study. A year later, Morgan, with Ely's assistance, was adopted into the Hawk Clan and given the name "Tayadaowuhku," meaning "Bridging the Gap" or "One Lying Across," supposedly because the Senecas believed he would help bridge the Indian and white worlds.[4]

Into the late 1840s, Morgan continued to return to the Parker homestead in Tonawanda. As Spencer Parker recalled some years later,

"Mr. Morgan used to come to talk over the old times so that he could write a book about the Senecas. He told the old folks a good many things, and helped them in many ways. He gave my grandmother her first set of dishes, and knives and forks. We never had real cups or plates before but only wood and bark dishes and carved wood pitchers."[5] The book, published in 1851, was *League of the Ho-de-no-sau-nee, or Iroquois*. Arthur would later write that both his granduncle Ely and his grandfather Nicholson had major roles in the production of the volume and that his great-grandparents, Elizabeth and William, were Morgan's "principal informants."[6] The book was definitely a family affair, with two of Ely's siblings posing in traditional costumes for the book's frontispiece.[7] Typically, however, Ely is recognized as the key Parker involved and is often spoken of as essentially a coauthor. "Parker was not merely Morgan's instrument, but his efficient co-worker, and the fortunate conjunction of these minds wrought much more than either could possibly have accomplished alone," one observer wrote.[8] Morgan himself recognized Ely's contributions. His dedication in the book reads:

TO
HÄ-SA-NO-AN'-DA
(Ely S. Parker)
A Seneca Indian,
This Work,
The Materials of which are the Fruit of
Our Joint Researches,
Is Inscribed:
In Acknowledgment of the Obligations, and
In Testimony of the Friendship of
THE AUTHOR

Nevertheless, it was Morgan's name that appeared on the book's spine and front page, and it was Morgan who would become the leading figure of nineteenth-century anthropology—not his Seneca informant and collaborator. Scott Michaelsen, a professor of English, argues that the very nature of anthropological inquiry essentially requires a native or local mediator. In this sense, all anthropological texts are coproduced even though coproduction is rarely an uncomplicated relationship. Michaelsen points out that the power dynamics between the outside anthropologist and local Native often create an unequal relationship; in Ely's case, Morgan "was holding over him the promise of various state

The frontispieces of Lewis Henry Morgan's *League of the Ho-de-no-sau-nee, or Iroquois,* portraits of Levi Parker and Caroline Parker Mountpleasant in Seneca dress.

posts as a civil engineer on the New York canal system. More than one Morgan letter combines a request for detailed information with a report on progress toward Parker's postings."⁹

Significantly, the relationship Henry Morgan and Ely Parker developed was not wholly unique for early anthropologists, who often depended on Indian informants who lived in the cesuras of their local communities and the outside world. For example, the important anthropologist Alice Fletcher had a similar relationship with her key informant, Francis La Flesche. Fletcher depended heavily on La Flesche's connections and knowledge, historian Joan Mark points out, and though solicitous when the young Omaha man once asked to be named on a report's title page, she felt affronted on another occasion when he, not she, was invited to present a paper at the American Association for the Advancement of Science. "She needed Francis La Flesche," Mark observes about Fletcher, and yet for many years "it seems scarcely to have occurred to her that he could and perhaps would like to be something more than her assistant."[10]

Morgan was not unkind or unhelpful. In addition to helping Ely's career and offering the Parkers some cutlery, he actively fought the Ogden Land Company's criminal claims, meeting with politicians in Albany and even traveling with Ely to Washington, D.C.[11] He helped Ely's siblings Carrie, Nicholson, and Newton receive an education at a state normal school.[12] Morgan's motivations were certainly complex but genuinely well intentioned. After the dedication to Ely in *League*, his first sentence in the preface expresses his sincerity: "To encourage a kinder feeling toward the Indian, founded upon a truer knowledge of his civil and domestic institutions, and of his capabilities for future elevation, is the motive in which this work originated."[13] But good results do not necessarily follow from good intentions.

Arthur unquestionably revered Morgan.[14] He considered Morgan the "father of American Anthropology," among the "greatest scientists of the world," and the *League* was "the profoundest ethnographic study of the American Indians ever produced up to this time [1907] ... a classic."[15] In 1909, when Arthur planned summer fieldwork, he explicitly compared his endeavor to Morgan's research: "I am collecting notes for a work on Iroquois ethnology and culture history that I am vain enough to hope will out-Morgan Morgan."[16] Thus, Morgan, like Ely and Nicholson, inspired Arthur, setting the standard for success. Arthur's efforts resulted in *Iroquois Uses of Maize and Other Food Plants*, which was in fact a wonderful volume investigating indigenous ethnobotany. The book summarized a decade of Arthur's knowledge gleaned from Iroquois in New York and Ontario, offering rich observations and detailed descriptions, insightful notes, and absorbing illustrations. However, Arthur was conspicuously influenced not only by Morgan's Iroquois ethnology but also by his theory of the evolution of human society. "It was Lewis Henry Morgan who first opened the gateways to a scientific study of the Indian," Arthur claimed, "and who from this study pointed out the laws of social evolution by which mankind has risen step by step from primitive ignorance to civilization."[17]

The *League* is a masterpiece of ethnology, written at a time when the anthropological genre did not yet exist. Interwoven throughout the descriptions of Iroquois social organization and material culture, however, is the beginning of Morgan's theory of social evolution, a theory that represents his most powerful and dubious influence on anthropology and the image of American Indians.[18] Although Morgan does not fully delineate this theory until 1877 in his *Ancient Society*, he argues in the *League* that all human groups have moved or are in the midst of moving through distinct hierarchies of organization: economic (hunter, pastoral, civilized), political (monarchical, oligarchical, democratic), and religious (measured by belief in a single supreme being: Greeks, Iroquois, Christian). The Iroquois were thus ranked somewhere in the middle of the hierarchy, and white Christian Americans were at the pinnacle.[19] Later anthropologists such as John Wesley Powell considered the *League* the "first scientific account of an Indian tribe," but it was Morgan's ideas of social evolution that greased the skids of anthropological theory in the late 1800s.[20] As Powell, himself a major proponent of social evolution, wrote in 1880, "Monarchies are temporary phases of government in the evolution of mankind from barbarism to civilization; and these monarchies with their attendant hierarchies, feudalisms, and slavery, appear only as pathologic conditions of the body politic—diseases which must be destroyed or they will destroy—and hence disappearing by virtue of the survival of the fittest. Hope for the future of society is the best-beloved daughter of evolution."[21]

Given that late-nineteenth-century social evolution seemingly denigrated Native societies, why did it hold such appeal for Ely and, more, for Arthur? Anthropologist Nancy Lurie is right to point out that "for the most part, individual Indians with whom the early scholars worked, such as Morgan's associate, Ely Parker, seemed to agree with the White opinion that the Indians would lose their distinctive identity, but they were motivated to record their native heritage for posterity."[22] Arthur, too, definitely thought the days of Indians were numbered and that the best he could do was try to salvage what remained. As he wrote in 1907 as much about himself as about his Seneca family,

> Time has slipped by. The Iroquois have become in a measure anglicized. Robbed of their forests and hiding places they have been pushed back in small corners called reservations and have yielded up through necessity their old-time ways, and the modern substitutes for their ancient usages are often pitiful caricatures.... This exhibition of departed glory is pitiful and pathetic.... Ultramodern

Indians will not be found on the reservations but out in the strenuous white man's world struggling side by side with the pale invader as college students, teachers, nurses, clerks, accountants, engineers, electricians, newspaper men, athletic trainers, bandmaster, musicians, doctors, philologists, anthropologists and what not. It is late, far too near the hour when a new epoch will dawn and there will be no more red men as such. Yet in the short time that remains it is our purpose to save at least a part of the tattered fringe of the ancient fabric that was.[23]

Lurie's reply to the question of Indian advocates better explains Ely, who worked with Morgan before the theory of social evolution was fully realized and when no alternative social theory was readily available to him. But Arthur came of the anthropological age when Franz Boas was just launching his crusade against racial determinism and unilinear evolution. We know in fact that Arthur met Boas and that the professor even encouraged Arthur to study at Columbia University. Despite all this, social evolution, even with its polemics and racist overtones, remained for Arthur the more appealing theory.

Loyalty can explain much. Arthur in large part modeled his professional life after Ely, a translator between cultures. Morgan, as Tayadaowuhku, similarly was a man dedicated to bridging two communities with his research, writing, and political activism. In a public address in 1919, Arthur even said that Morgan was in fact a relative, fictive kin.[24] Although said jokingly, the statement underscores the close kinship—even if not born of blood—Arthur felt for Morgan. "The Parker home was in a measure the spot where a new American science was born," he would later write and not without justification. "The family has ever felt responsible for recording and preserving the fame of its race."[25] He reportedly disliked Boas because the Columbia professor "regarded L. H. Morgan as a non-person."[26] Arthur could no more subvert Morgan or his theories than he could subvert his own father or grandfather or, for that matter, himself.

Beyond loyalty, it is also important to understand that Boas was in truth no viable alternative for Arthur. As Hanzel Hertzberg eloquently argues, the theories of social evolution and Boas's brand of historical particularism said very different things about the "Indian problem" and Indians in general.[27] Evolutionary theory created a framework that explicitly explained the relationship between Indians and whites.

Not only was the social, political, and economic improvement of Indians possible; it was predicted. Evolution offered a prescription for the ills Indians faced. Eminent ethnologist Fred Eggan observes that "Morgan was vitally interested in the future of the American Indian, and—unlike many of his contemporaries—he believed that the Indian had a future. Through his association with the Iroquois, he was one of the first scholars to see the problems of the Indians from their point of view, and to discuss the alternatives to extinction."[28] As Morgan himself wrote, "The development of national intellect depends chiefly upon external, reciprocal influences, and is usually proportionate to the vitality and motive which the institutions of a people possess and furnish."[29] Thus, positive reforms for Indians could be effected through institution building and constructive policies.

Boas, in contrast, believed anthropology should be based on objective scientific research that recorded small, authentic Native cultures on the verge of extinction. Boas and his students did not care a great deal about the relationship between Indians and the dominant society: the goal was to record as much as possible as soon as possible. At the turn of the twentieth century, Lurie points out, "in general, anthropologists appeared to have accepted the Indian's misfortunes as the workings of providence rather than the result of calculated policy they could question and oppose as scientists and citizens."[30] As anthropologist Faye Harrison has observed, because the Boasian paradigm of "salvage ethnography" emphasized exotic and narrow ideas of American Indian culture, "the specific forms of racism assaulting Native American reservation communities and the consequent processes of cultural change occurring in those settings were not adequately, if at all, explored."[31] In contrast, Arthur, witnessing the Senecas' struggle for sovereignty and survival for his entire youth, cared intensely about the social welfare of Indians. Boas's new language of cultural relativism and antievolution could not easily be reconfigured to the Parker family's fight to "advance" the Indian "race."[32] It might be said that the challenge Boas presented to the concept of race probably appealed slightly to Arthur. Boas untangled biology, language, and culture, which were long assumed to be inseparable. For Boasians, however, the "most aboriginal" was also the "most Indian," so Arthur as a potential Boas student could not easily have reconciled an identity that was legitimately Indian *and* American.

"Morgan's evolutionary ideas," according to Joy Porter, "allowed Parker to think of assimilated Indians like himself as progressive, as people in advance of their contemporaries. It was a positive way of seeing 'Indianness' and Indian culture. . . . Parker was able to use Morgan's validation and explanation of Iroquois and Indian culture as 'scientific' support for his own acculturated position."[33] Social evolution, although certainly not perfect, at least made room for an individual like Arthur who wanted to be all at once a real Indian, a real American, and a real anthropologist. As the years passed and Arthur grew older, he did become skeptical of some of the general tenets of social evolution, but he remained loyal to his predecessors and always recognized their collective effect on his life. "The influence of Morgan and my great uncle have been with me since childhood," he wrote, "and their example has been a tradition that has spurred me to carry on where they left off."[34] He always remembered his lineage, his kin both biological and fictive. Morgan, an expert in kinship, would certainly have appreciated Arthur's fidelity.

The American Red Man

In 1851, the same year Morgan's *League of the Ho-de-no-sau-nee, or Iroquois* was published, Arthur's grandfather Nicholson Parker wrote an eloquent paper titled "The American Red Man."[35] Nicholson was perhaps in his early twenties at the time and still a few years away from graduating from the Albany Normal School. It is uncertain whether he wrote this essay as part of a school assignment; given its passion, maybe the words were a private outpouring of Nicholson's thoughts and beliefs. A surviving flyer for the presentation testifies that Nicholson was giving public lectures by 1853, so perhaps the essay was read in public, as indicated by its concise length and apparent non-Indian audience.[36]

Nicholson begins by observing that a ceaseless power propels the universe's natural and social elements. It is "an august truth," he writes, that "without and within is force, resistless force, moving spirit and matter, moon and stars onward. Under this power, man and worlds must be alike pushed off the stage of existence, to make room for others." In what we can now interpret as an evolutionary mindset, Nicholson states that each entity is unable to resist that which is to replace it. "System rushes on system," he writes, "generation on generation, and nation on nation, an everlasting battle; a fearful war, in which the defensive must ever surrender, some expiring with a low, melancholy wail, and others breathing their last in a loud, warrior shout." In other words, the changing social landscapes are like the ocean's tides—as predictable as they are unassailable. These cosmic forces are materialized in the wars wrought by colonialism, the result being the Euro-Americans' dominance and the Indian peoples' infirmity. "Were this people wronged? You do not feel disposed to investigate the subject," Nicholson both asks and answers for an Anglo audience. "If wronged, then wrong is the very divinity of the inevitable laws which produced their ruin."

The conqueror is not without obligation, however. Nicholson suggests that there is the question of "the doing of justice to the characters of those whom the law forced you to destroy; the rescuing of their names from oblivion, and the placing of them within their proper sphere of history." Comparing the Euro-American colonialists to Saul, who famously chronicled the "deeds of every nation which he conquered," Nicholson writes that justice demands conquerors not forget those whom they despoiled. This peculiar argument clarifies how the burgeoning science of social evolution could simultaneously lament and celebrate the passing of so many Native American communities. The forces of the universe have destroyed the American Indian, it seemed to say, but that does not mean that they should be forever extinguished from memory, for they made no mistake of their own doing. We all are the victims of fate.

Nicholson also emphasizes that a legitimate history of the American Indian will help illuminate at least two points of confusion. During the centuries of colonialism in North America, Native peoples were often portrayed as being pointlessly cruel and brutal. This caricature balances that of the Noble Indian. Nicholson argues that although cruelty cannot be denied, such behavior is a reasonable response to the discordant conditions of imperialism: "His brethren carried into captivity, his wife and children bound in the chains of slavery, his fields destroyed, his hunting grounds harried, his dwellings burnt, his wide and beautiful country wrested from his grasp, and he driven forth without home, without food, without shelter. These! These changed his nature and sometimes made the man a demon." Ultimately, Nicholson says, whites have been much crueler than Indians: "The whites have deeds to answer for, far more bloody than the natives of America. Witness Jena: attest it St. Bartholomew: speak to thou inquisition! And what of the guillotine? Where is there an Indian Attila, or an aboriginal Robespierre? History answereth not. Oh! It is very modest of you to speak of Indian cruelty! And more easy too, than effective."

A second confusion is the lack of credit given to the intelligence of American Indians. Nicholson recommends that a history of great leaders, such as Red Jacket and Pontiac, would ably illustrate the "intellectual character of the red man." As further evidence, he offers the Indian conception of nature to illustrate "the superiority of the Indian mind," which is also demonstrated by the Indian conception of heaven "with its One Divinity, the all gracious, all potent, all omniscient, eternal Great Spirit, a heaven of beauty with its blue streams and singing birds." Nevertheless, Nicholson in the end predicts the complete and final destruction of Indian peoples. He envisions amity at last in the wilderness of North America, but a peace that arrives only by the death of the weak. "Peace! Peace everlasting," he writes. "A few more years, a few more massacres, a few more sighs, and not a descendant of that people will stand upon the soil of his fathers. The very grave of the warrior will be nameless, his dust mingled almost without memorial with the universe atoms. The tides of life will rush over the silent realms of death, and the deep sea-like voice of other generations rise where a lost people have not even left an echo. And you the arrogant, what of you? Look to the *inevitable necessary law, destiny*. In three thousand years may not two nations slumber, where but only one now lies in the icy pall of unconsciousness." The essay is closed with a sprawling signature: "Ge-wah-go-wa (alias) Nicholson Parker."

Nicholson was a great influence on Arthur. Young Arthur used to spend hours with his grandparents, particularly at the foot of Nicholson as he alternated between Seneca and English, sharing Seneca folktales and reading Shakespeare. Nicholson passed away in 1892, just as Arthur moved from his home east to the suburbs of New York City. And yet Nicholson's lasting influence on Arthur is seen in this essay, written when Nicholson was himself just a young man. For both grandfather and grandson, the great injustice was not the destruction of Native peoples, for they considered it their unquestionable fate, but the erasure of their existence in the memory of humankind. Indians, both men felt, are intelligent and strong. They would, even must, change to the ways of whites, but that did not mean the world had to forget their origins, their lifeways, their history—in sum, their humanity.

A Noble Race! But They Are Gone

The interest in ancient objects and earthworks spread across New York as settlers began migrating westward following the American Revolution. This interest notably coincided with the dispossession of many Iroquois communities, punished by American forces for their alliance with the British, their resistance to American hegemony, and their control of desirable lands. As early as 1799, Captain Charles Williamson wrote that in southwestern New York could be found evidence of cultivated fields and the remains of ancient forts with ditches and gates. Williamson believed the French had built these villages for defense, but contradictorily wrote that he did not "recollect that the French had ever so great force in this part of America at so early a period, for these forts, from very large decayed timbers lying in them, and large timber growing over those fallen down, must be at least two hundred years old." He also stated that these forts must have had many occupants, for "great collections of human bodies are found in them." He concluded that "an accurate examination of this country, by men of observation and science, might throw light on the history of this part of America."[37] Even a century before formal archaeological work was to begin in western New York, colonists already believed that the history of this region could be elucidated only through science.

As settlers continued to push into western New York, ancient relics and earthworks were exposed by both accident and exploration. Around 1850, some fifty miles south of Irving, for example, workmen uprooted a tree stump to discover a mass of human bones; and when another stump was removed in a nearby town, a cache of 167 arrowheads was found.[38] Intentional excavations are known from as early as 1822, when in the vicinity of the Cassadaga Lakes, some twenty-five miles south of Irving, a "mound was excavated and a large number of human skeletons exhumed," and at the same time a little farther south at an "old Indian burying ground ... as many as fifty skeletons were disinterred on one occasion." In 1870, still closer to Irving, "a large grave was opened, from which a great number of human skeletons were exhumed. These were the bones of individuals of both sexes and all years, from infancy to old age."[39] Many earthworks in the path of construction or new farm fields were simply flattened, as when in 1840 a "sepulchral mound" more than ten feet tall was "entirely obliterated," and another mound reportedly thirty to forty feet high was demolished, although not before a local resident "found beads, arrow-heads, and other Indian relics within this mysterious embankment."[40]

The fate of these objects and bones is largely unknown. Some relics probably decorated the shelves of local farmers' homes and businessmen's offices, and others were undoubtedly sold to collectors with "curiosity cabinets." Many of the human bones simply disintegrated on being exposed to the air. "An attempt was made to preserve a portion of these remains," one digger wrote around 1851, "but by exposure to the atmosphere they crumbled into a fine powder."[41] These bits of evaporating bone and harvested arrowheads were taken from the flattened mounds without guilt because it was believed that these places were the abodes of a race of people lost to time. Throughout the nineteenth century in America, the "mound builders myth" was a heated debate about who had constructed the great mounds throughout North America, a debate that in part was used to justify the appropriation of Indian lands and resources.[42] "The concept of the vanishing American disarticulated Native American heritages for nationalistic and scientific purposes," Randall McGuire explains. "Both the notion of the Indian as a fallen noble savage and the mound-builder myth used the Indian past to legitimate the White nation."[43] This justification is evident in western New York, as when one writer in 1879 reinforced the myth of distant ties: "This much, and no more, may be set down as reasonably certain, that these earthworks were reared by a people who preceded those found here by the first European visitors; but whether they were of Aztec, Toltec, Phoenician, or Egyptian origin, or whether they were descendants of the lost tribes of Israel, as some have supposed, is a question which will probably never be solved."[44] Such statements reinforced the legitimacy of American exploration and colonization, for if no one could prove these places belonged to a particular people, then it followed that they rightly could belong to anyone.

Nevertheless, by at least 1860 some writers expressed the conviction that certain ruins were plainly the homes of ancient Indian peoples.[45] However, apparently few believed that the Iroquois tribes of the colonial period and those still living in the area had any connection to the region's more distant Indian history. Yes, these places were made and lived in by Indians—but Indians long past. One writer in 1876 argued that although the area's ancient occupants were Indians, Iroquois traditions offered no clues to solve the mystery. The origins of the Iroquois, although unknown, were also uninteresting, he stated, for given "the monotonously recurring revolutions incident to the history of a barbarous people . . . it is doubtful whether it would afford us much instruction or entertainment."[46] Curiously, the writer ended his argument with a few lines of poetry that in this context can be read as either ironic or particularly insincere. This fragment of poetry may suggest an awareness of the intemperance of disturbing ancient graves—a common habit in western New York by the late 1800s. The romantic poet William Cullen Bryant, although uncited, wrote the rhyme in 1832:

> A noble race! but they are gone,
> With their old forests wide and deep,
> And we have built our homes upon
> Fields where their generations sleep.
> Their fountains slake our thirst at noon,
> Upon their fields our harvest waves,
> Our lovers woo beneath their moon—
> Then let us spare, at least, their graves.

Aspiring Anthropologist

In the same year Arthur moved to White Plains, his grandfather Nicholson and grandaunt Caroline passed away. Their deaths surely underlined for Arthur the changes in his life as he entered his teenage years. "Parker did not write about the effect on him of this separation of death and distance, but it must have been considerable," Hazel Hertzberg has surmised. "A New York City suburb was a very far remove from the rural life of western New York and his circle of kindred and community at Cattaraugus. We know very little about this period of his life. But it may be guessed that in White Plains he first felt the full impact of being an Indian yet not quite Seneca, a situation he shared with his father."[47]

Nevertheless, we know that Arthur was a sharp student; an 1892 report card attests to his acuity with an average grade of 93 percent in arithmetic, geography, physiology, grammar, spelling, reading, drawing, and deportment.[48] He graduated from White Plains High School at the age of sixteen and was soon ushered into Centenary Collegiate Institute in New Jersey. "He is one of the best lads I have known. He is a good student, fond of reading the most valuable books, conscientious, faithful steadily to his duties of any position where he may be placed," Arthur's pastor offered in an 1896 letter of recommendation.[49] After several months in New Jersey, Arthur transferred to Dickinson Seminary in Williamsport, Pennsylvania, laying the foundation for a career in the ministry. He felt some ambivalence about being there, however, as he wrote to a family friend in 1900. "My appetite for knowledge is very sharp and I intend to eat all I can while I have the opportunity, for what is life unless we can constantly learn?" he opined, but then acerbically added a few lines later,

"Beauty, beauty everywhere, but where, oh where is the RED MAN who owns it? and who are these usurpers I see?"[50]

On school vacations, Arthur would also return to his parents' home, now ten miles north of White Plains in Pleasantville, outside New York City. As his mother wrote in a formal though loving letter in 1900, "My dear son—Your precious letter came to me in due time. So glad to hear that you are feeling well. Hope you will be thro' your examinations alright. Sorry you had to give up Greek. Pa had a short note from Dr. Gray. He spoke very nicely of you. We shall be most happy to have you home with us once more. . . . Your loving mother, Geneva H. Parker."[51] Arthur also continued to return regularly to Cattaraugus with free passes provided through his father's railroad job and otherwise maintained his relationships there by sending back presents to friends and relatives.[52]

Arthur's broader interests are also apparent at this time. In 1900, he published several stories, including a fictional tale set in ancient Egypt titled "The Triumph of Woman's Wit," published in the *Dickinson Union*.[53] In May 1899, he was given a one-year permit, issued by the American Museum of Natural History, to collect "wild birds, birds' nests and eggs for scientific purposes."[54] His interest in natural history seems to have only been intensified while he was living in the city. When still a teen, he helped to organize "a group of boys who explored the fields and woods and then returned to the home of their Sunday school teacher . . . to read papers or to discuss what they saw out of doors."[55]

Even as Arthur was studying at the seminary in 1901, he wrote to John Wesley Powell, the prominent anthropologist and director of the Smithsonian Institution's Bureau of American Ethnology, requesting copies of various reports. Powell wrote back: "In reply to your note of October 23, I have to express regret that the regular edition of the Thirteenth Report of this Bureau is entirely out of print, though a few unbound copies remain; and in view of your strong desire to utilize the contents of the Report, I take pleasure in sending one of these unbound copies to you." At the end of the letter, Powell added, "It is a pleasure through you to renew memories of General Ely S. Parker and Nicholson H. Parker, both of whom I knew agreeably," which explains in part why Arthur was given such kind consideration.[56] Such connections would prove to be important for him in the years to come.

These bits of documents suggest a growing uncertainty about Arthur's commitments to the ministry. His indecision about his future is ultimately closely tied to the miscellany of his past. "What began as the two cultures of White Plains and Cattaraugus created an ambivalence that Parker was never able to shake," William Fenton writes. "He is a naturalist one moment, a divinity student the next, aspiring anthropologist, then Indianist."[57]

My Dear Professor

In 1899, Arthur was hired on a part-time or occasional basis as an "archaeological assistant" at the American Museum of Natural History, a post he would hold for four years.[58] In that era, the museum was thriving, along with many other cultural and educational institutions throughout New York City, as the museum sponsored more than a dozen annual expeditions and held major exhibits that drew public acclaim.[59] It was an electrifying time to be in New York and witness the birth of modern science. "Back in New York as a spindling youngster, stringy as a rawhide strap," Arthur recalled some years later, "I began to rub elbows with explorers and museum men. I helped boil heads from Mexico, unpacked vile smelling hides from the Arctic and washed bushels of specimens, some of which I catalogued."[60] As early as 1901, he also began taking part in excavations on Long Island for the museum.[61] Not yet twenty years old, he was working in one of the nineteenth century's great anthropological institutions. He was most awed not by the musty exhibits that constituted the front of the museum, but by the men he met in back: "It was in remote offices down long halls that I met the awesome Gratacap, Bogoras and Boas, the obliging Dr. Allen and Frank Chapman, the friendly Dr. Putnam and the genial Bumpus. These men were never too busy to identify pottery, fossils or birds' eggs brought in by a wondering youth. There was a thrilling world back of the scenes. It smelled of spicy dust and moth balls, but mostly of mystery and greatness."[62]

Of all the anthropologists who surrounded Arthur during those impressionable years, Putnam warmed most to the young man. Mentorship from a powerful figure was necessary for professional attainment at the turn of the twentieth century, when few universities offered degrees in anthropology. As Joan Mark notes, during this era "a would-be anthropologist needed to win the approval of a recognized authority (it was usually F. W. Putnam at the Peabody Museum or John Wesley Powell at the Bureau of American Ethnology) who would then supervise his or her work and provide jobs, institutional support, research funds, and publishing outlets as needed."[63] The lack of such mentorship opportunities—for example, for Francis La Flesche—often prevented politically unconnected Native American informants on distant reservations from joining the ranks of the growing discipline.

Frederic Ward Putnam, by almost any standard, is among the preeminent American anthropologists.[64] In a career spanning five decades, Putnam published more than four hundred works and helped inaugurate the American Anthropological Association and the Archaeological Institute of America. He established anthropology programs at Columbia University, the University of California at Berkeley, and the American Museum of Natural History and played key foundational roles at Harvard University and its Peabody Museum of Archaeology and Ethnology. Just as significant, he helped introduce anthropology to America as the science of humanity in his role of chief of Department M (ethnology, archaeology, progress of labor and invention, isolated and collected exhibits) for the 1893 World's Columbian Exposition in Chicago.

Over his long career, Putnam mentored dozens of aspiring researchers, including numerous women and a few Native Americans, including Antonio Apache (Chiricahua Apache) and William Jones (Fox). By the late 1800s, when Arthur would have first met him, Putnam was able to guide students from his multiple academic posts: starting in 1894, he spent three weeks of each month in Cambridge as professor of anthropology at Harvard University and curator at the Peabody Museum and one week in New York City as curator at the American Museum of Natural History. Putnam was a fatherly figure to many of his acolytes, particularly in the early 1900s, when a group of young followers became known as the "Putnam Boys." Arthur was a part of this group, which also included M. Raymond Harrington, Alanson Skinner, and Frank G. Speck. All four became professional anthropologists and remained fast friends throughout their lives. Skinner went on to a respected career at the Museum of the American Indian and the Milwaukee Public Museum, and Speck spent his life working in Philadelphia at the University of Pennsylvania.[65] The group found its way into the salon of Harriet Maxwell Converse, or "Aunt Hattie," as she was affectionately known. Converse, a friend of Putnam, spent her later years studying the Senecas. She was adopted by the entire Seneca Nation and secured the friendship of tribal leaders, who allowed her to attend ceremonies and entrusted her with sacred objects.[66] She clearly felt close to Arthur. Converse's connections helped Arthur secure his first full-time job as an anthropologist, and when she died in 1903, he became her literary executor.[67]

Arthur also became close with Putnam. As Hertzberg writes of their relationship, "If Parker's grandfather Nicholson served as a model of a man living in and between two cultures, Putnam became Parker's model of the scientist; and there can be little question that his career profoundly influenced Parker's own."[68] Even though Boas encouraged Arthur to attend Columbia University, Arthur purposefully chose to follow the museum path set by Putnam.[69] The choice, however, was fateful because as anthropology became increasingly professionalized in the 1900s, Arthur's lack of formal university training would haunt him.

Putnam's close relationship with Arthur can be seen in the very first correspondence between them.[70] The letter was written in October 1902 and begins, as would nearly every letter Arthur would write to his mentor, "My dear Professor." Parker, with much gratitude, is writing to thank Putnam for a check of seventy-five dollars, apparently from Putnam and an unnamed second benefactor, which would enable him to pay his college tuition. In hindsight, it is ironic to know that this money given to Arthur for his theological studies only strengthened his ties with and feelings toward Putnam and anthropology. Putnam would soon write to Parker asking him to spend the summer excavating a site in a familiar landscape in western New York: the Cattaraugus Reservation. For now, Arthur only expresses his gratitude and promises to do justice to those who have invested in his future. In closing, he emphasizes to Putnam his Indian heritage. "I am unable, my dear Professor, to express my thankfulness—as I look over my words I find them weak," he wrote. "A man of my race once said, 'The white man speaks his thanks by the words of his lips. The Red Man feels his thanks in his heart. His heart has no lips.' The former statement may not be wholly true but the latter certainly is—in my case."

These Silent Memorials

In 1847, New York governor John Young asked Lewis H. Morgan to gather together objects for the Cabinet of Natural History located in the state capitol. Morgan agreed, and a call was soon sent out "to our fellow citizens asking for their aid in furnishing relics of the ancient masters of the soil."[71] The next year Morgan sold his own personal collection to New York and began making collecting trips. At first, his views of his charge are somewhat unexcited. "If the specimens in our museums and private cabinets were at once brought into one collection, they would excite universal surprise by their variety and singularity," he wrote. "Such a cabinet would, it is true, contain but little to instruct; would seem to enlarge but slightly the bound of human knowledge, yet it would be all it pretended—a memento of the Red Race who preceded us. If the scholar of after years should ask of our age an account of our predecessors, such a collection would be the most acceptable answer it could render. It would enable the Red Race to speak for itself through these silent memorials."[72]

Morgan thus at first saw Iroquois objects as little more than memento mori—relics to remind later generations of the passing of New York's Native peoples. This argument is little different from Nicholson's call to chronicle the deeds of the conquered. By the late 1840s, Morgan began regularly sending back dozens of ethnographic and archaeological objects to Albany. As he became more involved in the work that would lead to the *League*, however, he no longer considered these things mere "mementos." They were now "specimens" of science that would elucidate human evolution. Morgan quit collecting for the state in 1851, with the publication of the *League*. After a hiatus from anthropology for six years, he began again but focused quite exclusively on ethnography.[73] The collection of rare objects would come to form the core of the New York State Museum when it was founded.

The Parkers are yet again linked to Morgan through his collecting. Of the $215 allocated to him by the state, nearly all of it was used to purchase objects from the Parker family.[74] More than a half-century later, in 1904, the New York State Museum hired Arthur to begin his own collecting forays among the Iroquois on behalf of the state. This position, tenuous at first, eventually set Arthur on a sure career path in anthropology when he proved himself as a collector and was hired as state archaeologist of New York. He then not only occupied Morgan's former post, but also became the official caretaker of Morgan's collection of nearly five hundred matchless Iroquois artifacts. A decade later, when almost every object was consumed in an accidental fire, Arthur was inconsolable for weeks. But as a young anthropologist just starting out, he would not have known this future. Then, he must have seen himself linked to Morgan more than ever: linked by connections to the Parkers, their common intellectual commitments, and their shared labors.

The Indians Would Not Let Them

One day sometime before 1889, a Seneca man named Henry Silverheels living near the town of Irving on the Cattaraugus Reservation started digging a hole near his house, a pit to winter his store of harvested potatoes. I imagine Silverheels, not a young man then, working slowly but methodically, listening absent-mindedly to the crunching sound echoing each time his shovel bites into the earth. He pauses a moment to wipe the sweat from his forehead, perhaps to look over his land thick with trees, a gentle wind sweeping the red and orange leaves into an autumn snow. As he goes back to work, the next strike abruptly stops short, and he hears not a crunch but a *ting!* rent the air. He stops, his shovel still partly wedged into the ground, and then slowly bends down on his knees. Gently brushing the dirt from the bottom of the hole, a shape appears at first like an apparition, uncertain and vague, but as he continues brushing the dirt away, he sees it is a pitted and encrusted metal knife. Curious almost in spite of himself, he digs on, soon finding pits with stone points and walls that appear to have once been some kind of fortification. As the sun begins to set, he is only half surprised to uncover a skull encrusted with dirt, an Indian he imagines killed after this fort was besieged long, long ago.

When exactly Silverheels found this ancient village and burial ground is unknown, but in an account of the event recorded in a diary stored at the Fenton Historical Society, Marcus B. Sackett, an Irving resident born in 1830, indicates that Silverheels was digging a cellar when he unexpectedly came upon a fort and soon discovered projectile points, knives, and eventually human remains. Sackett notes that not far from the house was discovered a burial ground, in which "years afterwards when it was dug open many skeletons were found."[75] This statement most certainly refers to the Parker and Harrington excavations of 1903, although the site was also apparently known to W. M. Beauchamp some years earlier and was published in 1900.[76] In an unpublished version of the Silverheels Site report, Harrington wrote that different Senecas told him that Henry was "digging a pit in which to winter his potatoes, had unearthed human bones, and had found others later while grading a road from the terrace to the flats."[77] In this report, the young archaeologist makes no reference to the trouble he and Parker had with the local Senecas when their work first began, but Sackett is not so coy. Years, perhaps even several decades before Harrington and Parker arrived, shovel and pick in hand, the Senecas had made clear that their ancestors should not be disturbed. "The Irving folks wanted to excavate at the time the place was first discovered," Sackett recounts, "but the Indians would not let them."

Part III

The Summer of 1903

4
Vast Unexplored Treasure Fields

Would I Forget Greek and Hebrew

During breaks and between semesters at Dickinson Seminary, Parker sped back to New York to pursue his love of anthropology. In addition to laboring in the American Museum of Natural History's dank storage rooms, he was given the chance to dirty his hands excavating ancient sites. On Long Island, he dug shell middens at Oyster Bay and Shinnecock Hills in 1901 and 1902, and later ventured farther west to the Mohawk and St. Lawrence valleys.[1] From the first, his status as an archaeologist was in part defined by his Indian heritage. As one 1902 article reported, with "A. G. Parker, a full-blooded Seneca, being one of the assistants, some remarkable aboriginal discoveries have been made during the past few weeks on Shinnecock Hills, Long Island . . . and here, by the directions of the Indian above mentioned, who knows all the traditions of his race, 'find' after 'find,' utterly unexpected and valuable, has been dug up."[2]

Although these expeditions were carried out under Putnam's watchful supervision, the work itself was directed by Mark Raymond Harrington. Raymond, as he was known among friends, was a year younger than Parker, born in 1882 in Ann Arbor, Michigan, where his father was a professor of astronomy and meteorology.[3] In his peripatetic youth, Harrington lived in Washington, D.C., when his father was the first chief of the U.S. Weather Bureau. Later the family moved to Seattle, where Raymond took canoe rides with the local Siwash people and learned some of the Chinook language, and then to New York, where he began his first tentative arrowhead-hunting expeditions and diggings.[4] When his father disappeared under the influence of a mysterious mental illness, Harrington dropped out of high school. But soon, with Putnam as a kind of surrogate father, he began his apprenticeship in archaeology at the American Museum of Natural History in 1899.[5] Impressively, while still a teenager, he was leading expeditions for the venerated museum throughout New York, further illustrating Putnam's propensity to encourage and sponsor aspiring researchers. Putnam's first letter to mention Harrington reports, "Young Harrington who I gave to explore some caves near Westchester had good luck. He is now on a second trip there."[6] The student archaeologists conducted some of the earliest stratigraphic excavations in North America (including at Shinnecock Hills in 1902), using what has recently been dubbed the "Harrington-Peabody technique," contributing to the development of a method that would become fundamental to archaeological science.[7] They also mixed ethnology with archaeology, studying the fading Indigenous cultures of Long Island.[8] Harrington suffered from stuttering, which in part may explain why he preferred the solitude of research and would come to depend on Parker at times as the unofficial spokesman for their shared work.[9]

By 1903, Parker's interest in anthropology was pulling him away from a life in the ministry. He likely had to give little thought to an invitation from Harrington and Putnam to join an expedition that summer. As Parker later recalled, Harrington asked, "Would I forget Greek and Hebrew and the origin of the Decalogue for a few weeks and undertake an exploration with him?"[10] The invitation came, no doubt, as recognition of Parker's devotion to the American Museum and confirmation of his growing friendship with Harrington and Putnam. Unlike previous expeditions, however, this summer's fieldwork would take Parker to a familiar landscape—the Cattaraugus Reservation, the place of his family, his roots, his own history. An underlying motivation in the invitation was likely the knowledge that Parker would provide the researchers with a singular entrée into the local community.

Putnam's enthusiasm for the expedition, as was the case for all museum directors and curators in the early twentieth century, was driven by the nearly insatiable desire for ever more objects. When the Peabody Museum opened its doors in 1866, it had a meager fifty artifacts on its shelves, a miscellany of "crania and bones of North-American Indians, a few casts of crania of other races, several kinds of stone implements, and a few articles of pottery."[11] When Putnam became the Peabody's director in 1874, the institution cared for eight thousand items, and just four years later he had grown the collection to thirty thousand objects.[12] As a later Peabody director, Stephen Williams, would write, "It was the gathering of specimens, a literal filling up of space, that was the concern of the first directors. They spoke with pride of the sheer numbers of accessions."[13] Rather than purchasing extant collections from private

Arthur C. Parker (*left*) and M. Raymond Harrington (*right*) as young men. (Courtesy of the Autry National Center, Southwest Museum, Los Angeles, photo no. P.11342)

collectors, Putnam sought a more systematic means of building a scientific collection, which at first depended on a web of amateur excavators. Toward the end of the 1800s, the "Peabody Museum Method" was in place, which emphasized scientific rigor and thorough methodology.[14]

This approach helped to transform the collecting of cultural objects from entertainment to science, "from delighting in the world's strange offerings ... to an attempt to master and control the world's diversity through new forms of conceptualization."[15] With the 1903 expedition, Putnam wanted both to build the museum's collection with wonderful things and to conduct an expedition grounded in scientific exactitude.

The invitation to explore for "a few weeks" soon turned into plans for a four-month expedition. A budget was submitted to Putnam in early April, titled "Estimate for four month's expedition to Ripley, Chautauqua Co., Cattaraugus Reservation and Alleghany Reservation, all in New York State":[16]

Salary M. R. Harrington @ 50.00 per mo.	$200.00
[Salary] A. C. Parker @ 40.00 per mo.	$160.00
Provisions @ 15.00 per mo.	$ 60.00
Cartage	$ 10.00
Transportation, etc.	$ 45.00
Land rent and digging rights	$ 15.00
Photographic supplies	$ 10.00
	$500.00
Outfit	
"Manhattan" Camera, a good, modern machine	$25.00
Photographic outfit	$10.00
Tent and accessories	$15.00
Camp outfit, including chests	$10.00

M. R. Harrington [and] A. C. Parker

Using the Peabody Museum's Henry C. Warren Fund, Putnam sent the first of a series of checks—for sixty dollars—to Harrington for supplies to be purchased.[17] By the evening of May 1, 1903, the two young researchers were on a train heading west. For Harrington, it was his first trip into the Seneca heartland, although it certainly would not be his last. For Parker, it was the first day of an exciting scientific journey that would, as he perhaps dreamed, launch his career. But the trip was more than an expedition for him: it was also a homecoming.

A Very Fine Earthwork

Just as Lewis Henry Morgan's ethnography on the Iroquois had been a Parker family affair, the 1903 field season would also come to depend on

Arthur's relations. Unlike Morgan, who had the good fortune and luxury of a tightly knit Parker clan all situated in one place, Arthur was in a more tenuous situation because the Parker family was now spread thin. The generation of Arthur's grandparents was no more—Ely, Nicholson, Caroline, and Levi had passed on in the mid-1890s. Arthur and his own parents had been urbanites, living just outside New York City for more than a decade.

Some aunts and uncles still remained on the Cattaraugus Reservation, though. Arthur and Raymond used Minnie C. Parker's and Sherman Parker's addresses for receiving mail at various points that summer.[18] And it would be Arthur who would identify the expedition's focal point, a buried fort just a stone's throw from his childhood home. As Harrington would later write, "To Mr. Parker is due the credit of furnishing the information which [led] to the selection of this particular locality for exploration, and it was his knowledge of the region that made possible the speedy discovery of a suitable site upon which to work."[19] Arthur, too, would later relate to colleagues that the summer's ethnographic work was helped by his family connections.[20]

The first weekly report to Putnam came from Harrington on May 8, 1903.[21] Harrington's exuberance saturates the page as he emphasizes the photogeneity of the sites as well as the abundance and beauty of the objects already discovered. He details how after arriving at Cattaraugus they examined many sites on the reservation, but eventually identified "a very fine earthwork which will show well in a photograph or model." They first placed a number of small test pits—"post holes"—into the site and soon discovered that cultural materials were in a stratum about a foot thick, with the uppermost layer disturbed from plowing, but the lower layer intact.[22] Harrington explained further that they had secured permission from the landowner to investigate the site and had begun excavating a thirty-five-by-eight-foot trench, then he gave a list of the objects discovered thus far:

> many stone points
> broken pottery pipe
> much decorated and plain broken pottery
> animal bones
> adult skeleton in poor condition
> fine pottery vessel (broken with same)
> adult skeleton in fair condition
> absolutely *perfect flawless pottery vessel*, beautiful shape, found with same

View of the Silverheels Site, 1903. The man in the distance is probably Parker.
(© 2008 Harvard University, Peabody Museum 2004.24.2931)

    infant skeleton with broken small pot and a few European trade beads
    a skeleton as yet partly uncovered
    a pottery vessel that can be restored
    engraved perforated tablet with incised figure of man
    celts
    charred corn, etc. etc.

"The site has been a fort of the Ka Kwa or Erie tribe shortly after the coming of the first white traders, who doubtless furnished the beads found with the skeleton," Harrington continued, referring to a group of people who lived around Lake Erie up until the mid-1600s and were closely allied with and eventually joined the Senecas neighboring to the east. "All the other objects found here are aboriginal." Even after signing off, Harrington seemingly couldn't help but add in his uneven handwriting: "Saturday P.S. *Another* skeleton found."

    The two archaeologists set up their field camp adjacent to the earthwork, as indicated by maps they would later draw. Young adventurers on a shoestring budget, Parker and Harrington piled their equipment in one tent and shared another tent except for when the rain made camp life unbearable, in which case they would retreat to a nearby boardinghouse.[23] Although they never complained about their situation—and indeed they seemingly relished it—a year later Harrington would mention to Putnam, "Parker and I found great difficulty in caring for the specimens in the two [tents] we had last year as it was; for we had to find some place for our trunks, our beds, the photographic outfit, the ethnological specimens, the provisions and the dry wood, axe, spades, etc. to say nothing of ourselves."[24]

Sore about Our Digging Up Bones

That Harrington and Parker were excavating human remains did not escape the local Seneca community, which since at least Henry Silverheels's first discovery when he was digging a pit to winter his potatoes, had been protecting the cemetery from despoliation. It is not known exactly what was said or what exchanges took place, but some Senecas expressed their displeasure to Parker and Harrington about the disturbance of the burials. Perhaps the young archaeologists were not altogether surprised, given that the previous year, while excavating on Long Island, they had experienced a similar problem. "The Shinnecock Indians have entered protest against the excavating going on at Sebonae," a brief newspaper article reported in 1902. "The bones of some small papoose were recently unearthed, and word was sent to M. R. Harrington in charge that 'he would lose the friendship of the tribe if he dug up any more bodies.'"[25]

Removing graves was odious to Senecas and other Iroquois because they perceived the excavation of objects and the placement of them in museums as quite literally stealing from the dead.[26] As archaeologist William Engelbrecht, among others, has explained, because Iroquois traditionally believe that a spirit remains with the bones of the deceased, to upset the bones is to threaten unsettling the ancestors. This is a problem for both the deceased and the living they may haunt. "Not surprisingly," Engelbrecht concludes, "Iroquois often view the excavation, study, and curation of skeletons of their ancestors in a negative light."[27] Although these beliefs may not have been expressly articulated to the young researchers, it was nonetheless these beliefs that underpinned Seneca resistance to archaeology.

"You have doubtless received my 1st weekly report by this time," Harrington again wrote to Putnam only several days after his first letter from the Cattaraugus Reservation was mailed. "I wish you would send me that letter of introduction pretty soon. Please make it in the form of a certificate with as much pomp and red tape as possible, to impress the Indians, some of whom are getting sore about our digging up bones. If you could quote a law or a decision that it is not illegal to dig up unmarked pre-historic burials, that would come in handy also." The request for a formal letter of introduction had been made several times previously, the implication being that a fancy-looking letter would quell whatever concerns the Indians might have; the solution, then, involved feigning to an imagined authority, which would presumably silence any dissenters, instead of listening to and addressing the community members' concerns. By the time Harrington wrote this letter—only five days into the work—he and Parker had already excavated thirteen pits, disinterring four adults and two infants.[28]

Although it likely was not illegal to dig on the Cattaraugus Reservation or for that matter in unmarked burials—this was three years before the Antiquities Act of 1906, which would require a permit for digging on federal and Indian lands—Harrington and Parker probably should have secured formal permission from those responsible for the Cattaraugus Reservation. Had they bothered to ask, they likely would have received authorization because Indian agents and others in the Office of Indian Affairs often tacitly or explicitly supported the use of myriad "resources" on reservations.[29] But permission was not always assured. Two field seasons later, in the summer of 1905, when Parker obtained a "lease" from a tribal member to excavate on his land, he wrote to Indian Agent R. B. Weber asking him to "certify" the lease between his museum and "an Indian land holder and make it legal." Weber curtly responded with just two sentences: "I can only say that leases of reservation lands require approval of Congress, and the President, to be effective. I have no jurisdiction in the matter."[30]

The Senecas' objections must have provoked a crisis for Parker. Here he was returning to the reservation—home—after a decade, with only a few visits in between, undoubtedly proud of his accomplishments, proud that he was being paid to study and preserve Indian history by one of the most prominent anthropological institutions of early-twentieth-century America, and within days of his putting shovel to earth a portion of the Cattaraugus community made plain their displeasure: they did not want

Vast Unexplored Treasure Fields   73

The walls and ditch of the Double Walled Site. The man in the foreground may be Parker. (© 2008 Harvard University, Peabody Museum 2004.24.3155)

Parker disturbing their ancestors. The crisis Parker had to resolve was the clash between Seneca concerns for the dead and an archaeological science that dismissed all claims of legitimacy other than its own. The crisis thus must have been not only political (*could* he ensure the excavations would continue), but also moral (*should* he continue the excavations into the burials). Parker wrote the next letter to Putnam: his decision was perfectly clear.

After itemizing the most recent finds—including four new burials, three of which were children—Parker reported, "Most of the Indians are friendly and much interested and have told us of a number of sites." He and Harrington were led to an unrecorded site with a double-walled earthwork. But then he added, "Some of the Indians are angry and jealous of our work. These are the more ignorant class—and will be probably silenced by some official looking document which Raymond suggested." With this letter, Parker committed himself to the scientific endeavor of his age, a work that would unfold with social and political blinders. In closing, he emphasized again the scientific promise of their work.

"Our prospects are splendid," he wrote, "and if what we have found is any indication we shall send back a good showing."[31]

These events would set a pattern in Parker's professional life; they set in place a moral foundation that dictated that science was the penultimate pursuit. All other claims that impeded science would have to be belittled and dismissed: *silenced*, as he wrote. If Parker seems cruelly indifferent to his own community—which, on the contrary, he cared a great deal about—it is important to recall that in the early 1900s there was no theoretical or methodological model that would have allowed him to balance scientific inquiry equitably with a community's deeply held concerns.

Nevertheless, the consequences of such decisions is manifest not only in Parker's life, but in the Northeast's development of archaeology, which would continue for decades as if science had an inherent right to Indian burials. To this day, many Northeast tribes continue to fight battles over the control of ancestral burials. As Richard W. Hill Sr. has remarked, the argument of right that archaeologists have used to excavate "unmarked" burials discriminates against many Native peoples who do not traditionally use markers recognizable to most Euro-Americans. "We do not believe in the use of permanent headstones to mark the graves of our ancestors, but state law makes a distinction between cemeteries and unmarked burials," Hill explains. "Our burial sites deserve to be considered hallowed ground whether they are marked or not. There has been a double standard in dealing with our people and non-Native remains. Non-Native grave sites are often afforded more protection than Native burials. . . . Our dead relatives deserve the same right to an eternal resting place as do all other races and religions."[32] It is sadly ironic that Arthur C. Parker, the first Native American archaeologist, working in his own community, did not challenge this legacy of conflict and the scientific tradition of callous disrespect.

Several days after Parker's letter was sent, an extravagant "letter of introduction" on Harvard letterhead with a raised seal came from Putnam. It read:

THIS IS TO CERTIFY
That the holder of this document, Mr. M. R. Harrington, is representing the Peabody Museum of American Archaeology and Ethnology, a department of Harvard University, and is carrying on an exploration for the museum, assisted by Mr. A. C. Parker.

All the specimens collected during the exploration and any objects given to Messrs. Raymond and Parker will be sent to the Peabody Museum, where they will be carefully preserved, properly labeled and catalogued, and placed on an exhibition for all time.

Any aid or courtesy extended to Messrs. Raymond and Parker will be highly appreciated and thankfully acknowledged.

F. W. Putnam
Professor of American Archaeology and Ethnology, and Curator of
  the Peabody Museum,
Harvard University[33]

The letter seemingly worked to quiet the conflict. "We have had no trouble with the Indians, and all except a few sore-heads have a 'good heart' toward us," Harrington responded to Putnam several days later, unsubtly belying his disparagement of Seneca concerns. "I expect no trouble whatsoever." The Senecas likely interpreted the letter as a permit—because it was possibly presented to them as such, with Parker himself misleadingly referring to the letter as a "permit" in a note to Putnam. Parker soon wrote to Putnam again, concurring with Harrington's appraisal that the crisis had passed: "We have gained the full confidence and friendship of many whose influence is valuable and trust all will be plain sailing."[34]

A Great Mass of Wonderful Material

Parker once wrote a short essay titled "American Anthropology, Its Scope and Its Problems," likely thoughts put to paper in 1902.[35] Even at age twenty-one, he displayed the quintessential Parker writing style: the essay is as intelligent as it is passionate. Importantly, this essay gives us a sense of what motivated Parker in his work and sheds light on his vision for anthropology—a vision that, like his writing style, would be with him throughout his life. In it, he posits that anthropology is at base a historical science that examines all cultural phenomena to illuminate humanity's evolution, both its unity and diversity.

"One of the most fascinating studies in the world is history," the essay begins, "its great aims [are] to delineate the evolution of man from the dawn of society, to enlightenment, to set forth his struggles for some unknown higher thing, to show his mistakes and his successes that posterity may profit." However, because history as conceptualized in the early 1900s depended on written documents, it is necessarily incomplete as such. Anthropology fills the gaps between those texts that document the human experience and then also extends back into the ages in which writing had yet to emerge.

Parker observes that our imaginations—myths and fables—previously filled in these gaps. That is to say, our conceptions are often factually wrong, and so we must instead depend on an independent and objective science to truly understand our origins. "Man's conception of his primeval propagations has been obscure and confusing," he states. "Anthropology supplants history and myth and drawing its data from archaeology tells us the scientist's version of the story." Parker, as was his wont, tends toward sycophancy and compliments the progress already made. "Scientific investigation in Europe began somewhat earlier than in America, but within our own lands, within the last 20 years it has taken tremendous strides guided by such men as Cushing, Powell, and Brenton," he writes. "American Anthropology took its rank as a pure science and under such masters as Holmes, Starr and Putnam its position is assured. The universities of Chicago, of Harvard and Pennsylvania have adopted courses in the branch and are turning out skilled men for the new profession."

This emerging science defined itself by disregarding dataless *curios*, instead focusing on *specimens* with scientific integrity. "Curios have been relegated to the store room and cellar," Parker boldly opines. "They are of no value. Only a specimen with complete data now finds a place on a Museum shelf, for it tells a story. It satisfies scientific inquiry instead of only as curiosity." Nevertheless, Parker cannot completely escape the language of antiquarianism, for these specimens are treasures to be pursued and cherished: "Both of the American continents are vast unexplored treasure fields, full of the richest material for the anthropologist." And in another section he expands further: "While Anthropology is engaged in solving the problem it is bringing to light a great mass of wonderful material. It is reconstructing the lives and times of races who flourished before Columbus was. From fire pit or sacrificial mound are brought domestic materials, their fabric and their thread, and even charred food of all kinds is brought to light. There is a certain fascination about the science which holds its devotee spell bound for he deals in the tools and the trinkets of tribes of men who lived when mankind was in his infancy." These statements emphasize further why it was difficult for Parker to see the Silverheels cemetery as little more than scientific treasures that rightly belonged to the noble scholar—even though on some level he must have realized that his anthropological prizes were also the earthly remains of his own ancestors.

In Parker's view, an anthropologist is a polymath in a pith helmet, for, he emphasizes, the anthropologist "must record the languages of native peoples, study their customs, religions, and folk lore. The Anthropologist is at once supposed to be philologist, ethnologist, and archaeologist, a botanist, zoologist, and numerologist, a photographer and an artist, and most of all a diplomat, a scholar, and a laborer." Such an image reflected no doubt how Parker already saw himself by 1902: an aspiring polyhistor dedicated to the mysteries of human society. It is little wonder that he embraced his charges in the 1903 expedition: with every interview of a Seneca elder, every bone collected and photographed, every day that the stubborn mud had to be scrubbed from under fingernails, Parker no doubt believed himself one step closer to being a full-fledged anthropologist.

"But of what use is all his work?" Parker rhetorically asks of the anthropologist. "His labor is to solve the riddle of man in America, and all his archaeological and ethnological material goes to shed light upon the two great problems, practically one—the unity or diversity of prehistoric man in America and his origin on the continent, for these questions have never been solved." To conceptualize human history, he asserts that a framework of evolution is needed, thus again aligning himself with Putnam. It is through evolution that we can understand history and, indeed, the questions at the heart of human history. "Anthropology leads back as far as traces of man are found and pictures him in all the successive stages of his evolution and brings them within the light of history." He adds, "Still, Anthropology has not finished its mission. It still is asking whence, whether, and *what* is man?"

The Silverheels Site

The excavations at the Silverheels Site proceeded by way of a series of trenches placed adjacent to one another in the ancient village, which was situated on the edge of a terrace, more than thirty feet straight above a marshy bend in the floodplain of Cattaraugus Creek. Once fortified with an earthen embankment and wood palisade, the site was by 1903 visible only as "a nearly obliterated curved bank of earth" and a scattering of pottery, lithics, ground stone, and fire-cracked rock on the surface.[36]

The first trench was abandoned, as the field notebook kept by Harrington and Parker relates: "May 5, 1903, Along the Reservation Road on the Cattaraugus Reserve, Chaut. Co. N.Y. On the H. Silverheels property 1½ miles from Irving, a trial trench was dug parallel with the bluff but abandoned because not warranted by indications."[37] A new trench—labeled Trench 1—was begun, running east to west, and almost immediately the first pit was discovered, layered in stained earth and charcoal and containing pottery fragments, lithic debitage, and fish bones. More pits were soon found in the trench, and within the first few weeks the two men recovered arrow points, whole pots, a celt, a clay dog figurine, animal bones, charred corn kernels, blue and red trade beads, wampum beads, burned wood, sheet copper, an iron knife, and a serpentine pipe carved into the shape of an owl.

The name for the ancient village was first given rather offhandedly, announced by Parker in a letter to Putnam after the first full week of excavations. "During the week first passed we have obtained some very interesting specimens on the Silverheels site, on Cattaraugus Reserve," he wrote, although he and others would also occasionally call it the "Silverhill Site."[38] Harrington would later explain that the name was coined in tribute to Henry Silverheels, who had first come upon the fort and burial ground: "In a low knoll forming part of the embankment through perhaps natural, stands the house of the late Rev. Henry Silverheels, an Indian preacher of some note, now occupied by his daughter and half-breed son-in-law, John Kennedy, who works the land within and about the ancient enclosure. We named the earthwork the 'Silverheels Site' in honor of its former owner."[39]

Over the course of the thirteen-week field season, Parker and Harrington would excavate thirteen trenches, some taking several weeks, but others only several days. The two labored six days a week, taking breaks only on Sundays, holidays, and rain days. Over the course of the summer, they excavated about 6,325 square feet—an area larger in size than one and a half basketball courts—digging as deep as 5 feet.

Although field notes and letters often refer to the site as an earthwork, fort, or fortification, the young archaeologists must have known within the first week of excavations that their trenches were situated over a burial ground. By the end of the summer, they would excavate, study, and gather scores of human bodies; they did not move their trenches to different areas of the site to expose architecture or refuse middens, but rather left them at the end of the terrace where day after day they exposed human remains and funerary objects. This focus on the graves was the norm of the age, for graves provided the two things archaeologists of the early twentieth century wanted most: tantalizing artifacts and human bodies. Objects were desired to pack the museum shelves, and the bodies were needed to elucidate the history of the Indian race. Historian Robert E. Bieder notes that as early as the 1700s French medical scientists had begun to transmute the body into scientific object: "Depersonalized and desacralized, the body became data. It was redefined symbolically, politically, and scientifically and was seen more as a specimen for observation than as the temple of the soul."[40]

By the 1830s, American researchers sought to explore the temperament and intelligence of the different races: not surprisingly, their findings perfectly matched social preconceptions of racial hierarchies. In 1839, Samuel G. Morton published *Crania americana*, which attempted to demonstrate scientifically the inferiority of Indians (among other races). Aside from the political implications of such findings, a dire consequence for Indians was the looting of their gravesites. With the flowering of craniology came a need for craniums to study: army officers, Indian agents, traders, and others were enlisted to gather Indian skulls from both ancient and recent graves. By the 1860s, scientists began taking an interest in the whole body as an indicator of evolution. "The short forearm of whites, as compared with those of blacks and Indians, was seen as a mark of evolutionary advancement," Bieder explains. "The bodies and bones of Indians became condensed stories of evolution, inferiority, and migration."[41] Early anthropology museums with their self-appointed missions to understand and document human evolution soon became mausoleums—the repositories of Indian remains. By the 1990s, it was estimated that in the storage rooms of just those museums subject to NAGPRA lay fragments of over two hundred thousand Indian bodies.[42]

As is evident from their letters, neither Parker nor Harrington conceived of their work as sacrilege, but rather in opposite terms, as science. For them, science was not about the testing of hypotheses, experimentation, and validation; it was about systematizing how archaeological objects were collected and studied. They achieved this goal by methodically laying out trenches, keeping detailed notes and photographs, and carefully labeling objects for their permanent preservation. As Putnam wrote in his first letter to Harrington that summer,

> Keep on sending the boxes as fast as you can, a few at a time, for the specimens are much safer here than in your camp. While you, of course, label everything from Grave 1, Grave 2, etc.; or Ashpit 1, 2, etc.,

I think objects obtained from some grave or some ash pit should be sent at the same time, to avoid possible misplacement or loss. Also whenever you make a print from one of your negatives, number it to correspond with your notes. You have sent me three prints of skeletons as found with associated objects, but you have not marked either of them as to grave or locality. This you should do, no matter if you have marked duplicates to keep with your notes. I always like to have everything of the kind labeled and I wish you to be very particular about labeling everything as found, and not trust to your memory for a single hour.[43]

The process of recording was the means by which objects moved beyond the state of mere thing of curiosity, a *curio*. The fact that fragments of an adult skeleton were excavated in Pit 99, thirty-six feet from the beginning of Trench 13, at a depth of thirty-one inches, was not hugely important for the analysis of the site; it predominately became a way of exhibiting precision in an analysis. Thus, detailing objects didn't help with archaeological interpretation so much as transform Indian objects into scientific specimens.

Assisted by Parker

The "permit" that Putnam sent to Harrington on May 18 served its immediate purpose of resolving the conflict the young archaeologists were having with the disquieted Senecas. The letter was also important because it announced and advertised the nature of the expedition itself. As Isabelle Burtan notes in her thesis "Silences at Silverheels," with this letter Putnam's vision for the Peabody Museum was rendered unambiguous, "to preserve, categorize, label, and display 'for all time': a grandiose vision of what a museum should be."[44] As such, the letter was an announcement of the project's power relations, a document to define the relationship among the community, the museum, and the field archaeologists. In this light, it is perhaps not entirely surprising that neither Harrington nor Parker was happy with Putnam's presentation of the expedition.

First, Harrington was displeased that the letter refers to him as "Mr. Raymond" twice, a peculiar error given that Harrington had worked for Putnam for four years by this point. "I received your very welcome letter and the document in due course," Harrington wrote after receiving the letter. "I am sorry to say there is an error in the letter. It speaks of me as Mr. M. R. Harrington in the beginning, which is correct, but it speaks of Messrs. Raymond and Parker in two places thereafter instead of Harrington and Parker. Will the error impair the value of the document?" Putnam replied three days later, "I am sorry that I did not notice the mistake in typewriting the document sent to you; but Miss Mead [Putnam's secretary] has made another copy which I send to you enclosed."[45]

Harrington notably said nothing of Parker's complaint. It might be that Parker said nothing to Harrington, keeping to himself a brewing anger. It might be too that Harrington did not show Parker the "permit" until the middle of June, although as observed earlier, on May 30 Parker indicated to Putnam that the storm over the burials had passed. Whatever the case may be, on June 12 Parker boldly—*boldly* given that he was but a twenty-one-year-old tyro on his first major expedition for one of the period's most preeminent anthropologists—reported his grievance:

My dear Professor:
In regard to a little personal matter; In the paper which you sent Raymond I notice you name me as an assistant. When I considered the proposition of the expedition I understood that I was to be a co-laborator. I indeed dislike to be named an assistant. The reason is this; I had known of the sites on the reservation and located many myself and I guided Raymond to the one on which we are now working having known it as an Indian site for years. We both do the same work and Raymond recognizes me as his co-laborator and for my future benefit I should like to be officially known as such. Of course I don't care as far as the "paper" you sent goes but I dislike the collection to read "M. R. Harrington assisted by A. C. Parker." The more just way I think would be to put "and" between the names.

I merely make mention of this matter because of the name "assistant" in the credentials you sent. I really have little doubt that I shall be called a "co-laborator," but I was afraid the mistake through oversight might be carried out in future papers.

It is with exceeding reluctance that I mention this little thing but for my future success I have deemed it wise to do so. Trusting that this may be after all but false alarm.

I am, Respectfully,
Arthur C. Parker[46]

It is difficult to imagine that Parker at this moment was not thinking of his granduncle Ely S. Parker, famously known as Lewis H. Morgan's informant. Morgan himself wrote that his early work on the Iroquois could not have been completed without Ely's collaboration, insights, and assistance, and yet it was Morgan who became the celebrated anthropologist, and Ely would remain the inconspicuous collaborator. Arthur must have been asking himself at that moment in June 1903 whether he would be considered a bona fide anthropologist or only an Indian informant. This letter lays his resolve bare: he wanted to be an anthropologist. Several weeks later Putnam sent the letter of introduction—revised again—to read, "That the holders of this document, Mr. M. R. Harrington and Mr. A. C. Parker, are representing the Peabody Museum of American Archaeology and Ethnology."

Nonetheless, Parker's concern was not misplaced. Although the Peabody Museum's ledger consistently records Silverheels materials as collected by "M. R. Harrington and A. C. Parker," some of the accession cards credit the collector as "Harrington, asst. by A. C. Parker."[47] A summary of American archaeology published in 1905 reported only, "Mr. R. Harrington: work in New York (Cattaraugus Res.), 1902–04."[48] Later writers similarly mention the research done at Silverheels as if it were only Harrington's endeavor.[49] Even Parker's biographer, historian Joy Porter, reports, "Since Parker had grown up there [in Cattaraugus], Harrington selected him as his field assistant, and he spent time from that summer to the next assisting on several expeditions in southwestern New York."[50] Although Harrington and Parker shared the work equally, and Parker was indeed instrumental in "arranging" for the site to be excavated, it is significant that Harrington was paid a higher salary than Parker—fifty dollars per month compared to Parker's forty.[51] Was this disparity a mark of experience? Harrington, after all, had formally worked for Putnam a year longer. Or was it a subtle mark of racism? It is not farfetched to surmise that when the fieldwork first began, both Putnam and Harrington on some level thought of Parker as more Indian informant than aspiring archaeologist.

The seeming disjunction between race and profession would plague Parker for much of his life. In the years immediately after 1903, he would often be called "Dr. Parker" and "Professor Parker"—titles that in truth he had not yet earned. So far as can be told, however, he did not correct such errors, and it seems he encouraged them. I do not think he committed these acts of omission because he was a dishonest man, but because it must already have been so difficult for him to prove himself—to prove that an Indian could be a scholar—that he must have appreciated whatever symbolic help he could get, even if the help came in the form of confusion. Parker desperately wanted people to believe the patina of his life matched the bedrock beneath, the great man within.

The Search for Pure Truth

Parker often wrote of how science provided for him not merely a professional occupation, but more, a guiding moral value. The merits of science became a part of his life at an early age. "In the early [eighteen] nineties I browsed in the laboratories of the great New York physician, Dr. Salisbury," Parker would reveal in 1939, "looking at his skulls and other anatomical specimens, wondering what caused man to have such strange fragments in his framework."[52] In his late teens, when he had moved to New York City, he had been able to expand this interest with an introduction to formal museum work: "Then came an even more fortunate time when I was permitted to examine the skeletal material at the American Museum of Natural History, to discuss the 'bones' with Bogoras and Hrdlicka, and finally to have some systematic guidance from Professor F. W. Putnam of the Peabody Museum of Harvard." Such experiences also help explain why by the time he was unearthing graves at Cattaraugus, he was well used to handling human bone.

Parker consistently emphasized, even decades later, how formative these early brushes with anthropology were for him. But he also recognized that the ministry could have been a viable career and pointed him in a direction that would enable him to see anthropology not just as a hobby, but as a much more meaningful endeavor. "These were the years of the sinking in of ideas, of the molding of a career which was much more tinctured by philosophical as well as scientific thought," he wrote. "But for a while philosophical considerations swept me from my future course. I investigated philosophy and religion and soon began to wonder why the pursuit of pure truth should not be enough, with all labels and departmentalized names stripped away." Thus, for Parker, anthropology was an expansive science whose goal is nothing less than to reveal truth itself.

Perhaps in part because of his religious background, Parker pursued anthropology with the zeal of a missionary, a convert's unbendable faith and confidence. His interest in religion, as he wrote, was more philosophical than spiritual, but his writing is at times inflected with religious imagery. Even before he arrived in Cattaraugus in the late spring of 1903, he had found one theme that fused scientific integrity with moral righteousness, a theme that would stay with him throughout his life. Private collecting of artifacts, he would proclaim, is a terrible transgression, a crime against the moral code of science.[53]

A Sin Against Science

Some four months before Parker and Harrington landed in Cattaraugus, Parker wrote a brief letter to Putnam about the proposed expedition:

> My dear Professor:
> In reference to my doing archaeological work, it would be of great-advantage if I could have a letter of introduction or explanation from you dated at either New York or Cambridge. I think you will see how it would be a great help in securing attention and courtesy. It might be well to explain to you that I am not trying to make a private collection nor do I wish to retain any fine specimen which I might discover, on the contrary I wish to turn such specimens and all specimens over to you subject to your disposal for I think private collections a sin against science.
>
> An announcement of your department at Harvard would also be duly appreciated. I know that you are very busy but trust that my request may not appear impertinent.
>
> Respectfully,
> Arthur C. Parker[54]

It was prescient of Parker to anticipate that locals would charge him with excavating for his own profit. However, he was wrong to think that a letter from Putnam on Harvard letterhead would protect him from such rumors and allegations. Even after Putnam had sent the letter of introduction—the "permit"—Parker wrote on May 30 to say that a new problem had emerged for him and Harrington. "Most of the Indians here are fairly well educated and some wealthy as farmers go, and their objections to us seem to be that we are making our fortunes—taking out thousands of dollars worth of 'relics.'"[55]

This problem was compounded by the fact that Parker and Harrington were themselves commodifying the very things that they told the Senecas held no commercial value. Ironically, on the very day that Parker mentioned to Putnam that the locals believed they were making fortunes, Harrington wrote to Putnam asking the professor if he would like to buy two collections. "Mr. Herman C. Markham, a friend of mine here, has let me have his local collection to sell. It was all picked up just west of Ann Arbor on and near his farm, and is a typical collection of the stone art of this vicinity, illustrating practically all the materials and even the rare forms. You can have these, and a few things I have picked up for $10.00. I enclose a list. Do you care for them?" Then, in the next paragraph he added, "My cousin down in southern Tennessee has shipped me a lot of archaeological material and has opened a mound, but the specimens have not yet reached me. Would you be interested in these?"[56] Strangely, for Harrington and Parker there was no contradiction between their buying and selling of artifacts and their admonishments against private collecting.

The difference from Parker's perspective was that he (and Harrington and Putnam) were collecting for science, to preserve and exhibit artifacts "for all time," to borrow Putnam's bold phrase. Hence, Parker was not against collecting per se, but rather against collecting that was done only for personal profit. Nevertheless, the people at Cattaraugus in 1903 likely did not understand this fine line between institutional and personal collecting, and it was probably not fully articulated to them. Indeed, the line was often blurred as Parker and the others both railed against the destruction done to sites by private collectors and yet contradictorily encouraged private collecting by purchasing looted objects, objects with obscure proveniences, and objects without scientific merit.

"There is an old Indian here," Harrington wrote Putnam on May 10, "who has four celts, an adze of stone, two *old* wooden corn-pestles, and an old wooden spoon with a bird figure on the handle. He also has a turtle shell rattle half made and part of an iron tomahawk. He wants $5.00 for the lot. Shall I get them?"[57] The old man was George D. Jimerson—Dondeh or Tahadondeh—who, Parker noted, "lived on flats back of Silverheels farm. He was a mystic and a medicine man."[58] Several weeks later Putnam replied to Harrington in the affirmative. "I think it is desirable for you to buy anything of special interest that the Indians offer at moderate prices." Then Putnam revealed that the purchase of such items was less for science and more for diplomacy. "The several articles you have mentioned which you can get for $5 you would better secure. More for the sake of doing something to help secure the good will of the Indians than anything else; although some of the old things, like the spoon and wooden pestle will be important to add to our collection. But do not pay high prices for things, and buy very, very little, unless you feel that we should have the specimens or that it would be a good thing to buy it for the above reason."[59] This instruction belies Putnam's interest in purchasing objects for building up his institution's collections: as early as the 1880s, Putnam, as anthropologist James E. Snead has documented, "cultivated residents of important archaeological regions to conduct local fieldwork and shop the results to Cambridge, reserving for himself and his small staff the responsibility of analyzing the new collections."[60] Parker soon reported that the items were purchased for five dollars, and for good measure they threw into the deal a cowboy hat he had gotten from New York City.[61]

Yet again, on July 1, Harrington conveyed that he could buy several more items, including a large turtle shell rattle and two masks of the Senecas' False Face Society. "All of which are used in ceremonial dances," he wrote. "I can also get many other things used by the Seneca Indians of the Pagan district of this Reservation." In mid-August, the masks were gotten and sent to Cambridge.[62] And even as the archaeological fieldwork was coming to a close, Parker was still offering Putnam more ethnological objects for purchase, including "a pack strap in process of manufacture, commenced 60 years ago by an Indian woman born in 1737. It is woven in moose hair patterns which I can read. It is certainly a fine ethnological specimen."[63]

Although the majority of objects first purchased on the expedition were ethnological, after the summer more artifacts from archaeological contexts were purchased. To the Senecas supplying the researchers, there likely was little difference between these anthropological categories. One supplier for Parker and Harrington in later years was John Kennedy, Henry Silverheels's son-in-law, who lived on the property during the 1903 expedition and was helpful to the archaeologists. "Last night John Kennedy on whose land we are working struck some bones while pulverizing down on the Cattaraugus Creek flood-plain, on a slight rise of ground," Harrington recorded in the field notes for May 26. "These were part of the contents of an ossuary, examined today.... Bones were of all ages, children to old people. Selected bones only were taken."[64] In the next letter to Putnam, Parker mentioned the discovery of the ossuary but made no mention of Kennedy's role in that discovery (although Kennedy is recognized in the final site report).[65]

At the beginning of 1905, Parker wrote to the obsessive and fabulously wealthy collector George G. Heye to offer items in a "splendid collection" that Kennedy had in part procured. Kennedy later wrote directly to Parker, saying that some boxes were waiting for him—presumably with collected artifacts—and he had come across another site while on a hunting trip. He had noticed the soil was black around an embankment and so had started digging, soon finding beads, a knife, pottery, pipes, and copper fragments. "I am going to work there a little," he wrote.[66] We also know from letters that after Parker and Harrington left the Silverheels Site, Kennedy continued to dig the site on his own, with the archaeologists' tacit support.[67]

Several years later, in November 1907, Harrington wrote to Parker asking if he had yet seen John Kennedy's "new collection," and if so, whether it was any good. On Christmas Eve, Parker in turn wrote to Kennedy, rather harshly reprimanding him for mixing up his new position at the New York State Museum and Harrington's work as a "Commercial Ethnologist" in New York City for his own company Covert & Harrington. He emphasized to Kennedy that he had no intention to compete with Harrington, but that he would be ready "to take the relics immediately at your figures." Using the same kind of language in Putnam's 1903 "permit," Parker emphasized that surely Kennedy would "far rather have [his] specimens in the State Capitol where the State can exhibit them" as the "collection would be written up and [he] could have the satisfaction of having a report, illustrated, of them."[68] Parker's presumption was that all people cared about exhibiting, analysis, and publication as much as he did. But Kennedy's main interest was money. He offered the artifacts to Parker because he thought Parker would pay a higher price. Harrington, in a letter written several days later, settled the mess of the "Kennedy Affair," as he called it:

> I had thought of clearing out the place my self (digging), but as I was pressed for time Kennedy agreed to dig with help and sell me the stuff at prices that I could afford to pay. I bought one batch which I have disposed of, and was to buy the present one—the customers were even picked out (before I heard from you). The first I knew of the Sai ya ji's double dealing, was when I heard he had sold you two of the best things. Then, yesterday I got a letter from him saying that he has added 50 percent to his price, and I answered telling him the deal is off. So if you want the stuff—go ahead and get it. I would have

given it up to you before as a courtesy but for my necessity of earning a living. There is nothing in it now for C & H so we take no further interest in it.[69]

Despite Parker's obvious distrust of Kennedy, he still purchased the collection for ninety dollars.[70]

Parker's language remained high-handed through the years: he would not "purchase specimens where complete data is lacking."[71] And yet in 1913 one collector donated two hundred looted artifacts, "four boxes of Indian relics—the cream of my collection," to Parker for his museum's stewardship.[72] Another exchange of letters in that same year suggests that Parker, as New York State archaeologist, purchased for four hundred dollars a salmagundi of artifacts, most with only elusive provenience.[73]

Tales of Vampire Skeletons

As the excavations on the Silverheels farm progressed into the stormy summer of 1903, there was little doubt that the focus of the young archaeologists' efforts was gathering human bodies. Parker's intimation on May 30 that the Senecas' main complaint was that the archaeologists were getting rich seems false or at the least misleading when seen against the backdrop of Sackett's diary, which records that Senecas had first objected to the excavation of the site when Parker was still a child playing along Cattaraugus Creek.

Two decades later, when Parker published his book *Seneca Myths and Folk Tales*, he admitted that the Senecas' disquiet ran deeper than worries over money. "To our camp came many Indian friends who sought to instruct Mr. Harrington and myself in the lore of the ancients," he related about the expedition of 1903. "We were regaled with stories of the falsefaces, of the whirl-winds, of the creation of man, of the death panther, and of the legends of the great bear, but in particular we were blessed with ample store of tales of vampire skeletons, of witches and of folkbeasts, all of whom had a special appetite for young men who dug in the ground for the buried relics of the 'old-time folks.'"[74] One of these storytellers was George D. Jimerson, who must have felt ambivalent about the excavations, considering that he sold objects to the young men and yet also told of vampire skeletons. Years later still, Parker would write that the Seneca homeland was beloved and sacrosanct for Senecas: "To them it was a holy land where the bones of their ancestors were buried."[75]

Even in 1903 Parker likely understood the deep social and spiritual value of human gravesites to the Senecas. As he grew up, his family surely related the importance of the rituals of burials, and he himself knew something of death, having been old enough to witness the passing of Caroline Parker Mountpleasant, Ely Parker, and Nicholson Parker, among others. At the least, he had read Morgan's *League of the Ho-de-no-sau-nee, or Iroquois* and so had learned that "respect for the dead" was a key element of Seneca faith. Senecas, like all Haudenosaunee, Morgan reported, incorporated complex burial rites, including inhumation and a practice of leaving the body exposed before gathering the bones and placing them together with the remains of other deceased family members. The gravesite itself remained vital because the spirit could revisit its body. "As before observed," Morgan wrote, "the spirit was supposed to linger for a time about the body, and perhaps revisit it. In consequence of this belief, a superstitious custom prevailed of leaving a slight opening in the grave, through which it might reënter its former tenement. To this day, among a portion of the Iroquois, after the body has been deposited in a coffin, holes are bored through it for the same purpose."[76]

Despite this knowledge, Parker remained impervious to the dead. His callousness came in part from his scientific training, which dictated that human remains were specimens above all else. But he also had easily adopted the views of his era that drew a distinction between Indian specimens and Anglo remains. "We have been digging up old Indians for the last six weeks and are having great luck," he wrote in a 1907 letter. "We find lots of 'em too. Rate of ten a week. They are good Injuns too, for you know that they say the only good Indian is a dead one."[77] Because of Parker's own personal history, he was thus strangely writing as much about himself as about the people he was exhuming. Although perhaps such writings illustrate a measure of self-loathing, more to the point they illustrate the degree to which Parker desired to be a bona fide scientist, and scientists of the day—Indian or not—had to see the Indian body as a mere object of study. Parker seemingly felt he had to adopt the scientific norms of his generation even if it came at the price of denigrating his ancestors and himself.

It was this difference in perception of the human body and soul that was at the heart of the conflict between the archaeologists and the local Senecas. For the archaeologists, the objects they were studying were specimens, whereas for the Senecas they were the sacred containers of ancestral spirits. Even after being presented with Putnam's "permit," the Senecas continued to be uneasy about the project. "To-day we were honored by a visit from Bishop Walker, member of the Board of Indian Commissioners or some like board," Parker reported to Putnam a month into the work. "He appeared much interested. The Senecas have great faith in the Bishop and as we were uncovering a skeleton and explaining why we did so and as he approved, our position is absolutely secure, though it may have been for some time past."[78]

5

You Boys Have Dreamed

Notes Made in the Trenches

By the middle of July 1903, Harrington and Parker had fallen into an easy routine. They continued working six days a week, digging pit after pit, conscientiously recording their findings into the field notebook. The notebook today resides in the Peabody Museum's archives, a ginger-colored, cloth-bound notebook, frayed at the corners.[1] On the front of the notebook is a large water stain, faint evidence of the notebook's once doubling as a coaster for a cool drink. On the back of the notebook in large bubble font and underlined is the name "Parker," although the first page dramatically announces in a sprawling handwriting: "Silverheel [sic] Site 1903, Notes made in the Trenches, M. R. Harrington, A. C. Parker, For Peabody Museum, Harvard University, Cambridge, Mass."

The notebook suggests that Parker and Harrington did equal work; of the total 8,854 words in the notebook, Parker wrote 4,322. The notebook also proves that the two dutifully documented their work, and taking Putnam's admonition not to trust anything to memory for even an hour, they wrote increasingly descriptive entries as the summer wore on, as two entries, both penned by Parker, demonstrate:

> *May 9*. Pit 13 in center of Trench 1 at 55 ft from beginning, at 27 inches down was found a skeleton probably male. Skull perfect. In usual crouching head up position. Lower arm bones and hand bones gone. Only a few scattered sherds and chips found in grave dirt. No remains of any object buried with body found. No charcoal above skeleton. PHOTO.

> *July 24*. At 25 ft from the beginning of Trench 10 was found a grave, Pit 75. The top of the skull was 43 inches from the surface. The skeleton was of a male. The bones were in good condition. The skeleton lay on its right side headed west and facing south, and in the usual doubled position. In the right side of the skull at the temple were

Parker excavating a trench at the Silverheels Site in 1903. (© 2008 Harvard University, Peabody Museum 2004.24.2930)

holes, evidently produced anciently by a wound. In the nose was found a long red bead and in one ear were some blue beads. The accompanying objects were near the face, a small pipe of clay on the right arm, 7 large beads of copper, probably native copper. Around the face small blue beads and at the neck long red beads.

The notebook's writing is flatly descriptive, a pretense to the detached, objective coolness befitting two aspiring scientists. But in the letters to Putnam, the excitement of discovery—even after weeks in the trenches—is palpable. Harrington and Parker continued to talk about how "perfect" this or that object was and to add postscripts to the letters relating the most recent discovery, wanting Putnam to know about every find. The field notes and the camera documented the excavations, which for the excavators defined their work as a scientific endeavor.

As the muggy heat of July arrived and settled over the site, several visitors came to break up the monotony and to add more prestige to the excavations. First came a former U.S. Indian Affairs commissioner, then, wrote Parker, the "President of the *Seneca Nation* visited our 'diggings' and saw us uncover this last named skeleton." By midsummer, the biggest problem for Harrington and Parker was the rain, which made the trenches too muddy to work, prevented the photographic prints from drying, and threatened the artifacts and equipment with mold.[2] They reported rain almost weekly. In typical form, they still managed to make the most of it. "This week our work has been much disturbed by rain but by working between showers we have managed to get somewhat of a showing," Parker proudly wrote to Putnam in one weekly report. "When it was too muddy in the trenches to work we spent our time on the flat below us and made a systematic examination of an old village site. The entire site has been plowed and the rain washed up quantities of pottery and chipped points, broken celts and pitted stones. We also have uncovered four skeletons."[3]

Justice Is All I Ask

I imagine John Kennedy's blood was boiling.[4] He had been hearing rumors all week that the two archaeologists on his land were making a fortune, but he wasn't making a cent, though he was offering plenty of hospitality. He had tried to be friendly to the two researchers, even showing them some bones that he had found down by the creek. He let them live on his land and do their work, spoiling part of his good field. But they kept a polite distance. He especially didn't understand why Arthur was acting that way: Kennedy knew just about all Arthur's family and remembered him growing up not far down the lane. And now when Kennedy went into Irving, those at the general store and men he met in the streets in Gowanda told him that the Harvard folks were taking advantage of him.

Kennedy went out of his house and stormed across the yard to the edge of the terrace at the border of his fields, where the trenches were growing more numerous every week. Harrington was on his hands and knees in a trench, and Parker sat huddled over a notebook beneath the shade of a nearby apple tree. Kennedy paused a moment. They, absorbed in their work, did not notice he was there. He watched as Harrington brushed the dirt away from a skeleton. The body was lying on its left side, with the legs drawn up. The bones were crumbling slightly with each brush, leaving a smear of white mixed with the dark brown earth. The earth smelled rich, like the full scent of wet moss. Slightly above the skeleton was a whole jar and next to that an iron hatchet. Kennedy thought to himself that the things were beautiful, and for a moment he forgot his anger. He continued to watch on as Harrington cleaned off more bones near the head that looked like a wolf's jaw and the upper portion of a large bird, perhaps a blue heron. Then, Harrington stopped and stood up, gazing at the skeleton. Next to the trench lay a mahogany box, from which he took out a camera. Pulling out the contraption's accordion-like back, he paused and pushed a hinge near the camera's small lens.

Kennedy cleared his throat. Harrington turned, surprised to find Kennedy hovering by the trench's side.

"I was in Irving today," Kennedy began with more anger in his voice than he intended. "White folks told me you making a lot of money."

Parker raised his head, listening, though he remained sitting in the shade. "Now, that isn't so . . ." Harrington stuttered before being cut off.

"White folks are saying—they telling me all over—you getting thousands of dollars' worth of stuff out of my land," Kennedy replied. "I ought to get a share of it."

Parker now came over to where the other men were standing. "What are folks saying?" he asked.

"Said I should get three thousand dollars for digging rights," Kennedy said, a tight smile on his lips.

"But even if you sold everything we've dug, separately, it w-w-wouldn't bring more than one hundred dollars," Harrington said, growing visibly upset. He quickly counted up the numbers in his head and realized that three thousand dollars was the equivalent of his salary over five years. "And we've expended much more money than that just getting them!"

"I could dig here myself and get the relics," Kennedy retorted.

"But you never even would have dug here before we came—even if you had suspected the specimens were here," Harrington said. "You're only saying that now because we've come here and done all this work."

"Those relics are worth money," was the reply. "Just today they said they'd give me five dollars for a pipe. White folks want to hire my ground so they can dig. Like you."

Parker interrupted, "But we were here first." He looked at Kennedy with narrowed eyes. "You know that."

"You were, that's right. And it's fine with me if you stay," Kennedy said, "but you should give me what's right."

"When we left Cambridge, we only took fifteen dollars for land rent," Harrington said, "and that's for the whole summer."

Kennedy stared at the ground for a moment, looking at the skeleton, the pot, the hatchet, the animal bones. "That's too little," he said at last, shaking his head. "I want at least twenty-five dollars."

"Well, I'm sorry, John. We just don't have that," Harrington said, but feeling relieved that the price went so quickly from three thousand to twenty-five dollars.

Kennedy thought again a moment and said, "I'll write that Professor Putnam on your permit then. He'll give me what's right. He'll know justice. He knows these relics' worth."

"Well, you go ahead and do that, then," Harrington agreed. "I'll write him too and ask him to give you what's yours."

This exchange we know almost word for word because of letters from Harrington and Kennedy and the field notes Parker was keeping that day. Kennedy did write Putnam, telling the professor, "Justice is all I ask" and thus only for fair payment.[5] (As an aside, Kennedy was himself hardly a man of perfect justice. Parker later wrote: "Black man named Henry Baltimore (a hostler) and his 'gypsy' wife Mary Polo lived near Nicholson Parker; and every now and then in the noisy night old John Kennedy would come from Gowanda, the trading town, and just to show his spite or knowledge of tradition would shout: 'Injun first, white man nex', dog nex', nigger lasht—Whoop.' The next hostler wasn't a negro.")[6] Harrington wrote to Putnam, too, explaining the problem by saying that Kennedy was being tricked by "some jealous white men."[7] Parker largely stayed out of it, although he must have written of the problem to his old family confidante Harriet Maxwell Converse. She wrote to their mutual friend Joseph Keppler that Parker and Harrington had been "driven away from their 'find'" and that "John Kennedy has taken a bribe from some White people who are to drive the boys away"; she also mentioned that if they had requested her assistance when they arrived in Cattaraugus, she "could have asked permission of the council."[8]

Putnam's written response, if any, to the problem is not preserved in the archives, but we know that in the end twenty-five dollars was paid to Kennedy. However, it seems that Kennedy, for this amount, restricted the area the archaeologists could dig in. A sketch map of the site was sent to Putnam; scrawled in Harrington's handwriting next to the map is written, "P.S. John Kennedy is not going to let us dig outside the boundaries of our present trenches, only back of them. The land outside he says has been 'spoken for.'"[9] Kennedy presumably planned to sell the digging rights for the rest of the site to others, and in fact he would later excavate portions of the site to sell its relics.

Parker—perhaps the summer wearing him thin after working and living with Harrington so closely—pinned the blame for the fiasco squarely on Harrington and took the opportunity to promote himself. "The land question has been settled and we have a signed statement from Mr. Kennedy," he wrote to Putnam. "My advice is to *always* secure land in the first place after making a preliminary examination, rent it, paying in advance and then dig. In this way, all trouble would be avoided and should I ever be given the funds of an expedition this would be my policy."[10]

The Bear Clan

Although Parker had articulated a Seneca identity for himself in the years before 1903, he was in fact not a formal member of the tribe because his mother and grandmother were white. This fact situated him in an ambiguous social space where he was neither fully Anglo (having a Seneca patrilineage) nor fully Seneca (having an Anglo matrilineage). Amidst the controversies of his return to his natal home, he received what he must have for many years longed for: adoption into a Seneca clan and the honor of a Seneca name.

"It may interest you to know that I have been made Chief of the Bear Clan by the Tonawanda Band of Senecas," Parker wrote to Putnam in late August. "I need only installation to make my claim good."[11] He was adopted into the clan and, following Seneca lineage laws, was given the name "Gáwasowaneh," a name he started using immediately among close friends such as Joseph Keppler.[12] As anthropologist Elisabeth Tooker explains, "By Iroquois custom, personal names are 'owned' by the matrilineal clans. A child receives a 'baby' name belonging to his clan then 'not in use,' a name that had once belonged to an individual who had died or who had given it up in favor of an 'adult name.'"[13] Parker's new name translated as "Snow Snake," which referred to a game in which long staffs (the snakes) are launched down an icy trough for the greatest distance.[14] Putnam offered his hearty congratulations.[15]

Given the controversies Parker had sparked on the reservation over the course of the summer, it may at first seem peculiar that the Senecas would bestow upon him this sign of acceptance. It is perhaps significant that it was not Cattaraugus, but Tonawanda, a community at

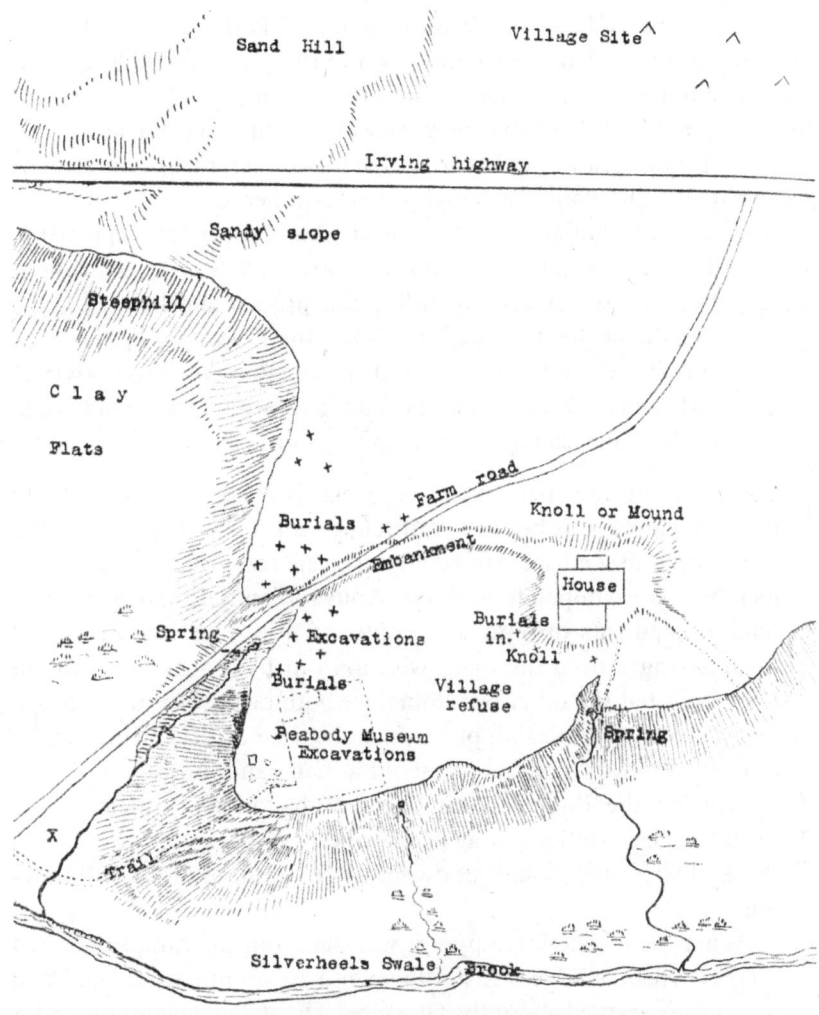

The Silverheels Site, showing the excavations on the end of the terrace. (Adapted from Parker, *The Archaeological History of New York*, bulletin nos. 235 and 210, printed with permission of the New York State Museum)

which Parker was not excavating graves, that accepted him into the Bear Clan. At the same time, Parker was also recording folk medicine and folk tales from a Tonawanda man named Gahweh Seneca, who perhaps helped introduce him to the community, and it was at Tonawanda that the Parker family had long held strong connections because William and

Elizabeth Parker, Ely S. Parker, and Nicholson Parker had lived much of their lives there.[16] It is thus important to recognize that at least some Senecas embraced Parker and wanted him to succeed. It is also likely that accepting Parker into a clan was a way of trying to bring him closer to the community, a way of ensuring that he would remain connected to his birthplace and would keep their interests at heart.

In addition to initiation into the Bear Clan, Parker also reported to Putnam that he was admitted into the False Face Society, a religious organization whose "object was to benefit, protect and help all living things of earth," as he described it.[17] More than twenty years later, he would write about how this came about, a scene that involved both Harrington and George D. Jimerson, the man from whom they had bought various artifacts in exchange for five dollars and a cowboy hat:

> One cold autumn night many years ago Jisgogo [Harrington] and myself lay upon our bunks in our tent on an Indian reservation. We were weary after a hard day's effort to locate some ancient pit deposits in which we hoped to find numerous Indian relics, such as pipes, pots, implements of bone and knives of flint. Our feet were tired from having shoved the spade with too much enthusiasm. Without knowing what the other was doing, we both began to move our feet as if dancing. This was simply to relax the tired muscles. Then one of us began in a low tone to sing an old Indian dance tune.
>
> Outside the door sat our friend Tahadondeh [Jimerson], or Wood's Edge. He looked at us and thoughtfully watched our feet. Presently he came in and sat down, while we snoozed off, still moving our feet.
>
> When we awoke for supper it was dark, but the campfire blazed merrily. Wood's Edge was still there and apparently troubled. "You boys have dreamed about the false faces," he stated. "Now you've got to join the False Face Company. You needn't look so dumb; I saw your feet dancing. Now I've got to make a mask for you both." Upon inquiry we learned that when one dreams of the mysterious masks and dances in his sleep, the power of the faces is upon you.[18]

Although Parker almost seems to make light of this sign of acceptance, it must have been the crowning moment of the summer. The timing of the initiations was hugely significant because they came just as his career in archaeology seemed ready to be launched. With the summer coming to a close and his first expedition completed, he must have felt that he could have the two things he wanted most. He could pursue a career in archaeology and keep hold of his Seneca heritage. He could be himself—an anthropologist and an Indian.

The *Buffalo Express* Desires a Story

As the summer wore on, the presence of the two archaeologists on the reservation was hardly a secret. Visitors included high-profile community members, and as John Kennedy related, even Anglos in the surrounding towns were well aware of the excavations. The return of a Parker under the visible tutelage of Harvard University surely offered plenty of grist for the local rumor mill.

A new dilemma thus presented itself to Harrington and Parker: Should they actively promote their work or try as best they could to keep it quiet? On the one hand, they feared that publicity would bring unwanted attention to their work, which was already stirring up controversy; on the other hand, they bemoaned that the locals did not understand the true intent of their research. Furthermore, they worried that others would take credit for their efforts.

"Shall we let newspapers have information or not?" Harrington wrote to Putnam in mid-June. "Shall we write the stories for the papers or grant interviews to reporters? If white collectors get in here as they are trying to do they will get all the newspaper credit of the whole thing." A week later, amidst the "digging rights" dispute and while some Senecas were still expressing displeasure about the graves being disturbed, Parker wrote, "The *Buffalo Express* desires a story from us but I have refused until a later date as all publicity ought to be avoided now." Nothing was mentioned about the newspaper again until the end of August, a week before the excavations closed for the summer. "The *Buffalo Express* has requested that I give them a short sketch of our expedition and I enclose a story which I have hurriedly written for your criticism," Parker wrote. "It ought to be returned to me at the earliest possible date as the newspaper has been waiting for it since June. I wrote them I should have it to them early in September. Of course I receive payment."[19]

Putnam assented a week later: "I return the mss with this and have no objection to your giving it to the Buffalo paper if you and Harrington have agreed upon the matter. It was understood that neither of you were to give out articles for the press until the work was over and that you and Harrington should agree as to writing for the papers. So long as no more work is to be done on the site, you are both at liberty to give out general articles such as the one sent me, only you two must agree to who shall write for this paper and who for that."[20] He also requested that Parker send him the published article.

Neither the draft of the story nor the published article survives in the archives with Putnam and Parker's papers. And despite a systematic search of the microfilmed 1903 autumn issues of the *Buffalo Express*, the article could not be found in its pages. For some unknown reason, Parker's article was most likely never published. Nevertheless, this exchange is significant because it illustrates an ambivalence about archaeological knowledge in the public sphere. Even as the young archaeologists complained that they were poorly understood by the local townspeople, they also feared the consequences of informing them. On the one hand, Harrington worried that others would get credit, but on the other Parker fretted that news of their digging burials would spread even farther. Rather than working to correct such perceptions, the archaeologists instead elected to keep their endeavor mostly quiet.

Parker would soon learn much more about newspapers, first during a brief stint writing for the *New York Sun* and then as their favored subject. In the archives in the New York State Library is a scrapbook brimming with articles from the early 1900s.[21] Many faded clippings feature Parker's lectures and research, giving him the attention and legitimacy he deeply desired: articles in the *Dunkirk Observer*, *Postville Autograph*, *Rochester Herald*, *Albany Argus*, *Albany Knickerbocker Press*, *Brooklyn Eagle*, *White Plains Argus*, and the *White Plains Reporter* announcing in bold print "Work of Ga-Wa-So-Wa-Neh" (n.d.), "Prehistoric Relics Unearthed at Ripley" (1906), "Indian Burial Place" (1906), "Indian to Talk to His People" (1910), "Where Hiawatha's Laws Still Govern" (1910), "Seneca Discusses Indian Lodges" (1911), "A Few Thoughts about Indian Life" (1911), and "500 Attended Lecture" (1911). For the aspiring scholar in 1903, however, the relationship between archaeology and the press was still uncertain.

Closed for the Season

On the back of a letter sent from Harrington to Putnam on August 1, Putnam scribbled to his secretary, Frances G. Mead, in his nearly indecipherable handwriting, "Miss Mead should Parker write that he can continue the work with likelihood of good results through Sept. At cost same as now—*less* Harrington's salary. Please let him know that *I wish him* to do so and for him to go on with it."[22] Putnam was in Berkeley, California, at the time, and so it was not until nearly three weeks later that the message was conveyed to Harrington, who himself had already expressed plans to take classes in the fall semester at the University of Michigan.[23]

Parker, though, had his own plans. "I am very sorry that I shall not be able to do so on account of business in New York," he replied. "I am an applicant for a position as lecturer for the Board of Education and preparation will necessitate my presence in New York City."[24] Nonetheless, the invitation to carry on their work was a true compliment to Parker, a mark of Putnam's trust and a sign of Parker's arrival as a researcher capable of leading his own expedition.

As August came and the end of the season neared, the excavations did not slow at all. On the contrary, one senses that Harrington and Parker were racing to complete one hundred burial pits. They reported: August 10, pits 87 and 88 are dug; August 15, pit 93 is discovered; August 24, pit 95 is excavated. Then, on the last day of fieldwork, working on a Saturday through a downpour, Harrington recorded, "August 29. Much rain. Pit 100, an ash pit, found just beyond Pit 99." Of these one hundred pits, sixty-five were burial pits or graves.[25] On the next work day, August 31, all the last specimens and remaining field equipment were packed and sent to Cambridge—three boxes of archaeological specimens, one box and one bundle of ethnological specimens, one camp chest, one bundle of poles, and one box of negatives.[26]

"The work is closed for the season," Harrington reported. "Be sure and have the camp chest opened *at once* and the tents thoroughly dried and aired, as they are very wet after the past weeks rain, and would mould and be destroyed in short order if left in the box. I enclose key of camp chest. It would also be advisable to open box #35, containing ethnological specimens and dry the contents, and to also open the bundle and dry the ethnological objects in the hollow of the wooden mortar." The letter reveals that they were collecting up to the very end. Harrington purchased ethnological artifacts, including a ladle, corn pounder, and leader's pole, all associated with the False Face Society. In their final days, they continued to gather objects from the excavations as well: "During the past week we found among other things, a folded skeleton with a crushed pot, another with a jar containing bone tubes, beads etc., an infant skeleton with a small jar, another skeleton with a broken jar and a number of round stones; and a few crumbs of bone with a beautiful pipe in the shape of a human figure." Harrington finally noted that they went over budget, but, he added with a shade of pride, by only $1.47.[27]

From Putnam's perspective, the expedition was no doubt a success, although he was strangely reserved in his Peabody director's annual report. "Fortunately we were able, during the past summer, to secure the services of Messrs. M. R. Harrington and A. S. [sic] Parker, young men whom I had trained in connection with the American Museum of Natural History," he wrote. "From the graves explored we received several skeletons and a fine lot of pottery vessels, also characteristic pipes, stone and bone implements, ornaments, and many other objects.... While the young men were on the Cattaraugus reservation they secured from the Indians a small ethnological collection."[28] The project's success was also reported in the country's leading journal, *American Anthropologist*.[29] Indeed, after nearly four months of work, 863 new objects and human remains were waiting to be cataloged and added to the Peabody Museum's shelves.[30] Of these, 51 were ethnological objects, and 812 were from archaeological contexts—including 98 human bodies.

At the close of the season, Harrington and Parker went to New York City and then after months of constant companionship parted ways. Putnam, in a letter, intimated that Parker was perhaps considering going to Columbia University. "So you have decided to enter Columbia," he wrote, though he perhaps was mistaking the interview Parker mentioned as a desire to enter the university. "I think this is a good step and you will have my sincere wishes for your success," Putnam added, no doubt feeling a bit stung to imagine Parker under Boas's hand. Whatever opportunity Parker was pursuing in New York, it did not pan out, and by November he was writing to Putnam seeking employment.[31]

After Harrington left New York, he briefly stopped by Cattaraugus to watch the Green Corn Dance, then traveled on to Michigan. "Mother and I have settled in Ann Arbor for now, with most of our furniture, in a very pleasant house," he wrote to Putnam in early October, "and I have entered the university, taking up French, English and General Biology, which comprises Zoology and Botany taken simultaneously. I have entered as a special, but hope to pass up the entrance requirements and graduate, and to this end, am taking Geometry. In addition, 20 hours per week must be spent in the University museum, where I have a position as assistant at a salary of $15.00 per month."[32]

Sifting Basket (Seneca)

The letter of introduction, or "permit," that Putnam sent to the Cattaraugus Reservation in 1903 proclaimed that the objects collected during the expedition would be "placed on an exhibition for all time." Although such language was no doubt in part merely a ploy to assuage angry Senecas, it also reflects the mindset of an age in which anthropologists believed they were saving Native American cultures—both from the farmer's destructive plow and the ravages of cultural change.

By the early twentieth century, public exhibits were a central part of the anthropology museum's mission. In fact, Putnam played a key role in this process, first as head of the ethnology department at the 1893 World's Columbian Exposition, in which he and Boas undertook the colossal venture of gathering ethnological objects from seemingly every corner of the Americas and organizing and displaying them for the public. The sensational success of the exhibits was hugely important in establishing anthropology's promise: its potential to capture the public's imagination and the possibility of developing the field into a bona fide scientific discipline. Putnam's influence grew outward from the exposition like roots through loose soil. As the exposition's anthropology exhibit became the Field Museum, he had a hand there, and in 1894 he was appointed curator at the American Museum of Natural History. With positions in museums and at Harvard University, he began training museum scholars, and by the turn of the century "so great was his influence that in almost every museum where anthropology had a place there could be found a Putnam-trained student."[33]

Although science-oriented museums in the United States had been displaying antiquities and ethnological objects since the 1880s—including the Peabody Museum, the American Museum of Natural History, and the United States National Museum—these early exhibits were almost always dependent on objects obtained by gift and by the purchase of earlier amateur collections. The exhibits of this period were thus organized by types of objects or geography. By the time the Silverheels collection arrived in crates in the Peabody's storerooms, however, a more systematic and informed style of display was in place, in large part due to the undertaking of research-oriented collecting expeditions and the methodological rigor Putnam insisted on.[34] Still, the exhibits of this period were obtuse. Most often they were organized by "culture areas" or chronology; when the exhibits were labeled, it was as if book text were simply transposed to the display case. The large numbers of objects left on display, many without interpretation, emphasized the "empirical approach" of the period because "the student was supposed to bring to the exhibits his own orientation, and to draw from them his own conclusions."[35] Putnam's approach to museum display—influenced greatly by his mentor Louis Agassiz of Harvard University's Museum of Comparative Zoology—focused on the objects' geographic location and historic contexts.[36]

As the objects from Cattaraugus arrived in Cambridge, they were unpacked, cleaned, labeled, and cataloged. These procedures were important steps in the process of transforming objects into specimens of scientific quality—things neatly categorized and stored in logical order. Most of the artifacts were left in storage rooms; however, some were exhibited. In the fall of 1904, Harrington corresponded with Putnam about a Mr. Willoughby's redrawing of Harrington's Silverheels Site field map for an exhibit, and Putnam mentioned in his annual report at the end of the year that the Silverheels collection was then on display, although it is unclear which Silverheels objects were put out for public view.[37] At some point, the exhibit was taken down, but a few objects remained on display. Notably, the objects shown were the ethnographic items originally collected, in Putnam's words, "more for the sake of doing something to help secure the good will of the Indians than anything else." These objects included a sifter basket, salt basket, sacred tobacco basket, and husk face mask.[38]

The Peabody Museum's main exhibit hall itself became a relic with time; it changed little in seventy years, remaining after 1910 as "rows of glass-fronted wooden cases, crowded with artifacts, arranged by linguistic group in a vague culture area approach, with brief labels."[39] A few renovations took place in the 1950s; then the entire exhibit hall was redone and opened in the spring of 1990. The goal of the new exhibit was to "explore ways in which North American Indian and Eskimo groups responded to Western contact" and to tell "the complex story of how Native Americans came to be who they are today."[40] The presentation of this story was organized by "culture areas," almost precisely the same conceptual organization for museums that Putnam had promoted a century previously. Eight galleries were dedicated to illustrating ten culture areas. Since 1990, the exhibit has changed little.

If you were to visit the gallery today, you would enter the darkened room that presents the northeastern culture area. Among the first display cases you would see is one titled "Northeast Lifeways," holding a dozen or so artifacts. At the bottom, not far from your feet, sits a basket, tilted upward for you to look in. You would more likely just walk past it, but if for some reason your curiosity is piqued, you might find the label that describes the only artifact collected that summer in 1903 left on display today:

Sifting Basket (Seneca)

After corn was pulverized and ground in a mortar, a basket such as this was used to sift the meal. The shifting basket was integral to the process of making corn bread. This basket is made of ash splints arranged in a twill weave. The very small standards are paired and tied at the top. The base is square and has feet that were formed by pressure when the basket was wet. It was collected by Mark R. Harrington on the Cattaraugus Reservation, New York, in 1903. (03-32-10/62630)[41]

Although the exhibit underscores the museum's commitment to public education, in essence this institution, like most anthropology museums, remains in a sense a glorified storeroom. It houses some two million ethnological objects alone, with more than seventy thousand from North American Indians; the exhibit includes some five hundred things.[42] Today, the archaeological materials from the Silverheels Site are not in the Peabody Museum proper, but rather in a colossal storage facility nearby, a nondescript brick building camouflaged by trees and next to an even more blank-looking cement building. After a digital password is entered, the alarm turns off, and a thick metal door on the side of the building opens. Within is a cavernous space stacked floor to ceiling with artifacts. Along a row of metal shelving with bulky wood boxes are the materials from Silverheels. In the drawers, neatly organized within small boxes and plastic bags and resting on cushions, are animal bones, pottery fragments, arrow points, and pipes.

In this space, surrounded by so many things, the Silverheels Site collection is dwarfed, a mere fraction of the museum's seemingly endless holdings. Although small in size and number, however, the objects hold a power still for the visitor who knows their history. These things were first created and cherished centuries ago, then protected by Senecas for decades, then exhumed by two young men whose professional ambitions were fueled by a genuine love of the past. These things sparked

The Peabody Museum Annex storage area, with the Silverheels Site collections located in the photo's middle ground. (Photograph by author, March 29, 2006, with permission of Harvard University, Peabody Museum)

imaginations and careers; they were uncovered, touched, and sent here with the belief that they would remain in this place until they turned to dust. These were the things that made Arthur C. Parker a professional archaeologist.

These things also came from a place where the people did not forget their ancestors and did not stop caring for the earthly remains of their forebears. Nearly one hundred years after Parker and Harrington sent the bodies and the funerary objects eastward, the remains went back in the other direction. Although some objects are still kept in the nondescript storage room, most of what was collected at the Silverheels Site was returned to the Seneca tribe in 2002 through the NAGPRA process. It is debatable whether Parker would have approved of the repatriation.

The Most Ambitious and Best Paper

Shortly after Harrington arrived in Ann Arbor in the fall of 1903, he found himself short of cash. He was living in a one-room apartment with his mother and had many "unexpected expenses" from moving and then for various class fees. "So I am writing and doing all sorts of things to 'raise the wind,'" he wrote to Putnam, not hiding a hue of desperation. "I want to know if there is any report writing of last summer's work, from the notes turned in, or any thing of that sort that I could do for the Peabody or the American Museum to earn a little money." A month later, he would offer to sell Putnam artifacts he had collected at Cattaraugus: two dollars for a bark tray, five dollars for a False Face Society mask. "I bought these for myself, but as cash is so short I fear I can not afford to keep them and believe I had better offer them to some museum; and I naturally begin by asking you," Harrington explained. "Do you want them? Please let me know very soon as I need the money badly."[43]

By the end of November, not only had Putnam purchased the items for the Peabody Museum, but he had also offered to pay Harrington to write a report for the Silverheels Site. Given Harrington's financial straits, Putnam even paid an advance. "Thank you very much for sending me part payment in advance on the report," Harrington wrote. "I intend to make it the best and most complete I ever did [sic] wrote. I realize its importance to my future when published, and I am going to take every precaution to see that it is all it should be. I have my outline finished and about ¼ the Report done in rough draft. All other articles will be laid aside until this one is finished."[44] Several weeks before the end of 1903, Parker sent Putnam his own report, "The Aboriginal Occupants of the Silverheels Site," for which he was eventually paid ten dollars.[45]

In the spring of 1904, Harrington sent his complete, hand-written report to Cambridge, titled "Exploration of an Iroquoian Stronghold, Erie Co., Western NY, Silverhill [sic] Site, 1903." Putnam expressed his pleasure at the article. "Your report was duly received and I have read every word and compared with photographs," he wrote. "I am very much pleased with the report and think you have put it in good shape and made a good readable paper. Of course a number of photographs will have to be illustrated to be printed with the report. I shall go over it carefully again and have illustrations made of many of the specimens, so as to give a clear full account of the exploration and what was found."[46] Putnam explained that Parker's account would make for a good appendix, which he wanted to use in addition to another appendix summarizing the skulls and skeletons recovered. With the letter, he enclosed a check for twenty-two dollars, the second half of Harrington's payment. The help that Putnam provided Harrington seems to have been crucial for the young man who was having difficulties. In the fall of 1904, Harrington wrote to the professor, "Whenever I think of you a lump rises in my throat—I confess it—and I long to see the Friend, who, in the darkest hour of my life, gave me the helping hand and saved me from—the depths. I can say no more."[47]

The higher payment for Harrington and the request for him to write the report was possibly more an act of charity than a rebuff to Parker. At the same time that Putnam received the Silverheels report, he took one of Parker's papers, "Use of the Bannerstone," and "fixed that up" and sought its publication in the *Bulletin of the American Museum.* He seemingly also published one of Parker's papers on the making of arrows. But the bannerstone paper was rejected: "the authorities there, who believe they know more than I do about archaeology, decided not to print the papers and returned them to me," Putnam grumbled.[48] It is difficult to tell whether Putnam was trying to help Parker get his first publications or to take Parker's work for his own profit.

Five years passed, and the Silverheels fieldwork remained unpublished. Then Parker asked Putnam if he could publish the reports under the auspices of the New York State Museum. Putnam agreed.[49] Still another seven years passed, however, before Parker was able to work on the manuscript. By then, he had started on a much larger work that was to be an archaeological study of the entire state of New York. Silverheels would be featured as one of a dozen sites that illustrated the breadth and depth of New York's archaeological history. But at this point the director of the Peabody Museum, C. C. Willoughby, unexpectedly asked for the return of the unpublished reports. Given that some fourteen years had gone by since the 1903 expedition, Parker could not have been overly surprised at this request. Nevertheless, because his report was "ready for the printer," he must have been panicked. He wrote back, explaining that he had a "mutual understanding" with Putnam that the New York State Museum would publish the materials. He generously included Harrington's original hand-written report.[50]

Willoughby replied with a proposal that Parker could publish—if he did so promptly—some of the other sites the Peabody Museum sponsored, but that the Silverheels report should be published through his museum. "I have been looking over the collections resulting from Harrington's explorations, and have come to the conclusion that an account of the work at Silverheel's [sic] site should be published by this museum," he wrote. "It should be well illustrated with good drawings and photographs from the specimens themselves, and with a few field photographs from the specimens themselves, and with a few field photographs. It would make I am sure a very attractive paper."[51] This response must have been doubly insulting for Parker. Not only was Willoughby taking back the Silverheels report for publication just when Parker's own book was nearly done, but still more than a decade later the Silverheels expedition was still being referred to as Harrington's expedition—the phrase *"collections resulting from Harrington's explorations"* must have echoed in Parker's head for days—as if Parker was not there or as if he was in fact the mere assistant he had refused to become.

Parker played elusive, it seems. His response to Willoughby is not preserved in the archives, but he apparently ignored the suggestion to have the Peabody Museum publish the Silverheels report. "Will you kindly read my letter of February 12 again?" Willoughby wrote in mid-March. "You apparently misunderstood a part of it, and did not answer my request as to how you felt regarding my proposition. Please let me hear from you again regarding this matter."[52] Nothing more of the matter was said in their correspondence.

Another five years came and went before the report was at last published. Parker's book *The Archaeological History of New York* was submitted to the printer at the end of 1917, but ostensibly because of a long printer's strike, it was not released until the summer of 1922.[53] Although perhaps Parker might be criticized for taking nearly twenty years to publish the report, a measure of praise is apposite too. After all, Putnam did nothing with the manuscript for five years, and Harrington, who was so often credited with leading the expedition, did not press for publication. Parker not only published the work, making it accessible to researchers for decades to come, but also made it much more relevant by situating it in a larger text examining New York history.

The Silverheels report appears as "A Midcolonial Seneca Site in Erie County" in Parker's book and is credited to M. Raymond Harrington. The writing, as was typical for the time, is largely descriptive.[54] Yet the report shows a unique willingness to draw on ethnographic analogy and makes clear the value the author places on Indigenous interpretation; for example, the Senecas interpreted a human figurine carved in bone as a "'ga-ya'-da' or image [that] was a very powerful 'witch' charm, and that similar ones had been often used by their men of magic," and a face on a effigy pipe "looked something like the modern Seneca ceremonial wooden masks or 'ga-gó-sa,' so much that the Indians considered the pipe a representation of a masker blowing ashes between his fingers as do the 'False-face Society' men of today." The report also conveys the commitment to the rigorous scientific methods to which the excavators aspired. Because the pits were excavated as discrete units and artifacts were systematically recorded as belonging to particular units, the report could offer some intriguing insights. Not only could the researchers compare grave types and their contents, but they could also make inferences about particular graves. For example, the archaeologists recovered only two "arrow-making outfits," and each was in a separate grave; the human remains in those graves were both of disabled men, allowing Harrington to surmise that "perhaps among these people arrow-making devolved upon those who could not hunt." Or, for example, they could observe that nearly all the wampum they recovered were found in the graves of women and children. Furthermore, by recording and collecting nearly all the observable cultural remains they came across, the report illuminated the more prosaic aspects of life at the site, what the Senecas ate and how they lived.[55] Although the rhetoric of archaeology as a science that focuses on *specimens* in large measure dehumanized the lives of the ancient Indians, at least the scientific method Harrington and Parker employed in some measure restored a sense of historical connection to contemporary Senecas and the personhood of those taken in boxes to the Peabody Museum.

The published chapter in Parker's book was little different from the hand-written report that Harrington completed in 1904, with one major exception: the report's main conclusion. In the report's first iteration, the main conclusion was that the site was occupied by an Indian group known as the Erie or Nation du Chat in the documentary record, a group the Seneca had "destroyed" in 1655. Given this firm date, the main question was whether the artifacts indicated an occupation before or after the mid–seventeenth century. Harrington rightly concluded that the trade items in the graves indicated that the Silverheels Site was occupied after European contact, but he wrongly surmised that "the present Senecas . . . did not come here until well along in the 19th century most of them about 1843, when they left the old Buffalo Creek Reservation."[56] Because no artifacts suggested the site was occupied in the mid-1800s, Harrington concluded that Eries must have built and lived in the site sometime before 1655.

In 1907, however, Parker wrote to Putnam, "For some time I have been growing suspicious of the Erie-ness of the Silverheel's [sic] site." With the letter, he enclosed a report in which he argued that after the Eries were extinguished, the Senecas quickly filled the void. "To have left so rich a hunting ground unvisited and without settlements is contrary to the known policies of the Iroquois and it is extremely probable that the Senecas to whom the territory naturally fell early had villages and defensive works there," he wrote. "Tradition has little to say of this occupation though there are a few faint glimmerings that might lead to the idea. Archaeology, however, sheds a more definite light on the matter and from the grave pits and refuse heaps in the Cattaraugus valley I am led to say that there is much evidence to support the statement that the locality was occupied by the Senecas soon after the Eries were driven from it."[57] A decade later, Harrington visited Parker to make their final revisions to the Silverheels manuscript.[58] On the original 1904 report, Harrington's conclusions were crossed out in red ink, and in Parker's handwriting a new conclusion written in the margins asserts, "The probabilities are, then, that the site was occupied by the Seneca after 1655."[59] This conclusion was the one published in the 1922 book. And thus not only was the Silverheels Site the place of Parker's first major archaeological expedition; it was also, as the science confirmed, for him a place of his own ancestors.

Alanson Skinner, Parker's close friend and one of the "Putnam Boys," reviewed *The Archaeological History of New York* in the prestigious journal *American Anthropologist* shortly after the book's publication. Although the volume includes several contributors—in addition to Harrington, Harrison C. Follett and Frank Hamilton Cushing authored two sections—it is Parker who gets credit for the book. Skinner is laudatory of Parker's theoretical interpretations and is only critical of his slapdash list of archaeological sites in New York State appended at the report's end. Overall, however, the reviewer piles the plaudits any writer would crave—and surely for Parker the kind of recognition he had yearned for since he wrote to Putnam to say that he was Harrington's equal. "All in all, this is the most ambitious and best paper hitherto published on the archaeology of the region and is likely to stand as such for many years to come," Skinner enthused. "It sets a standard of merit that American scientists may well follow in the study and discussion of the archaeology of any part of our continent. The State of New York is to be congratulated on having so able and erudite a student of its early inhabitants as Mr. Parker."[60]

Part IV
The Archaeologist Gáwasowaneh

6

IT IS KNOWLEDGE, SOLELY, THAT WE ARE SEEKING

Genuine Indian Trophies

By the late autumn of 1903, Parker must have felt that his world was coming undone. His long-time supporter and friend Harriet Maxwell Converse passed away.[1] The possibility of work or college in New York had fallen through, and it was too late in the semester to return to Dickinson Seminary. Even Putnam was of little help. He wrote to Parker saying that he could not promise a "permanent arrangement," although he tempered the bad news with the promise of funds for fieldwork the following summer.[2]

Parker was then living in White Plains, presumably with his parents, searching for work where he could find it. He sold stories to the *New York Sun*, a respected New York City daily begun in 1833.[3] He was trying to get a book of Indian legends published through Harper and Brothers.[4] He sold ethnological collections for estates.[5] He also found work as an ethnological decorator, becoming involved in the construction of the Hotel Astor, a new ten-story, five-hundred-room luxury affair that William Waldorf Astor spent seven million dollars on, including seven hundred thousand for furnishings.[6] Parker's charge was to decorate a "large Indian room" with four hundred feet of panel pictures showing "the Eskimo tribes, North West Coast tribes, Choshonean, Siouan, Iroquoian, Algonquian, Athapascan, Pueblo stocks and Mexican stocks" in their "Indian life—home, hunting, war ceremonies, etc., the scenery of the country in which that particular stock resides." In addition, "genuine Indian trophies" of various types were to be included, "the Eskimo *bay* being decorated with Eskimo material etc., the walls or ceiling painted with Eskimo designs, and the panels along the sides filled with pictures of Eskimo life, and so on with the other bays or sections." Parker felt that his task was not merely one of ornamentation. "The decorations will be hung in such a way that art and science will blend," he wrote to Putnam, "or in case of dispute the learning is to be in favor of science."[7]

In typical fashion, Parker undertook the decorating job with industrious verve, but perhaps his heart was not completely in it, as indicated by his stated preference to turn a hotel lobby into a science exhibit. At the same time that he was locating photos and objects for the Astor, he was in contact with the New York State Museum in the state capital, Albany, about the possibility of employment. He wrote first to Frederick J. H. Merrill, its director, about conducting an archaeological exploration for the state.[8] The proposal was passed to William M. Beauchamp, then the godfather of New York archaeology, who favorably reviewed it.[9]

The proposal to the state museum might have ended the possibility of working that summer for the Peabody Museum. In April, Parker asked Putnam if the Peabody Museum would support his "leasing and working ancient Indian sites in western New York" or, if not, whether it would be "right for me to enter into a contract with other parties."[10] In almost every way, Putnam's explorations at the turn of the century were just the beginning of scientific research in the Northeast, and he wanted the work to continue.[11] Nevertheless, Putnam replied more than a month later saying that he did not have the same amount of money as he did the previous year, and, anyway, if Parker had the chance to work for the state museum, he should instead pursue that opportunity. Putnam added that with the several hundred dollars available to him, he would be able to fund only Harrington's exploration. "I dislike very much to have you discontinue your work for the Peabody, but I do not see how I can help it," he wrote. "I hope you and Harrington will not get into any confliction and that you will each take distinct areas for your explorations."[12] Strangely, contrary to Putnam's letter, Harrington's 1904 proposal was for the same amount of money spent in the 1903 season—which included a ten-dollar per month raise for himself, although Parker's replacement, another "Putnam Boy," Alanson Skinner, agreed to work without a salary.[13] When Skinner was just sixteen years old, he had excavated a shell midden with Parker and Harrington in 1902 near Shinnecock Hills, Long Island.[14] In the end, Parker had to borrow money from his friend Joseph Keppler to make it through the autumn.[15]

Parker's disappointment would not yet end. Merrill's replacement at the New York State Museum, John Mason Clarke, wrote to Parker at the beginning of the summer to say that his preference was to purchase objects instead of paying for research expeditions that have unpredictable results.¹⁶ The news must have been doubly hurtful to Parker, first because it meant that he wouldn't do any fieldwork that summer and second because the purchasing of artifacts instead of their scientific recovery was contrary to his developing professional ethic. "I was informed that the State Museum disliked to risk their money on an expedition, fearing that the money invested would not be repaid by value of specimens or 'relics' found," he later seethed to Putnam. "They, therefore were going to use the money to buy curiosities such as they had not. Needless to say I was disgusted and did not hesitate to reply that I was not aware that scientific institutions of this day hunted for curiosities etc." With few options left, Parker then tried to "write, lecture, and criticize" for profit—not ways to get rich—and made plans to return to college in the fall.¹⁷

I Have Added to Myself

M. Raymond Harrington's first publication was in the *Journal of American Folk-lore*, a one-page article relating a story told to him by a sixteen-year-old Abenaki woman named Beulah Tahamont.¹⁸ She was then living at Lake George, in upstate New York, but was visiting New York City—likely the American Museum of Natural History—when she shared the tale with Harrington. Beulah and Raymond occasionally dated.¹⁹ Perhaps a kind of portent of things to come, the tale was about a marriage torn asunder by a husband careless around the dead. An Indian man and his wife camped under a witch buried in the branches of a tree. When the couple saw the grave, the wife wanted to leave, but the husband was indifferent and soon went to sleep. Late into the night, when the fire went out, she heard a terrible gnawing sound, like an animal chewing a bone, and became frightened and remained still in the darkness. When morning came, she turned to her husband and saw that he had been killed, nastily mutilated, one side of his body and his heart eaten away.

Perhaps on that visit to New York or perhaps on another, Beulah met Arthur. They were similar in age, and both came from families that had a foot planted in both the Indian and white worlds. Like Arthur, Beulah had the encouragement and support of Harriet Maxwell Converse.²⁰ Beulah was a child actress by the age of four, appearing in several silent movies, and her father, Elijah Tahamont, would later be brought to Hollywood in 1912 to be in movies as well as to lecture on Indian ways at road shows and circuses.²¹ Beulah, like her mother, was very beautiful; she posed as a model for a sculpture of Princess Wenonah in 1902.²² The sculpture still stands today in Winona, Minnesota. She was also very smart; she and her sister Bessie were the first Indian children to attend a New York public school (Public School 45), and she later attended college.²³ "It is predicted that if she continues in her exceptional educational progress," a 1901 article declared, "Beulah is destined to become the cleverest Indian woman of today."²⁴

Amidst Arthur's struggles in 1904, he married Beulah Tahamont. "I have added to myself a beautiful Abneki-Algonquin maiden from Sabreouis College, McGill University, Montreal," he effused, sharing the good news with Putnam. "Thus the Algonquins and Iroquois are connected in peace once again."²⁵ As their lives would often parallel each other's, Harrington, too, married that spring.²⁶ The marriage between Parker and Tahamont perhaps got off to an uneven start because the next winter we find Parker remarking to a colleague that he had now documented the Abenaki word for "contempt."²⁷

Beulah is elusive in the historical record. She is not often referred to at length in Arthur's correspondence, in most cases only a polite offer to accept or give kind regards here and there. Oblique references are occasionally made to her health, the first only a year after the marriage began. "My Beulah does not seem able to stand the damp climate and changeable spring weather here and although she has been very well, now she is quite ill," Parker wrote. "I am having every medical aid possible here, and await her recovery."²⁸ In late 1905, Beulah bore a son, Melville A. Parker. "I saw Parker and his wife at Cattaraugus," Harrington wrote to Putnam in passing. "They have a little boy about 1½ months old."²⁹ The Parkers would also get visits from the Tahamont family. "Bessie Bright Eyes is with us in Rensselaer," Parker wrote to W. S. Fannell about Beulah's sister living at their home just across the Hudson River from Albany, "and intends to study in the school there. At present I am giving her a little coaching that she needs, she never having attended school for lack of opportunity beyond a few grades. . . . Chief Tahamont and my good mother-in-law are in New York. They had a successful hunt in the north and brought us some venison." In the summer of 1907, Arthur was again ordering maternity clothes for Beulah. Their second child, a daughter, Bertha A. Parker was soon born. "Mrs. Parker read your letter with much pleasure and requests me to send her kindest wishes," Arthur wrote to Putnam at the end of 1907. "We have two little ones now and are very happy with them."³⁰

Within a year, Arthur's children were adopted into Seneca clans and given the names "Ga-nun-dai-ye-oh" and "Ni-ye-wus-ah (Ye-wus)."[31] Like Arthur and his own father before him, the children, with a mother who was not Seneca, would have a circumscribed position in Seneca life. But unlike Arthur, they would grow up with a sense of belonging to the Seneca community because they were adopted into it while still infants. Also Parker no doubt understood that his children, with a mother of Abenaki heritage, would be recognized fully as American Indians.

The Parker family was outwardly a happy one, living together even when Arthur was running an expedition. Arthur took his family with him into the field, first in 1906 at Ripley and then in 1907 at Sinclairville, camping out.[32] But something was amiss, though what exactly is hazy today. All was tranquil on the surface. We hear of Beulah spending the day in Arthur's office.[33] But then several months later she is away at Lake George, presumably with her family, and in early 1910 she is again ill. "I regret more than I can tell you that Mrs. P. was ill and unable to be the hostess as she would have liked to do," Arthur apologetically wrote Alanson Skinner. "She is up and around but is very far from being well." A month later Arthur would write to his landlord, "Owing to the ill health of Mrs. Parker and other reasons I have been obliged to vacate the house which I have hitherto occupied."[34] The "other reasons" are not known exactly, but it would seem by this time that the marriage was collapsing.

Beulah is mentioned several times in letters between 1911 and 1912, mainly that she is ill and unwell. "I write confidentially when I say that I sometimes fear for Beulah's mental health," Parker confided to Keppler in September 1911, "and I am never very sure what she may do to herself or to the rest of us. Last winter I had her in the hospital for some time."[35] Then, suddenly, like a phone line that abruptly goes silent in a storm, Arthur never writes of Beulah again. In 1912, Beulah went to Hollywood and appeared in a film by D. W. Griffiths.[36] Perhaps her desire to be in movies was the source of conflict, or perhaps it was merely an excuse to leave an unhappy home. At some point before 1914, there was a permanent split, and Beulah took the two children with her. Beulah and Arthur would never see each other again.

Memory of My People

Parker's intention to give up archaeology, even if for only a time, and return to college was short-lived. The decision to give up higher education was a gamble. In the late 1890s, as Parker began wandering the halls of New York's museums, practical hands-on experience was the key means of training the next generation of museum men. But by the early 1900s a shift from training in museums to universities was well under way. According to anthropologist Jay H. Bernstein, the factors pushing students away from museums in the early 1900s included the fact that museums weren't adequately training students and that whereas many philanthropists wanted museums to focus on classical antiquities, younger researchers wanted to focus on Indian tribes.[37] A crucial factor pulling anthropology to universities was a major shift in the role of professors with the introduction of a new German model in which professors were expected to be scholars and researchers in addition to teachers. There were also an increasing professionalization and specialization across disciplines—anthropology was successfully defining itself as a distinct field, separate from the classics yet an important branch of the social sciences.

Looking at his mentor, Frederic W. Putnam, Parker saw an exceptionally successful professor and curator with only a bachelor's degree. In 1904, little more than a dozen people had a Ph.D. in anthropology or closely allied field.[38] Only a handful of universities even offered anthropology courses.[39] But Parker's mistake was assuming that the past would repeat itself in the future. A Ph.D. would soon nearly be requisite for professorships and curatorships—for legitimacy as a genuine archaeological scholar. "Anthropology, previously an isolated field of inquiry without any institutional support, self-taught and practiced as an avocation of wealthy all-around scholars and hobbyists, was now an academic discipline," Bernstein outlines. "Standards of scholarship rose, and entry into the profession required university certification, specifically the Ph.D."[40] It was during this transition that Parker missed his chance to finish college and pursue graduate school, a decision that for years would come to haunt him. "I have always regretted that I could not take a course under your direction at Peabody," he would write to Putnam only several years after dropping out of college, "but I have treasured your suggestions and criticisms and am endeavoring to make the most of my knowledge."[41] Parker, already an ambiguous archaeologist because of his perceived race, would later also come to feel ignoble because he lacked advanced educational credentials. He allowed people to call him "Doctor" and "Professor" for decades, though he never formally taught and did not have an honorary doctorate until 1940; he would often be sure to bring up his early affiliation with Harvard University.

In October 1904, Parker wrote again to Putnam mentioning that he had an interview with Andrew S. Draper, New York's commissioner of education, to discuss securing a position with the state museum. "And now another thought comes to me: suppose the State does not accept my offer?" he wondered, ever the planner. "In this event could I expect any encouragement from the Peabody?" To this question, he added as explanation, "You see, live or die, I am trying, at any rate, to have the memory of my people preserved in a tangible form."[42] As Parker's pursuit of a career in archaeology becomes more anxious, he increasingly frames his desire with his Indian heritage. He expresses his interest in anthropology as a service to the Seneca community. This service, however, is not one of actively helping the struggles of the living community, but rather helping that it be *remembered* in the annals of history—a motive deeply embedded in the Parker clan that goes as far back as Nicholson's lecture "The American Red Man," which petitioned the American conquerors to remember Indian tribes they have destroyed.[43] In Parker's mind, archaeologists and ethnologists are slaves to the past. Anthropologists are memory keepers.

Traveling to Albany, Parker met with Draper to discuss "gathering and preserving to the state the traditions, folk lore, implements, or anything else relating to the New York Indian tribes."[44] The proposal was for Parker to purchase these items and have them preserved at the New York State Museum. He seemingly believed that the purchase of these objects was acceptable because they were to be mainly ethnological specimens rather than archaeological objects. In November, he received an official letter from Draper, offering an arrangement for six months at a salary of fifty dollars per month plus expenses, in which he would be charged with "gathering information from the New York Indian reservations concerning the ceremonies, festivals, rituals, religious thoughts, songs, speeches, etc., of the tribes," publishing this information, and collecting "any relics in the way of implements, dress, ornaments or manuscript which would help to retain for future generations the best information as to the characteristics and customs of the Iroquois." During the interview, Parker must have expressed sentiments similar to what he shared with Putnam. "You must bear in mind your statement to me that your motive is to preserve information of your ancestors, and work earnestly to that end," Draper concludes his offer letter. "If you do so, it will be a real service to the history of the State."[45]

It is not difficult to imagine Parker's heart beating faster as the words sunk in. "When I read this I emitted several war yells and offered tobacco to my great clan totem," he confided to Keppler.[46] At last, after nearly a year of bouncing from one failed effort to another in pursuit of a dream—a seed of hope planted as far back as when Uncle Ely Parker would talk of Lewis H. Morgan by the fireside when Arthur was still a child on the Cattaraugus Reservation—he would have a position of real use and the promise of steady employment. Not only that, but he must have been all too aware that the job he now had was nearly identical to the one Morgan himself held a half-century earlier.

Parker would later learn that it was Melvil Dewey, in honor of their mutual friendship to Harriet Converse, who had pushed for Parker's hire first in the summer of 1904 and then more successfully in the fall.[47] Dewey (of library fame), a man of some means, was personally to pay for the ethnological objects Parker was to collect—a kind of twofold donation, first to Parker for his employment and second to New York State, which would receive the objects gratis. Parker seemed to care little about where the funds were coming from: the main thing was the new opportunity presented to him. He jumped into the new task and thrived. Throughout the winter and spring of 1905, he collected all over New York, including stops at Cattaraugus, where he was able to visit with his grandmother and collect items from John Kennedy.[48] "I am exuberant in my work," Parker effused to Keppler in March that year. "It thrills me and yet sobers—I want to do much with it for the treasures I have found deserve a rich setting and sincere admiration." With this employ, he was also able to help his family. "It has been necessary for me to finance various Parkers directly—or indirectly near to me, who were in a bad financial condition, to pay up some old debts, to care for the expenses of sick people," he mentioned to Keppler in May.[49]

Parker's bosses were more than pleased. "I have read with interest the account of your work and both the Commissioner and myself are very heartily in sympathy with what you are doing," Draper's assistant wrote to Parker. "It will undoubtedly be of great value in correctly appraising the influences which guided the history of the Iroquois nation." They believed that Parker, as a Seneca, was obtaining information that was more authentic and had more depth than had been previously collected for the state.[50]

In the midst of Parker's collecting successes, John Clarke changed his mind and asked the young anthropologist if he might consider conducting archaeological excavations for the New York State Museum. When Commissioner Draper caught wind of the proposal, he at first asked

Parker to finish what he started, but then several weeks later recalled Parker from the field to begin undertaking plans for Clarke.[51] What changed Clarke's mind, why he now decided to support an expedition rather than the buying of relics, is unknown, but by the beginning of the summer of 1905 Parker knew he would again be working the earth with a shovel and pick. First, however, one of his main tasks was to obtain as many "leases" for excavation as he could with a budget of two hundred dollars.[52] Over the summer, he worked to get excavation leases, continued collecting ethnological materials such as several False Face Society masks, recorded Bear Society songs, attended the Strawberry Thanksgiving Ceremony to make notes, and participated in a healing ceremony, "faithfully shaking a gourd rattle, as a novice, in honor of the spirit forces that make the 'little water medicine' potent," he explained to Clarke's assistant, Howard Rogers.[53] Such multitasking would come to be Parker's standard operating procedure, his hands forever in many places at once. As Parker at last began excavating the Burning Spring Site in the Cattaraugus Valley, Clarke, obviously pleased with his industriousness, held out the possibility of hiring him full-time.[54]

Working through the winter and spring of 1906, Parker mainly collected objects, recorded songs on wax cylinders, and documented secret rites of the Seneca.[55] As summer neared, he obtained a lease from William Young to excavate the Ripley Site, located along Lake Erie, some forty-five miles south of the Cattaraugus Reservation.[56] Harrington and Skinner had explored the same site in 1904, and Parker wanted to dig there, most likely because he knew it was laden with artifacts and because he wanted to prove to Harrington that he was equal to the task of digging there. He and three men began excavating the site—an Anglo from Irving named Everett R. Burmaster, Parker's friend Jesse Mulkins, and a Seneca named William Blueskye, who had previously worked with Skinner; Beulah and their son were there, too, helped by a cook.[57] The focus, as at the Silverheels Site, was on skeletons. Parker and his crew reported to have excavated 101 graves.[58] "I am having the most astonishing luck I ever had in my life," he wrote to Keppler. "My trowel and shovel are veritable magnets. The most unique and beautiful things in clay and bone and stone seem drawn from the ground to them. You see the Great Spirit is giving me success." The work went fairly smoothly except for a falling out with William Blueskye, who quit on bad terms.[59] Parker published the work three years later, and it has been categorized as part of the early functionalist approach, a focus on "how artifacts were manufactured and what use had been made of them."[60] This approach often depended on ethnographic analogy, and Parker, with his concomitant interest in Iroquois living traditions, was able to produce with the Ripley Site report "an early attempt to delineate the entire culture of a group from archaeological remains interpreted in the light of ethnology," according to David Brose.[61] In many ways, the functionalist approach Parker took at Ripley set the theoretical foundation for his life's work in archaeology.

The other crisis that occurred while Parker was digging at the Ripley Site involved the lease with Young. Ironically, even though he had announced to Putnam in 1903 that he would always be sure to obtain full permission in writing before excavating, he now made exactly the same mistake as Harrington had with John Kennedy. "Mr. Young is unmarried, an illiterate and a degenerate," Parker explained flatly to Clarke. "Naturally then he is of a suspicious disposition and has no interest in educational matters. He would not sign the regular lease form which I read to him when I first asked for the property although he gave me to understand that he would sign for a year's time."[62] A week later the problem was resolved. Although Parker held the landowner in disdain, Young had what Parker wanted, and so even years later the two were still trying to strike deals.[63] By the end of the summer in 1906, Parker had deemed the Ripley excavations an unmitigated success. "I cannot here enumerate all that I have brought to light and science," Parker boasted to Clarke, "but I assure you that the specimens I have discovered especially in the line of pottery are unequalled by those found on any other single site in New York. I have even far outstripped the record I made in 1903 when Harrington and I took out a collection which we thought long would remain unrivaled."[64]

After his struggles, his persistence, and his tireless labor, in the autumn of 1906 Parker was at last offered the full-time and permanent position of archaeologist in the Science Division of the New York State Education Department. The first person he wrote to share the good news with was Putnam. "In this hour of success I wish to thank you most gratefully for the interest which you have shown in me since the beginning and for your influence which you have ever been glad to use in my behalf," he gushed. "Your help has been the great means that has lifted me into the goal of my ambition."[65] With this post, Parker was no longer an itinerant archaeologist. He had the credentials that he desired and the work ahead of him that he had dreamed of for years. At last, he was a bona fide archaeologist—and not just any archaeologist, but the first official archaeologist of New York State.

Horror Stricken

In the late autumn of 1905, as Parker was seeking to obtain new excavation leases for the New York State Museum, he was repeatedly rebuffed by his Seneca community. "Returning to the Cattaraugus valley I revived my efforts to lease certain sites but met with refusal notwithstanding that I offered every possible inducement," he reported to Clarke. "The sites that I wished were on Indian lands and the owners were horror stricken when the proposition was advanced. They did not wish the bones of the ancient of their race to be disturbed."[66] Only at the Burning Spring Site was Parker allowed to dig with a payment of twenty-five dollars. He did a cursory inspection of the Silverson Site as well, but the landowners, he told Clarke, "refused to permit more than superficial examination." The next year, in May 1906, he returned to the Burning Spring Site but was refused permission to excavate further. Several weeks later, he claimed he had secured a one-year signed contract with William Young, "a peculiar man," who held the land on which the Ripley Site was situated.[67] Young was a non-Indian who did not object to the disturbance of Indian burials.

These events are significant because they illustrate that the controversy of the Silverheels Site was not isolated. The Senecas' attempts to protect their ancestral burial ground on the Silverheels farm were the rule rather than the exception. Many if not most Senecas were horrified by the thought of archaeological study, and they made their revulsion unambiguously known by consistently refusing Parker permission to excavate. These events also show that Parker's reaction to the upset Senecas in 1903 was not an isolated reaction, a set of rash decisions made in difficult circumstances. Instead, his persistence in the face of such resistance reflected a deep-rooted attitude that he shared with nearly all archaeologists of his day. It is quite possible, too, that because he was able to find success at Silverheels in spite of Seneca objections, he felt he was right and justified in ignoring Seneca concerns.

Beyond Parker's immediate and self-centered interests, it is notable how easily his contempt of Seneca anxiety fit within his more expansive thinking about social evolution. He believed that those individuals who had advanced beyond savagery and barbarism lived their lives by reason rather than by superstition. Barbarians were backward thinking (and hence anti-science), whereas the civilized were forward thinking (and hence pro-science). The fact that Parker was himself of Seneca ancestry and yet was pro-science only served to reiterate and elevate his own social position at an advanced evolutionary state. That an Indian could be such a dedicated scientist showed that he was a shining example of how Indians could be lifted beyond the pall of savagery. Parker believed himself to be educated and progressive and thus able to understand and embrace the true value of archaeological inquiry.

The attitude Parker had held toward his kin in 1903 is again reflected in his frustrations to convince Senecas to allow his expeditions in 1905 and 1906. Yet even when rebuffed, he did not give up his convictions. Contrarily, he became more entrenched in them. He genuinely believed that anyone with a measure of intelligence would not knowingly thwart efforts to advance knowledge. His belief in the goodness of science fed his arrogance, even as the years wore on. Indeed, Parker believed that to find supporters of science, all one had to do was evaluate educational levels. As he wrote in 1907 to Burmaster, who was then helping to organize a systematic survey of the Cattaraugus Valley,

> It may be a difficult matter for you to explain to the Indians, who hold most of the land, I believe, the bearing of this problem upon American archaeology and anthropology in general as probably but few are sufficiently versed in the purposes of scientific research to grasp the meaning and import of such work. However, I think that there must be a few intelligent enough, and indeed, I am assured that there are, to co-operate with us in our investigations. There must be some in the vicinity of Irving, judging from our census of education, who will gladly help you in this study. Explain to the people whom you visit that it is knowledge, solely, that we are seeking and the material evidences of our knowledge. Comprehending this idea few will stand in the way of research but on the other hand gladly consent to the plan.[68]

The attitude Parker developed toward Indians who objected to archaeology eventually seeped beyond race, as seen in his spiteful comments about Young and in later interactions with others. "It may interest you to know that your refusal to cooperate in a scientific survey of this kind is unique in the history of this section of state service," he bullied one Anglo landholder in 1910, "but I feel sure that if you realized the scientific importance of archaeological investigations of the character we are prosecuting you would hardly stand in the way at the particular point which you happen to control."⁶⁹ The issue of permission may have started with race and remained infused with it, but over time it became more broadly about the righteousness and right of archaeology.

Do Curators Collect?

While Harrington studied at the University of Michigan, he opened a business in the spring of 1904 to help make ends meet. According to his new letterhead, the company was called "M. R. Harrington & Co." and specialized in the wholesale and retail of "genuine Indian work from all parts of the country."⁷⁰ As noted, Parker, too, engaged in commercial collecting and sales of antiquities and ethnological objects in the year after the Silverheels expedition. The difference became that after the New York State Museum hired Parker, he collected on behalf of the state, whereas Harrington continued to collect as a business to put himself through university. But the line between the two was not always so obvious.

In the autumn of 1905, Harrington wrote to Parker from New York asking him if he had any objects to sell. "If you have any chance to buy reasonably new or old Iroquois gagohsa or salable Iroquois objects of any sort which you can send me honorably, without doing injustice to your expedition," he wrote cautiously, "let me know and we will arrange some scheme by which you will profit as well as myself by the deal." Although Harrington is careful to emphasize that he would be interested only if Parker could do this "honorably," it was an awkward request given that Parker was at the same time employed for the state museum to collect the very objects Harrington desired. Indeed, Harrington's business no doubt conflicted at times with his own employment. Shortly after he wrote Parker, he reported that during his Christmas vacation, the Peabody Museum and American Museum were sending him on a joint collecting trip "to buy up old stuff for the museums" at Alleghany and Tonawanda.⁷¹

There is no evidence that Parker was collecting for his own profit on the side, but at some point that winter Dr. Clarke acknowledged the potential conflict of interest. He asked Parker if he had a private collection. "I beg to assure you that I have none at present," Parker promptly responded, "although some time ago I had a number of good specimens. In times past I have been in the habit of buying desirable relics whenever they were offered to me but I have always disposed of them to some scientific institution, never having made the business a matter of commerce."[72] He added that since he had begun working for the state museum, he had sold items only to the state, and he insisted on a firmly held belief that collectors should ultimately place their objects in institutions that can care for them in perpetuity. (In fact, however, Parker sold objects to Keppler and Heye in the spring and fall of 1905; and he would continue to sell objects, including grave goods from the Cattaraugus Reservation, to Heye into 1908.)[73] Almost twenty years later, this predicament was still in Parker's mind. "Museum men do not collect for themselves," he wrote definitely, perhaps then thinking back to his first days working for the state museum. "A curator who builds up a collection for his own cabinet lays himself open to heavy temptation. He also opens himself to criticism and suspicion.... No museum man should be the rival of his own institution.... To have a personal collection, therefore is unethical."[74]

A still deeper contradiction ran through Parker's collecting behaviors. Like the issue of curators collecting, this one would take him many years to come to terms with fully. The core problem was that for decades Parker did not recognize the ways in which his own collecting strategy contributed to the destruction of the very things he sought to protect. First, his excavations, at least in several instances, helped untrained professionals become aware of the economic potential of Indian antiquities. After the Ripley excavations of 1906, it was said that "Everett Burmaster made pocket money to pay for a weekend's entertainment of baseball and beer by excavating artifacts and selling them in the towns along the trolley route."[75] John Kennedy became involved in the antiquities trade after the 1903 Silverheels expedition. It is highly significant that both Harrington and Parker condoned Kennedy's culling efforts by purchasing objects from him for their respective institutions.[76]

Second, Parker would often bemoan the damage done by collectors and looters at one moment, but then in the next purchase objects that had been disinterred without concern for scientific integrity. For example, on July 12, 1906, he quoted a letter from Harrington that reported the widespread looting in Jefferson County, which had "produced a crop of phenomenally active local collectors and most of the sites are combed to death." Harrington noted that a certain Dr. Amidon's collection was a good example of such dubious collections. The next day, however, Parker received a letter from Clarke reporting that the New York State Museum had decided to purchase Amidon's collection for $175.[77] A year earlier Parker had facilitated the possible purchase of a spurious collection from a collector for his friend Joseph Keppler.[78] In 1908, he entertained the possibility of buying a few artifacts from a man who pronounced his business "buying and selling old mahogany and relics" obtained from miscellaneous sources.[79] Parker eventually decided that the prices were too high, and anyway, he hastened to add, for the state museum "it is not our policy to purchase specimens where complete data is lacking."[80] But then some five years later four boxes packed with two hundred artifacts without good context went to the state museum, and a year after that the museum considered buying a large collection for $400.[81] It seems that if a collection was unimportant to Parker, he would tell a collector that he did not want dataless antiquities. But then, in contradiction to his ostensible ethic, if the antiquities taken from unknown contexts were striking enough, he would buy them.

Perhaps one consideration that slowly began to change Parker's views on collecting was the growing awareness of the problem of fakes. Indeed, as numerous contemporary scholars have written, one key problem with the antiquities market is that when objects of dubious origin are bought and sold, it is all too easy for fake artifacts to enter into circulation.[82] As a result, collections can easily become perverted as imaginary artifacts are studied alongside authentic ones. In March 1914, Parker worked to encourage the New York State legislature to pass a law similar to one in Kentucky that outlawed the forgery of relics. "The intent of the bill is excellent and would prevent a great deal of abuse," Parker wrote. "There are a number of persons in the State who make the practice of imitating such objects and they are sometimes quite successful in deceiving purchasers. This results in a great deal of confusion to the scientific observer and needless expense in making special trips to study reported discoveries which turn out to be fraudulent."[83] Nearly a decade later, New York's legislature passed a law in which making or knowingly possessing forged antiquities was punishable by a fine of $25 to $200 and imprisonment in the county jail for up to ninety days. By 1939, Parker was publically writing about the "perversion" of archaeological data by forgeries.[84]

In the mid-1920s, Parker began to be more explicit in print about distinguishing those collections made from archaeological expeditions and those gathered by amateur relic hunters. "There is a vast difference between merely collecting 'relics' and archaeology," he argued in one article. "Mere collecting is often pure destruction of source information, while archaeology is the reconstruction of a vanished culture by means of careful observation and artifact interpretation."[85] Nevertheless, his commitments remained ambiguous. Only a year after this statement was published, Parker's museum accepted a skeleton procured by amateurs and then several months later a recreational collection so large it required a moving van to transport it.[86]

Another decade would pass before Parker finally decided that his museum would no longer buy antiquities from collectors or dealers. "For a full century America's treasure vaults of prehistory have been shamelessly looted," he proclaimed, conveniently dismissing any complicity on the part of museums. "The tragedy is that once destroyed these significant pages of antiquity never can be restored. The record is gone forever." Thus, in this same article in 1937, he announced that his museum, following in the footsteps of the Southwest Museum in Los Angeles, was no longer "interested in buying collections made by those unfamiliar with the technique of archaeology and whose field records are incomplete. It is interested solely in scientifically gathered information, the result of skilled hands and trained minds. We look forward with hope to a similar stand by other museums who are painstakingly restoring the broken pages of forgotten races."[87] And in 1938, he happily announced in the pages of *American Antiquity* that a group of Seneca chiefs proclaimed that whereas scientific archaeological work "adds to the sum of the world's knowledge," relic digging robs "America of the only remaining source of her pre-history and is an uncivilized affront to the memory of our forefathers."[88]

The Fruit of One's Labors

As Parker's career path became established at the New York State Museum, he was seen, as he certainly saw himself, to be wearing the mantle of New York's most revered anthropologists. "Following up the work of Lewis H. Morgan, who probably contributed more to initiating and advancing anthropological work among the Indians of the state than any other person," one observer wrote, "there were the writings of Beauchamp and the studies of Converse, while among the younger contributors may be mentioned Parker, the present state archaeologist, and Skinner."[89] Parker must have been proud when he read such statements confirming his dedication. Certainly, through his hard and innovative work, he was worthy of shouldering the legacies of Morgan, Beauchamp, and Converse.

In the months leading up to Parker's appointment as state archaeologist, when he was still working for Draper, he thrived in the role of ethnographer. With his family connections, he enjoyed special access to secret rites and was even given permission to record them.[90] He was also given preference to obtain ceremonial objects, such as "a dog pole in the mid-winter ceremonies" and the "famous Tall Peter silver crown" that certain collectors had purportedly been craving for more than twenty-five years.[91] Unlike in his experience with archaeology, in his ethnographic endeavors he was able to make more effective use of his Seneca connections.

It is little wonder, then, that after working at the Ripley Site over the summer of 1906 and publishing it the next year, Parker turned much of his energy toward ethnology and collecting.[92] A string of solid ethnographic and folkloric publications soon began emanating from his Albany office: *Iroquois Uses of Maize and Other Plants* (1910), *The Code of Handsome Lake, the Seneca Prophet* (1912), *The Constitution of the Five Nations* (1916), and some years later *Seneca Myths and Folktales* (1923), which was heavily based on research done between 1903 and 1906.[93]

Collecting anthropological specimens was also an important part of Parker's job. Five years after he began this tireless work, however, he quite literally saw nearly all of it go up in smoke when a fire broke out at the state museum. Parker was notified as the building was swallowed in flames, and he bravely ran into the inferno. "It was after the great roar of flame had swept through that my assistant and I got in," he would later write, "and amid the crashing walls, burning cases, and clouds of smoke, rescued much of great value in the Archaeological and Ethnological Exhibits." An impressive 10,000 objects were on display at the time, and most were utterly destroyed by water, fire, and the sandstone ceiling as it collapsed.[94] Many of the archaeological specimens were obliterated, although Parker was able to pull the Ripley materials to safety in time. Of the ethnological objects, the fire consumed 150 objects Lewis H. Morgan had collected before 1854, 350 objects from the Harriet M. Converse Collection, and some 200 "rare objects" that Parker had gathered over the previous six years. What survived were 50 Morgan objects in Parker's office at the time, Converse's silver collection, some wampum belts, and—inexplicably to Parker—all of the ceremonial objects associated with Iroquois rites.

The cost of the fire in terms of the collections lost was estimated at fifty thousand dollars, then an astronomical sum. But for Parker the damage was more than strictly material. Losing so much of the collection—which represented not only his own efforts, but also those of his anthropological heroes—was devastating. Depressed and perhaps suffering from smoke inhalation, he became physically sick. "The calamity made me rather ill for a time and I have not recovered from the shock fully yet," he wrote a friend weeks after the disaster.

> It was an awful experience, I assure you, to see the fruit of one's labors and the results of 60 years collecting by others shrivel up in a merciless flame. The most aggravating and the most discouraging feature of it all is that most of this material can never be replaced. The things are simply not to be had now. With the archaeological collections the case is slightly different. Although many of the specimens cannot be duplicated, collections fully as interesting can be purchased from private parties. This does not reconcile me, however, since what has been lost is so much information gone.[95]

In a letter to Keppler, he wrote morosely, "I was truly heart sick."[96] Such an emotional reaction shows us that for Parker, his work was not merely a job; it was his life. Notably, not a letter can be found in which Parker writes about his divorce or separation from his two children with such unabashed feeling, yet he openly grieved for the destroyed objects as if he had lost a part of himself.

From the ashes, like a phoenix, the new state museum opened in the fall of 1912. At the museum's reopening, the builders dedicated their efforts to an emerging ethic within the museum world to commit their work to education and civic engagement—shifting the museum ideal from storehouse to schoolroom. As Henry Fairfield Osborn, president of the American Museum of Natural History, proclaimed at the state museum's dedication ceremony,

> The old museum idea was that of a sanctuary or refuge, a safe deposit vault for curious, rare, or beautiful objects which might be lost or destroyed; the ignorant visitor was tolerated rather than attracted, the curator was a keeper, not a teacher. The new spirit within the natural history museum is the educational spirit, and thus is animated by what may be called its ethical sense, its sense of public duty, its realization that the general welfare of the people is the prime reason for its existence, that exploration, research, exhibition and publication should all contribute to this, that to serve a community the museum

reach out to all parts of nature and must master what nature has to show and to teach.[97]

Parker embraced this new mission wholeheartedly. For some years, he had been working on the design and construction of Iroquois life groups composed of reproduced artifacts from Tonawanda and Cattaraugus and wax models of living Indians.[98] The six dioramas were dramatically lit, a scene painted in the background, set within the darkened exhibit hall.[99] The result was a tableau that made visitors feel as if they had been transported centuries back in time and had suddenly happened upon a group of Iroquois going about their lives. More than two hundred thousand visitors saw the exhibit annually for many years; the successful installation, once "recognized as the finest exhibits of their kind in America," remained in place until 1976.[100] These dioramas embody, art historian Terry Zeller observes, Parker's recognition of the lay public's import, for he understood that the public visits museums not to consult collections as scholars do, but "to be *interested* without effort or fatigue."[101] Parker's novel approach was to move beyond taxonomic presentations of artifacts to the presentation of stories, using objects to express narratives visually. Thus, through his example and his writings, he was a central figure in creating the kinds of displays we recognize today, which seek to teach visitors about ideas instead of about mere things.[102]

The spirit of the museum as an institution that serves the public would stay with Parker for the rest of his life and even percolated into his anthropological writings, which would, with time, come to reach nonprofessional readers, children and adults alike. In many ways, Parker's efforts were expanding on the ideas of civic-minded thinkers such as John Cotton Dana and John Dewey, but Parker was unique in his unflagging attempt for four decades to realize the aspiration to make the museum, as he often said, a "university for the common man."[103]

Feeling the pang of empty shelves after the state museum's resurrection in 1912, Parker became increasingly involved in the region's archaeology. An article in the summer of 1915 reported that "a party headed by Arthur G. [sic] Parker, of Albany" was excavating a fort on the shores of Owasco Lake and had already "unearthed more than 100 relics."[104] In 1916, he took a lead in founding the New York State Archaeological Association and would later serve as its president. Today, the organization still prospers, with fifteen chapters across New York.[105] Later that same year he published an article in *American Anthropologist* that conjectured the origin of the Iroquois based on archaeological evidence.[106] Also around this time, he again returned to the Silverheels Site materials, working on the publication of his synthetic volume *The Archaeological History of New York*, although through no fault of his own it would not be published until 1920, first in a series of four New York State Bulletins, then as a two-volume compilation in 1922.

After Parker completed a biography of his granduncle Ely S. Parker, he again turned to archaeology, publishing increasingly in the field.[107] In 1919 and 1920, he and a crew began work on Boughton Hill near Victor, New York, some fifteen miles southeast of Rochester.[108] The site was thought to be a "Seneca capital" destroyed by the French in 1687. It was reported that Parker "discovered a good number of specimens," including pipes, a carved bone comb, some rare fragments of wood and fabric preserved by copper and brass artifacts, and numerous graves. During the next field season, he and Everett Burmaster explored chert pits and surveyed two large quarries in Coxsackie, just south of Albany.[109] In 1922, Parker went west again, this time to Canandaigua Lake, thirty miles to Rochester's southeast. There he focused on "excavating a remarkable prehistoric Indian Cemetery," which "yielded polished slate tubes, bird stones, two-holed gorgets, fossil ivory articles, and other unusual articles."[110] Ever focused on gathering numerous and spectacular objects, he thus predominately continued to concentrate his archaeological work on graveyards, wanting both human remains and their grave goods. It is noticeable, though, that he no longer sought to excavate on Indian land, and he never again sought to dig at home on the Cattaraugus Reservation. Indeed, he now did his archaeological research around Rochester and Albany, a great remove from his Seneca kin. His last excavations for New York State were in 1924 in the Cayuga Lake region, where he claimed to have found "the largest and longest occupied inland Algonkian sites in the State."[111]

Parker's archaeological work continued to be well regarded, even as some of his ethnographic research—for example, his book on the Iroquois Constitution—became controversial.[112] As the chancellor of New York University wrote to the president of the University of the State of New York when Parker's book *The Archaeological History of New York* came to his desk, "It is a most interesting publication, and even a hasty examination reveals the earmarks of such painstaking and thoroughgoing work as one likes to find in a government publication."[113] Although it has been observed that Parker's work of this period was born of a writing ethic that honored above all description, Parker was keenly aware of his reader's presence, often writing gripping passages.[114] Not many archaeologists of his day (or even today) would begin a report with such language: "Since the remote days when man appeared upon earth, he has been writing his own history. This writing has been, as it were, a tattooing of the brown skin of the earth mother, and the ages have covered the tracings with layers and obscured them."[115]

The Archaeological History of New York is highly descriptive of particular sites, but it is so in order to answer fundamental questions that may now seem obvious but were then unresolved. The book sought through archaeological study "to determine what races, stocks and tribes occupied this State; to discover what they made; what they used; how and where they lived; what of art and science they knew; and, even more boldly, to discover, perchance, what these autochthones thought and desired." Parker expansively framed New York's archaeology within the larger context of human history across the Americas, thus entering into dialogue with scholars throughout North America and beyond. Furthermore, he uniquely conducted an algebraic analysis of frequencies of artifact types within sites, archaeological cultures, and regions, illustrating the possibilities of archaeology as a "statistical science."[116]

Parker was not just churning out descriptive lists of artifact types; he was writing to change how people understood the possibilities of archaeology as much as New York's Indian history. He was thinking about archaeology along the cutting edge for the time, positively responding to American Anthropological Association president Roland B. Dixon's criticism of eastern archaeology as "woefully haphazard and uncoordinated ... sadly insufficient ... unsystematic and incomplete." Addressing the association, Dixon said that "we are today concerned with the relations of things, with the whens and the whys and the hows; in finding the explanation of the arts and customs of historic times in the remnants which have been left us from the prehistoric; in tracing step by step the wanderings of tribes and peoples beyond history, beyond tradition; in attempting to reconstruct the life of the past from its all too scanty remains."[117] Parker's work showed the potential of this new kind of archaeology.

Just as *The Archaeological History of New York* was rolling off the printer's press, the president of the University of Rochester wrote to Parker to tell him, "[We would like to] confer upon you the honorary degree of Master of Science in recognition of your work in the field of

Indian archaeology."[118] With this degree, Parker would receive on paper what he had long ago earned through his blood, sweat, tears, and ever-churning mind. Parker, now forty-one years old, would return to college for a day to collect his graduate degree. Nearly two decades after he first showed Harrington where Henry Silverheels had discovered an ancient fort when digging a hole to winter his potatoes, Parker must have felt that he had arrived at last.

More or Less Indian

The question of how Parker represented his identity in his work is important because it points to the problem a century ago of whether an Indian could become a bona fide anthropologist or would always remain in some measure an informant. To prove his worth and indeed even his superiority to Anglo scholars, Parker presented his different identities in different ways at different times. At one moment, he would sign his name "Gáwasowaneh" and draw attention to his Cattaraugus connections; at the next moment, he would practically deny having any Indian blood at all; but at the next, he would proudly connect both his genealogies by signing his name "Arthur C. Parker (Gáwasowaneh)." It is this multifaceted approach to his own identity that shows identity is not one thing only, but many things that are context dependent. That Parker manipulated his identities does not necessarily make him manipulative.

In the early part of 1906, as Parker was vying for a permanent position at the New York State Museum, he was under pressure to obtain objects and information that were truly unique and valuable. It was then that he wrote to Peter Sundown on the Tonawanda Reservation after hearing that Harrington had stayed with him and received his assistance. Parker explained first that he wanted to stay in Sundown's home and second that he wanted "to get a few relics such as brooches, gus-ha-ah, ga-ge-da, gais-ha, wooden bowls and in fact almost any old relic." He also explained that he had written down many old stories and wanted to get still more. He finished his letter by reminding Sundown—though Sundown likely already knew—that his grandfather, Nicholson Parker, had been born at Tonawanda. He signed off, "Arthur C. Parker, Ga wa so wa neh."[119]

More than a year later Harrington told Parker of a man named Enoch Schenendoah living just south of Syracuse in Onondaga Castle, New

York. "Mr. Harrington, Jis-go-go, was at my place yesterday and told me that you knew of an old Indian burying ground," Parker eagerly wrote to Schenendoah. "If you are sure that the burying place is a very old one and that no modern Indians were buried there I would be interested to see the place." His valediction was now simply, "Yours very truly, Ga-wa-so-wa-neh."[120]

Parker overtly claimed that his connections to Iroquois communities, both through his relatives' reputation and his own membership after initiation, gained him information and objects outsiders could not easily obtain. "I hardly expected that some of the more secret native orders would be willing to give me permission to enter their lodge ceremonies and make notes or allow me to take down the text of their rites," Parker wrote his boss in the spring of 1906, "but in several cases this permission was given and I have been able to get some of the rituals translated, though not as well as I shall be able later on."[121] Though this claim was largely true, Harrington, too, apparently had no trouble obtaining high-quality objects or gaining access to informants. (Harrington, it seems, even spoke some Seneca and wrote letters to Parker in the language.)[122] Other Anglo researchers had been adopted in the same way Parker was. Strictly speaking in terms of Iroquois kinship, Parker was no more or less a member of the community than Lewis Henry Morgan and Harriet Maxwell Converse were. Nonetheless, he had the distinct advantage of having close kin who were widely known and respected, as well as of having spent his youth on the Cattaraugus Reservation.

Parker suggested that being Indian offered more than just easy access to informants: it also afforded special insights into Indian culture and history. Prior to giving a public lecture in 1907, "The People of the Long House, the Story of the Iroquois Confederacy," illustrated in stereopticon before a group of "cultured ladies," he casually remarked in a letter to the organizer, "It might be stated as a matter of interest that the lecturer was born on a New York Indian reservation, the grandson of one of the chiefs, and was actually passed through all the experiences of an Indian of the fallen confederacy of the Five Nations." He was quick to add that just because he was of Indian ancestry did not mean the talk would be unscientific. On the contrary, he said, "it will be a study in ethnology from the inside."[123] Thus, Parker suggested that his bloodlines imbued him with a nearly matchless position in anthropology, for he was one of the discipline's few Native American scholars at the time, which enabled him to interpret the Iroquois world from within.

Parker did not always so boldly affirm his Indian identity. In 1906, after Putnam told Parker that he was included in an album as an "official" student of his, the young state archaeologist replied, "Perhaps there is just enough of the Indian in me to make me eternally grateful to the fellow who gives me a lift and godspeed."[124] Arthur C. Parker in such instances seemed to vacillate between being Indian and being barely so. As he wrote in 1909 to an editor of a magazine while pitching an article about the "real" history of the Iroquois, "I happen somehow (look me up), to be more or less of an Indian and also the State Archaeologist. I am supposed to know Red Skinned history more than skin deep."[125] His ambiguous self-representation of race was no doubt born from what was in fact an ambiguous social position—of being part Indian and part white, but not fully either. Real anger and resentment may also have been sources of this ambiguity. On one trip to Ontario, a reporter quoted Parker as he explained that the Canadian Iroquois were a "stronger and more intelligent people than their New York brothers" because they had "abandoned the ancient system of descent" and traced genealogy through the male line. "In New York a child born of a white mother and Indian father is denationalized and has no right to the claims of his father taking the nation of the mother," Parker said and then maliciously added, "Legalists point out that only animals, slaves, and some Indians, among them the Iroquois of New York, take their descent from the female line."[126] Parker no doubt harbored profound resentments.

Parker also had to be strategic about his ethnicity because of the unconcealed racism that pervaded early-twentieth-century America. Some newspaper writers seemed all too eager to make Parker play Indian to reinforce their readers' own stereotypes. One such article, printed in 1908, included an image of "Prof. A. C. Parker. The State Archaeologist in Indian Costume," showing a very young-looking Parker with a full war bonnet and a pipe. He is staring wistfully off in the distance. "The Indians are pretty well killed off in this section of the country and Albanians no longer fear the loss of their scalps. However, once in a while one stealthily skulks around and delivers a blow or two with a verbal tomahawk. And strange to say, the Indian is invited to do his worst," the article begins. "There was a pitched battle the other day at St. Paul's church and for an hour or more an Indian shot his flints into an audience of pale faces who entrenched themselves behind the protecting rows of chairs. The fray resulted in no serious damage and

Prof. Arthur C. Parker, the Indian who addressed the Men's Guild at St. Paul's church, escaped unharmed."[127]

One article after another was sure to mention Parker's ethnicity: "Mr. Parker knows his subject, as he is himself a Seneca Indian," "State Archaeologist and a full-blooded Indian," "Parker is by descent an Iroquois Indian of the Seneca Nation," "Ga-wa-so-wa-neh, or Mr. Parker," "He signs his letters 'Arthur C. Parker,' but in the quiet of his own home he prefers to be called 'Ga-wa-so-wa-neh'," "The speaker is a full blooded Seneca Indian and decidedly proud of his race," and "Archaeologist A. C. Parker, of Indian Blood."[128] It is easy to imagine the mixed feelings these articles might have inspired in Parker: on the one hand, pride that he proved a man of Indian heritage could become a successful scholar, but, on the other, unhappiness that he had to prove himself just because his patrilineage was Seneca. Also, given his many ambiguous statements—"more or less Indian"—he must have been disconcerted to learn repeatedly from reporters that he was a "full-blooded" Indian.

These pronouncements came at a time in America when many Indians were considered innately ignorant, savage, and worse. It was a time when the U.S. government was actively seeking to crush Native American cultural, economic, and political sovereignty through myriad programs.[129] Indian children across the country were forced to go to boarding schools for the express purpose of ensuring they would not grow up to be Indians.[130] Thus, Parker was succeeding both because of and in spite of his Indian heritage. Paradoxically, it was his Indianness that allowed him to succeed as state archaeologist, and yet it was his Indianness that also made him inherently unsuited for this position. Nonetheless, in the end, Parker made it work. His ethnicity combined with his profession helped make this anthropologist a success in many people's eyes. As one article published in 1915 praised, "No mistake was made in appointing Arthur C. Parker state archaeologist. A descendant of the Seneca chief, his knowledge of the Indian language and his prestige with the Indians on the reservations of this State have enabled him to make New York's collection of Indian relics the finest in the country."[131]

7
WE CAN'T GET AWAY FROM HISTORY

The Usefulness of Men

Into the 1910s, although Parker had given up conducting archaeological research on Indian reservations, he continued to maintain contact with Indian communities through political activity. For more than a decade, he, in typical fashion, worked tirelessly for pan-Indian causes and the welfare of New York's Native peoples. As early as 1911, Senecas and "old friends of the Indians" enlisted him to challenge how they were represented in a Rochester newspaper. "Our New York Indians have been systematically defamed by the press by various interests for several years," he fumed in a letter to the editor. "I refer you to an article in the *Buffalo Evening News* of Dec. 5th which depicted the Cattaraugus Indians as 'naked, poorly nourished and starving' and also the statement of the State Board of Health a year ago last May to the effect that the Indians lived in houses without floors etc. etc."[1] The next year he would begin his long tenure as secretary of the New York Indian Commission.

During World War I, Parker's main activity with Indian politics involved the Society of American Indians (SAI), which was conceived in 1911 when a small, elite group of scholastic Indian and Anglo advocates convened at Ohio State University on Columbus Day. They dreamed up an organization that aspired to stir in every Indian "the realization of personal responsibility for self and race, and the duty of responding to the call to activity."[2] The organization promoted a strong assimilationist agenda, which held that Indians must melt into America's ethnic stew while retaining the best of their Indian heritage. Its underlying ideology insisted that for Indians to endure beyond their almost inevitable extermination, they would have to adapt to the ways of their conquerors—a principle that was only a slight variation on the famous axiom of the time, "Kill the Indian and save the man!"[3] The SAI accepted and promoted the view that Parker himself had articulated some years earlier. "Mr. Parker said that the Indian knew that as a race he was doomed," a reporter summarized a talk Parker gave in 1908. "The doom is not physical extermination, but absorption. White men and women are continually intermarrying with the New York Indians and now the percentage of white blood is too large. Their hope is, however, that the distinguishing virtues, traits, and characteristics of the Indian which are so strong—hospitality, loyalty, veracity, eloquence, political ability and democracy, with many more attributes—will so modify the white race of the future that the Indian traits will be conspicuous."[4] In some measure, Parker hoped mainstream America would assimilate Native American virtues.

SAI members held that Indian identity was largely an internal strength, but in the external world Indians should embrace American citizenship, cultivate the skills and pursue the education needed to compete in capitalist society, and aspire to reach the evolutionary tree's crown. Parker wrote often for the SAI, passionately arguing that Indians must concurrently assimilate and retain their "Indian individuality."[5] The goal was to advance Indians to the position of civilized citizens so that they could productively contribute to their tribe, nation, and humanity: "the Indian should accustom himself to the culture that engulfs him and to the force that directs it . . . he should become a factor that directs it . . . he should become a factor of it, and . . . once a factor of it he should use his revitalized influence and more advantageous position in asserting and developing the great ideals of his race for the good of the greater race, which means all mankind."[6] Out of savagery into civilization was the idea.[7]

The group worked mainly outside of Indian reservations on national issues, opening an office in Washington, D.C., and launching the organization's mouthpiece, the *Quarterly Journal* (1913–15) at first and then *American Indian Magazine* (1915–20). It was successful in helping to establish a special Indian court of claims, improve health care on reservations, encourage Indians to fight in the Great War, and start a national American Indian Day. It also illustrated the possibility of creating a national pan-Indian organization by bringing together leaders such as Marie Baldwin (Chippewa), Gertrude Bonnin (Sioux), Sherman Coolidge (Arapaho), Laura Cornelius (Oneida), Charles E. Daganett (Peoria), Charles A. Eastman (Sioux), Albert Hensely (Winnebago), J. N. B. Hewitt (Tuscarora), Francis La Flesche (Omaha), Delos K. Lone Wolf (Kiowa), Carlos Montezuma (Yavapai), James Murie (Pawnee), Thomas L. Sloan (Omaha), Henry Standing Bear (Sioux), and of course Arthur C. Parker.[8] Ultimately, however, the SAI collapsed in the early

1920s, driven apart by "divisive religious issues, differences over the future of the Indian Office, and its failure to win a significant following among local tribal leaders."[9]

Many pages have already been filled with descriptions of Parker's activities in the SAI, where he was a central figure.[10] Although this work was extracurricular to his job as state archaeologist, his association with the organization is significant to his archaeology career in several ways. The SAI's philosophy of Indian betterment epitomized how Parker saw himself as a Native American archaeologist. "As self-made individuals committed to Indian progress," anthropologist Jeffery R. Hanson observes of the SAI leaders, "they espoused a national philosophy and platform that was modeled after their own personal history."[11] Shortly before the formation of the SAI, Parker gave a speech in which he argued that the degree of blood—whether an Indian is a "full-blood" or a "mixed-blood"—is irrelevant to a person's success. "It is not a question of the degree of blood but the question of individual competence that should count in determining civic or social status," he said. "Some quarter bloods are far more incompetent than some full bloods." Obliquely borrowing from Boas, Parker argued that it is the environment that shapes the person, not his or her "blood," and so each person should be judged individually on his or her own merits. "All mentions that the mixed blood is necessarily an inferior are wrong," Parker added. "Good Indian blood and good white blood have produced some of the finest Americans who ever lived . . . it is the manhood, the character, the usefulness of men that counts. It is his environment that determines his conservatism or progress, and not his racial blood."[12] Thus, Parker was saying that he wanted to be judged on the basis of his actions, not his blood quantum.

Parker was not denying his Indian heritage so much as drawing attention to how he had overcome the traits that might delay Indians at the evolutionary stages of savagery and barbarism. Indeed, as Hanson has noted, SAI members Hewitt, La Flesche, and Murie were Indians practicing anthropology; and Alanson Skinner and Frank Speck were nonvoting members.[13] All these anthropologists, like the SAI itself, embraced the tenets of Morgan's social evolution. But more, individuals such as Parker, Hewitt, La Flesche, and Murie themselves embodied the validity of social evolution, the possibility of Indians progressing to the top notch of civilization. Given Parker's personal and professional attachments to Morgan, he especially must have understood that the SAI and its successful Indian members could prove Morgan's anthropological theories to be true—theories that infused Parker's ethnography as much as his archaeological endeavors.

In addition, Parker believed that Indians should have a deep pride in their cultures and histories. "Each race should develop its own virile qualities and its own inherent virtues," he wrote. "For the Indian to cast aside all that goes to make him such and abandon all that his fathers have produced would be conducive of great harm. Without pride a race becomes dispirited, inefficient, incompetent, and the prey of stronger forces."[14] The SAI was one outlet in which Indian pride was developed, perhaps seen most plainly in the creation of a national American Indian Day.[15] For Parker, anthropology was a complementary outlet to recognize and celebrate the ingenuity and successes of Indigenous peoples. Even in the SAI's magazine, he sought to fuse politics with anthropology, including Indian folktales; he was intimating that Indian pride could be enhanced through anthropological study.[16] As he would write in his father's obituary in 1929, Frederick had inspired him to give "the Indians a new interpretation, and to draw from their teachings and customs the worthy things that would make the world hold the red race in greater esteem."[17]

Sadly, the uplift of one's own often comes at the cost of denigrating others. For the SAI and Parker, the target was often African Americans. As journalist Robert Allen Warrior has written, "In espousing a European-immigrant model for Native assimilation, Parker contended that African-Americans could not follow the same model because 'the African negro was a savage who was cruel to his own race and superstitious in the extreme.' Rather than becoming enlightened through their ability to reason, as Parker would have it for Native Americans, African-Americans could integrate only because of their 'natural servility and imitativeness,' which is 'evidence of feeble character and inferiority.'"[18] Some years later Parker's philosophy would turn darker still as he began to champion the eugenics movement.[19] Although he had long rallied against popular ideas of "fixed racial groups which were somehow 'pure' and whose 'mixture' would bring about social upheaval," ideas that underpinned eugenics politics, his ominous interest in this subject may in part have been brought about by his frustrations with the pan-Indian movement.[20]

In the early 1920s, as the SAI fell apart, Parker left the organization and pan-Indian politics altogether. Thereafter, his efforts in the betterment of Indian peoples tended to be either narrow projects, such as when the U.S. secretary of the interior appointed him chair of the Committee of 100—though, significantly, he had not sought the chairmanship—to investigate conditions on Indian reservations, or local projects, as when he secured federal funding during the Depression to create a program and museum on the Cattaraugus Reservation to revitalize traditional Iroquois arts and crafts and provide needed jobs.[21] Parker would never again become so ensconced in a major political organization, pan-Indian or otherwise. But after years of working into the night for the SAI—endless streams of letters and articles, of debates, arguments, and strategizing—he perhaps felt a bit like a soldier returning home after a losing campaign. He was likely just content to be back in the quiet of home and in the arms of his first love, anthropology.

Why Archaeology?

Parker's involvement in the SAI was his political effort to enhance the image of American Indians, and archaeology was his professional effort, as he wrote, to help hold the "red race in greater esteem." But he believed that the value of archaeology extended far beyond this, to individuals, the state, and indeed all of humanity.

In *The Archaeological History of New York*, Parker explains that archaeology can be vital in the healthy development of individual personalities. He quotes a successful businessman who claims that it was his hobby of hunting arrowheads as a youth that allowed him to develop his skills of observation and clear thinking. Hence, the wandering youth obtains "the zest of out-of-door exercise, bringing health as well as wisdom." Further still, archaeology benefits the individual, for "it is a human science, it awakens the imagination along logical lines, it teaches the use of resources nearest at hand, thereby developing ingenuity; it cultivates attention to small details, thereby stimulating observation; and as an outdoor study, it cultivates a keen appreciation of the land in which one lives."[22] In the end, archaeology leads individuals to a broader understanding and appreciation of the human race.

Parker spent nearly his entire career in publicly funded institutions, so he also articulated four main reasons why the state should support archaeological inquiry. First, archaeology is uniquely capable of explaining the state's ancient history. The archaeological sites of a state are "visual exhibits" for citizens to understand who lived in their home before the arrival of European settlers. Second, archaeological objects are a "vast reservoir of valuable knowledge." It is the state's duty to conserve and protect its resources. In addition, archaeological sites are "monumental exhibits." Demarcating sites and protecting them arouses the public's imagination and inspires scientific research. Monuments belong to the people of the state and should be protected for them. Fourth, archaeological collections have proven to be of lasting value. "Their value to science and art," Parker claimed, "is recognized even by those who are neither scientists nor artists."[23]

Parker's most expansive justification for archaeology was tied to his most passionate topic: anti-looting. For Parker, archaeology is the foundation of all human history as well as the basis for illuminating the foundations of human knowledge itself. If it is not merely the gathering of things, then it cannot abide careless destruction of an object by individuals bent only on wanting to possess the thing in itself. For Parker, the answer to the question "Why pursue archaeology?" was that collectors destroy, whereas archaeologists build valuable knowledge that would otherwise be lost to time.[24] For Parker, the shift from a focus on "relics" to a focus on "specimens" defined archaeology's professional development since the discipline's inception.[25] Relics are collected out of curiosity, whereas specimens are collected to solve scientific problems.

In the 1923 pamphlet *Method in Archaeology*, Parker outlines his philosophy.[26] He begins by positing that humans believe they can study humanity simply by virtue of belonging to the species. He claims, "No mocking bird in the ecstasy of song would conjure itself an ornithologist.... Yet, because man is man, somehow men believe that there is no other requirement necessary to be an archaeologist." As evidence, he offers this exchange:

> I once asked a poor, but happy, half-wit what he was doing in a cornfield. He answered, "You see, mister, I'm an archaeologist, and I'm pickin' up arrowheads."
> "Well, why do you pick them up?" I asked, to draw the fellow out.
> "Well, you see, mister," he answered, "I can't help it; they are so bright and shiny. I, I—, can't help it, really; they are so bright and shiny."

Merely collecting, he argues, does not make an archaeologist or a student of human history. Rather, an archaeologist is one who asks and tries to answer such questions as "What are the associated artifacts of each culture represented within the area of your explorations? What is the difference between the pottery of the gorget using people and that of the people who made clay pipes with concentric rings about the bowls? With relation to the position of the skeleton, where was each artifact from a grave found?" An archaeologist pursues these questions systematically, recording his excavations with field notes, photos, and the best of scientific knowledge. To demonstrate the difference further, he gives this illustrative example:

> Let us suppose that the great archives at Ottawa were destroyed by a mighty tornado, and that its priceless records of Canada's history were torn into millions of shreds and scattered like confetti over the province. Suppose, then that some dullard, wandering over the land in the after days, began to pick up all the letter "A"s that he could find, pasting them in an album. His collecting propensities then would cause another enthusiast to collect all the letter "B"s. Together they would go, with another who would be attracted by such a hunt, and pick up scattered letters from here and there, tearing them from already torn pages and pasting them in their albums. Their great joy would be in finding letters that they could identify, and in tearing them from the rest of the pages that they found unintelligible. Finally, these men would gather into a club and proclaim themselves Archivists, and to prove their right to the title would exhibit their albums of letters. "Ah, what a finely illuminate letter *A* that is," you would hear one exclaim. "It is different from this one I found, for mine has a duller point and is crossed higher up." Then would come the enthusiasts who would point out that the *A* men were not scientists at all, for a chosen group had discovered at least twenty-six different types of letters, each of which had two characters. This would be great discovery indeed, but what would it have to do with the history of Canada?

Thus, Parker suggests that archaeology is not merely about collecting As and Bs, but about putting the letters of history together to form a more expansive story of past lives and events. "Archaeology is nothing less than *pre-history*," he writes, "archaeology has ends in view far more important than the mere collecting of relics and specimens, and ... its aim is far more definite than that of only describing the 'relics' found on pit or mound. These 'relics' are to the archaeologist specimens of human handiwork, and illustrate some stage of culture. They are valuable, primarily, for what may be learned from them."

Although those who collect artifacts without documentation believe that they are somehow preserving the past, they are sadly mistaken, Parker explains. They are actually destroying the very objects they claim to care about. He argues, "The wrong is simply this: the bulk of archaeological specimens found by persons utterly unfamiliar with archaeology as a science [ends up in museums] . . . call[ing] attention to the fact that *the story of aboriginal man, which might be rescued, interpreted and preserved, is being actually destroyed in the most thoughtless manner.*" Ultimately, Parker argues that archaeology must become professionalized and built around questions of culture and history. First, museums "must acquire their specimens only by deliberate excavation." Second, untrained private collectors should not "do any excavating whatever." And third, archaeologists must conduct their excavations in pursuit of research questions such as "How came man to North America? What routes did he take? . . . What are the characteristic artifacts of each culture? How do these artifacts differ from those of other cultures? . . . What was the physical type of each group? What is known of their skulls and other bones? . . . What did each group know of, (a) agriculture; (b) hut building; (c) earth-works, as mounds, etc.; (d) quarrying; (e) stone working? . . . What are the various cultures represented within the area of our investigation? What have we done to map this area?"

Parker would eventually become so staunchly anti-looting that he would argue before the National Academy of Science, the Rochester Philosophical Society, and his museum patrons that archaeological resources should be nationalized so that sites, whether on public or private lands, can be excavated only by professionals. The United States, he argued, unlike countries such as Denmark, had "not yet awakened to the fact that a legal right may be a catastrophic moral wrong."[27]

For all his heated arguments railing against collectors, however, Parker at times showed a lucid empathy for the instinct to collect. He understood that the discovery of ancient objects is a complex moment that ricochets between the emotions and the intellect:

> One seldom recovers from his first surprise and delight upon discovering an arrow head. From it he receives a psychic inoculation that brews in his blood the pabulum upon which the chromosomes of his own starved instincts feed. In him is revived the spirit of his own remote biological past and his physical contact with his own ancestral life is completed, thus bridging the great gap—the long and

seemingly bottomless chasm, that separates yesterday from today. The cell entities that build the marvelous colony that in the aggregate makes the physical man thereafter have a refreshed memory and an intensified consciousness of the long struggle through the ages to their present attainment. The arrowhead, therefore, has a marvelous appeal to what is most elemental in man, and its influence lives as a potent subconscious power. This is the biological compulsion that lingers in the little flint artifact.[28]

Perhaps this discernment led Parker to engage collectors rather than merely to discount them. And perhaps, too, his desire for engagement was an instinct born in the Dickinson Seminary. Like a steadfast proselytizer among unbelievers, he was ready to preach directly to those who had sinned against science. In 1926, he bravely attended and gave a speech at a banquet held for twenty-six local amateur collectors in which the attendees brought "rare relics" to be "passed among the diners between courses for admiration and comparison." (The dinner menu mimicked the region's history, starting with "chicken broth of the Mohawks, passed on to Algonquin potatoes and concluded with Eskimo ice cream.") According to the newspaper article recasting the meeting, among these collectors Parker then gave a talk about how archaeologists alone are qualified to piece together the torn fragments of history. "Dr. Parker regretted that the excavations of this wonderful field have been carried out by laymen," the reporter recounted, "intent only on recovering the relics which often they do not long treasure." Parker lamented that within a generation "the soil will be barren for the trained archaeologist." He told the gathering that the county in which they were living, "now thoroughly ransacked by untiring and enthusiastic collectors of aboriginal sites," had been "robbed of its messages by the failure of trained archaeologists to open the pages of its story."[29] It's not difficult to imagine the collectors' awkward applause following this speech.

And yet through his plucky efforts and unstinting written arguments—and no doubt by the sway of his enthusiasm and passion—collectors were converted. "By hammering away at methods we have succeeded in inducing some of our amateurs to keep better note books," Parker proudly reported in 1928.[30] Of course, by even working with amateur archaeologists and interacting with them so closely, he risked being tainted through association. But he showed that as much as he disdained unscientific collecting, he, like any good missionary, was always ready to mix with the corrupted and tell them why their unscientific souls were in jeopardy.

The Office of Director

As the Roaring Twenties swelled, and there was a collective sigh after the Great War, Parker's career was in parallel recovering from a long, difficult decade. After nearly twenty years at the New York State Museum, he had at last built a solid national reputation as a "museum man," ethnologist, and archaeologist, and his efforts in politics, though not hugely successful, had earned him standing as a man intensely dedicated to the betterment of Indian peoples. He had even recently been admitted to the Masons and quickly rose in their ranks. "At the present writing, Mr. Arthur C. Parker, New York State Archaeologist, and a Seneca Indian, is undoubtedly the greatest living Iroquois, if not the greatest living American Indian," his friend Alanson Skinner extolled in one article. "He is distinguished for his knowledge of Indian affairs, from those of today to their archaeology. President Coolidge recently called him to Washington to serve on the Committee of One Hundred and the Masons of the State of New York have within a few months elevated him to the Thirty-third degree. It is probable that Mr. Parker is the first American Indian ever to receive this last distinction."[31]

On December 1, 1924, Parker formally resigned from his position at the state museum, ending two decades of service to New York State. Although this decision was in some ways a lateral career move, Parker had grown increasingly frustrated with a lack of support from the museum's administration as well as with a paltry salary. "My principal reasons for leaving here is that I have no help, no stenographer, and the 'powers' have no proper understanding of what archaeology and ethnology are," he explained. "I have some real plans and many subjects to complete. I have not the physical means of working here and so must go where I can work—and draw a salary that will at least half support me. I have had only the most pleasant relations with the Director and am sorry to leave him. Perhaps in a new location surrounded by a group of friends who know and appreciate the game, I can produce some of the things that are looking for expression." Director John M. Clarke was genuinely upset by the prospect of Parker's departure. "It is beyond my power to express how deeply I regret, personally and officially this change," he wrote glumly to Parker. "It may prove to be for the best interests of all concerned, surely for your private advantage, but I am blind to any good result that can come from it to our institution here." Frank Pierrepont Graves, president of the University of the State of New York, also expressed his great regret.³²

In the spring of 1925, *Science* announced that "Dr. Arthur C. Parker, since 1906 State Archaeologist of New York, has accepted the office of director of the Rochester City Museum."³³ This local museum recruited Parker because it sought a director to give it greater visibility in New York and beyond. Parker's reputation and even his early association with Harvard University were hugely attractive to Rochester's city leaders. Even more than twenty years later, the expedition of 1903 helped promote Parker to the directorship of a museum. "I know him to be one of the most outstanding men of science in America and that he has attained world-wide recognition both as an archaeologist and ethnologist, and as a specialist in museum science," the Municipal Museum Commission's president wrote in support of the hire. "I know him to have been associated with the Peabody Museum of Harvard, the American Museum of Natural History of New York and the State Museum of Albany, NY. He was trained under Professor Putnam of Harvard University, and was on the Harvard-Peabody staff in 1903."³⁴

"It is wonderful to be here in Rochester and see my plans expand," Parker wrote to Skinner shortly after arriving in Rochester. "Someday I shall have a real museum with all the appendages. It is a ten years' job and one full of joy. But of course there are drawbacks too."³⁵ The joys included having his own museum to run his way and being nearer to friends and relatives in Cattaraugus and Tonawanda. The drawbacks included taking over a museum that was badly organized and bloated at the seams with a hodgepodge of artifacts gathered with little sense over the years. The museum itself had only a vague purpose; it lacked a comprehensible organizational structure; its exhibits were unsystematic; and its staff was poorly trained.³⁶ In typical Parker fashion, he jumped into the work with vim and quickly turned the museum around. Reaching back to his early experiences in museums, he worked to meet the three objectives Franz Boas had laid out early in Parker's career, that the museum "furnish healthy entertainment . . . instruction and . . . the promotion of research."³⁷

As museologist Terry Zeller has outlined, Parker's work was concentrated in three areas.³⁸ First, Parker successfully promoted the museum to regional audiences. Through numerous newspaper articles, talks, and conferences, he convinced the denizens of Rochester that every thriving city needs a thriving museum. Along these lines, he was able to secure the museum's financial well-being. When the Depression arrived, the museum budget was cut by 70 percent, and even Parker was briefly laid off. Nonetheless, the museum came to flourish in the 1930s, and, now reinstated, he oversaw the construction of a new museum building, an "ultra-modern" granite building of three stories and some 1,100,000 cubic feet, completed in 1942.[39]

Second, Parker worked to create public exhibits and programs that would reach the broadest possible public. He supervised the construction of exhibits that aspired to teach museum visitors about their community's history. Within just four years of arriving, he had built an entirely new set of exhibits for the museum. Period rooms were made, such as a Seneca log cabin from 1813, as well as exhibits on local industry and science. The museum's hours were extended to 10:00 P.M. several nights each week, and it was open every day of the week. In 1930, Parker changed the museum's name to the "Rochester Museum of Arts and Sciences" to reflect the institution's new, broader educational goals.[40]

And third, akin to John Cotton Dana's work, Parker strove to have the museum serve the community in which it was centered. In 1926, he started an accessible monthly publication, *Museum Service*, and put his museum to service by creating the School Sciences Division, which distributed educational materials to local schools. By 1939, the program was reportedly reaching sixty thousand students a month. He wrote scripts for radio shows. He placed temporary exhibits in different buildings around town, such as City Hall and various high schools. He sponsored hobby shows; one in 1935 pulled in one hundred thousand people in just six days. At the height of the Depression, Parker created the Seneca Arts Project, which used various federal and local funds to employ some one hundred Seneca artists to craft artifacts, including reproductions of those Lewis Henry Morgan had collected for the New York State Museum and had been lost in the museum fire of 1912. Parker's goal was to benefit both the Seneca community (with employment and a revival of its arts) and the museum (by receiving the objects).

Parker's efforts were recognized nationally when he was elected vice president of the American Association of Museums in 1927, a position he would hold for more than a decade.[41] He was a wanted man, getting various job offers.[42] Parker undoubtedly relished the recognition, decades of work and a dream sowed a half century earlier in

Grandfather Nicholson's parlor finally coming to fruition. In 1935, he published *A Manual of History Museums* under the prestigious imprinter Columbia University Press. It was well received, influencing a generation of museum workers.[43] He is even credited with coining the term *museologist*. As Zeller convincingly argues, Parker was among "the most active, vocal, and articulate spokesmen of all time for the community museum with education and public service as its *raison d'être*," and as such he "deserves to be numbered among the outstanding pioneers in American museums."[44]

High Accomplishment in the Science of Archaeology

In 1940, Parker received an honorary doctorate from Union College for his work in the "arts of museum administration," but significantly also for his "high accomplishment in the science of archaeology."[45] Thus, it was his research in archaeology that at last gave him the seal of academic recognition that he had so long desired. Even with his intense administrative duties in Rochester, he maintained an active research program. One of his first archaeological projects as director reflected his populist goals for the museum. In 1926, he conducted a "paper survey" of Indian sites in eastern Pennsylvania in collaboration with the Wyoming Historical and Geological Society based out of Wilkes-Barre, Pennsylvania. The project involved sending out some thirteen thousand letters with publicity posters and questionnaires to "Historical and Patriotic Societies, Farm Bureau and Grange leaders, foresters, school teachers, Scout masters, and many hundred known individual collectors in the forty-one counties comprising the Eastern portion of the State."[46] In addition, newspapers wrote articles about the survey and asked individuals with knowledge about the location of archaeological sites to contact the society. The response was overwhelmingly positive. "The subject of the Indian is apparently more popular with the average citizen than is commonly supposed," it was reported. "The Society did not wait long for the response. The postman was swamped with replies, varying in interest and importance from 'Don't know nothing about these goods,' to the invaluable information turned in by amateur collectors and well-known historians. Photographs of rocks covered with Indian picture-writing, soon to be covered by one of the super-power dams, have been received. Old trails soon to be obliterated by railroad cuts and fills have been brought to the Society's attention."[47] Numerous maps were sent in as well. The information was dutifully recorded, and at the project's end a considerable 1,900 new sites were recorded.

More orthodox projects soon followed. In 1927, Parker's museum sponsored expeditions in Pennsylvania, Ontario, and New York, with intensive excavations at two sites, Levanna (Cayuga County) and Lamoka (Schuyler County).[48] At Lamoka, excavators put in a trench 28 feet wide and 225 feet long. The site, estimated to be two to four thousand years old produced more than five thousand artifacts for the museum and, Parker believed, presented evidence of cannibalism. The next year Parker and his crew returned to Lamoka Lake. In addition to numerous skeletons, "over ten thousands specimens of bone, antler, and stone have been brought in," he wrote proudly.[49] Excavations were also conducted in Pennsylvania and at Chautauqua Lake.

As Parker's workload at the museum intensified, he had less time for directing expeditions, so he began working with a young man named William A. Ritchie. In 1929, Parker only supervised Ritchie's work, done on behalf of the museum, although in 1930 Parker himself was able to go to Willow Point, near Binghamton, New York, to excavate twelve skeletons and visit some sites in Pennsylvania.[50] In 1932, the museum didn't sponsor any expeditions, but in 1933 Parker worked closer to Rochester, in the Genesee region, focusing on the "perplexing Iroquois-Algonkin cultural complex."[51] By the mid-1930s, Ritchie was given increasing responsibilities as Parker turned ever more to the work of the museologist. In 1934, Parker supervised Ritchie's explorations throughout New York: at a site near Canandaigua where "several thousand bone, stone, and pottery specimens, and two extensive cemeteries were found," at three Iroquois burial sites in Western Finger Lakes region, at sites in Genesee Valley, and at a site twenty-five miles south of Rochester, a Seneca cemetery, "which had escaped detection by collectors and expeditions from four museums during the past 50 years, [and] was located by the Museum party and 80 burials uncovered."[52] In 1935, Ritchie worked alone again, under Parker's supervision, at a "singular Algonkin workshop site" near Bainbridge, as well as at sites in the lower Susquehanna Valley, the Mohawk River, and the vicinity of Seneca Lake.[53] And in 1938, Ritchie was sent to excavate two large village sites on Oneida Lake in central New York, at which numerous artifacts and a "number of burials also came to light."[54] Parker's last active fieldwork came in 1936 and 1937, when, accompanied by Ritchie and a team of volunteers, he conducted surveys in the St. Lawrence Valley and a few excavations in various parts of New York.⁵⁵

Parker also continued to be involved in archaeology through his administrative work. In 1934, his museum hosted the Eastern States Archaeological Association annual meeting, at which numerous presentations were given, including "a series of papers on the field work of the museum's recent excavations at Alima and Canandaigua."⁵⁶ In addition, he served terms as president of the New York State Archaeological Association (1932), the Genesee Country Historical Federation (1935), and the New York State Historical Association (1945).⁵⁷

The archaeological research Parker conducted and sponsored while in Rochester illustrates his ambition to study and be associated with archaeology throughout New York. In this way, the final years of his archaeology career were a continuation of his synthetic book *The Archaeological History of New York* (1922). His active participation in the New York State Archaeological Association and later in the larger, more prestigious New York State Historical Association similarly underpinned his ambition to make the Rochester Museum of Arts and Sciences more than a city museum and to make his name synonymous with New York archaeology.

His archaeological endeavors in the 1920s and 1930s also exhibit his embrace of an outreach ethic, a dramatic change from his early expeditions. Consider, for instance, that in 1903 Parker strove to keep the Silverheels Site a secret from the press and again in 1905 was instructed to avoid the press, ultimately promising his employers to "jealously guard my material from all sources that would lead to premature publicity."⁵⁸ Such an attitude sharply contrasts with his "paper survey" of 1926, which enthusiastically recruited the public and press to help identify sites. Through the museum's exhibits, the inclusion of volunteers in fieldwork, his popular writing and radio shows, and his continuing commitment to a scientific archaeology, Parker in many ways anticipated the "public archaeology" movement that began in the 1970s and took off in the 1990s.⁵⁹ Indeed, a 2005 project that thought itself rather novel was remarkably similar to Parker's paper survey conducted eighty years earlier.⁶⁰ Thus, Parker's public engagement with archaeology came to reflect and reinforce his populist attitude regarding museums: the two went hand in hand.

Although these efforts show Parker's aspiration to connect with the general public, his work away from Indian reservations illustrates his avoidance of dealing with the issue of digging human remains. As noted earlier, in the 1930s Parker continued to be involved with Senecas at Cattaraugus and Tonawanda, but his archaeological research was carried out away from the prying eyes of New York's Indian communities. The fact that he and his protégé Ritchie continued to excavate burials indicates that his avoidance of Indian reservations was far from coincidental. Thus, Parker would not—and perhaps could not, given his enduring commitment to science's ascendancy—resolve a major conflict with his own community, a conflict that had begun with his first major expedition at the Silverheels Site in 1903. Despite it all, to the end he insisted on the right to take Indian remains in the name of science. The lesson he learned in 1903 was not to stop digging to respect his kin's wishes, but rather to keep his work on dead Indians quiet from the living ones.

Making the Most of It

On September 17, 1914, at age thirty-three, Arthur C. Parker married for the second time, to a seventeen-year-old woman named Anne Theresa Cooke, "an accomplished musician who had both charm and a commitment to community effort." Also from New York, Anne had a strong interest in regional history. Like Beulah, she would often accompany Parker during his archaeological expeditions.[61] It is unclear whether Arthur needed or simply enjoyed his wife's company in the field, but the presence and support of family was an important part of his work. Arthur had his third child with Anne, a daughter, Martha Anne Parker. Both mother and daughter were adopted into the Wolf Clan and given names, Yewanote and Gawenone, respectively, thus formally becoming part of the Seneca community.[62]

In marrying an Anglo woman, Arthur must have known that he was consigning another generation of Parkers to being Indian only partly but not fully. The marriage also perhaps further provoked his own ambiguities of identity; having an Anglo woman in his home and Anglo in-laws must have been a change from Beulah's presence only a few years earlier. But, then, who can say with matters of the heart? It would seem the couple truly loved each other: Anne would be with Arthur until the end.

Another marriage would also affect Arthur's life directly, though the marriage was not his own. At some point after 1904, M. Raymond Harrington dropped out of the University of Michigan and enrolled at Columbia University in New York City.[63] He received his master's degree there in 1908 after completing a thesis on Iroquois archaeology. Harrington's business with his friend Frank Covert, trading in ethnological art pieces, would lead him to a job with George Gustav Heye, the obsessive collector whose collection would eventually become the Museum of the American Indian and later form the core of the National Museum of the American Indian in Washington, D.C. Through the 1910s and 1920s, Harrington undertook expeditions to Arkansas, Tennessee, Nevada, Texas, and even Cuba.

Arthur and Raymond remained close friends.[64] In 1927, they would also become brothers-in-law when Raymond married Edna L. Parker, Arthur's sister. Raymond had not seen Edna for twenty-three years, but after bumping into her in Reno, Nevada, he hired her as an expedition secretary and tutor for his son, and then married her shortly thereafter.[65] The newlyweds moved to Los Angeles the next year, where Raymond was hired as director of research at the Southwest Museum.[66] A letter to Arthur from his father would suggest that Edna had at last found a measure of happiness with Raymond. "Edna is out in the desert now," he wrote. "I don't see why she don't stay in Los Angeles, and keep a home. It must be some task to look after everything for Raymond. But poor girl, she had over twenty years of—well, not life but in reality buried, and now that she is really living, she is making the most of it. She has a good boy in Raymond and he evidently thinks the world of her. So I can't blame her for living to the full while she is still able."[67] Raymond later became curator at the Southwest Museum and undertook work in the Depression with the Civilian Conservation Corps to salvage the "Lost City" that was to be drowned by a lake after the construction of the Hoover Dam. The myth goes that Raymond kept digging until the water was literally lapping at his feet. After Edna passed away in 1948, Raymond married again the next year.[68] He was eventually given an honorary doctorate by Occidental College in 1956. He continued to conduct archaeological studies in California and Nevada for the rest of his career. Just short of his ninetieth birthday, in the summer of 1971, Raymond died and was buried in the San Fernando Mission Cemetery.

Strangely enough, Raymond also ended up close to his good friend's former wife, Beulah. After Beulah's separation from Arthur, she moved to Los Angeles, where she would live the rest of her days. She appeared in several major movies as "Beulah Dark Cloud"; in a film version of Zane Gray's *Desert Gold* in 1919, starring as a Tohono O'odham mother; and then in the Western movie *The Crimson Challenge* in 1922. She produced and directed pageants, including one called *The Landing of the Pilgrim Fathers*, which was among the first plays put on in the Hollywood Bowl. She remarried, this time to a yard clerk at Western Pacific, "a half Swede and half Indian," and became Beulah T. Filson.[69] In 1928, she had a serious accident and was forced to retire from acting and directing.

In her long retirement, Beulah again accompanied an anthropologist into the field, only this time the anthropologist was her daughter. Bertha had become involved with the Southwest Museum through her stepuncle Harrington, and mother and daughter went on "ethnological expeditions" that collected "data on the lore, mythology, and early history of the California Indians." On one such trip in the early 1930s, Bertha and Beulah participated in a healing ceremony preformed by a shaman of the Maidu Indians in northern California.[70] Bertha had been troubled by a singing bird that came to her only at night, and Beulah had a bone fragment removed from her arm, which had been fractured earlier, perhaps in the career-ending accident. They visited again several years later, another adventure that included a feast of Indian bread, local raw salt, wild berries, fruit, and a rice stew with "dear" meat, which turned out to be the family dog.[71] A decade later, in the years just before Beulah's death at the age of fifty-eight in 1945, the two were still traveling together to conduct ethnographic interviews.[72]

The President, Dr. A. C. Parker

In the deep of winter, on Sunday, December 29, 1935, some seventy-five dedicated scholars gathered in Andover, Massachusetts, for the first annual meeting of the SAA, the Society for American Archaeology, held in conjunction with the meeting of the American Anthropological Association and the American Folk-Lore Society. The attendees sat through a swift business meeting and heard eight papers, including Herbert J. Spinden's "The Intermediate Period of Maya Archaeology," Carl C. Seltzer's "The Racial Anthropometry of the Zuni Indians, with Special Emphasis on the Relationship Between Archaeological and Physical Data in the Southwest," Arthur C. Parker's "Iroquois Effigy Combs," and Allen H. Godbey's "The Patina Factor in Archaeological Chronology." They also saw a black-and-white movie, *Pottery Making at Las Guabas, Coclé Province, Panama*. It was a productive meeting, according to the report that followed it, which also observed, "The President, Dr. A. C. Parker, presided."[73]

The SAA had been organized a year earlier at the Hotel Roosevelt in Pittsburgh, Pennsylvania, after the subscription dinner for Section H of the American Association for the Advance of Science (AAAS).[74] Carl E. Guthe, director of the University of Michigan's Museum of Anthropology and later, in 1944, director of the New York State Museum, opened the 1934 AAAS meeting and gave a brief history of the events and ideas leading up to the proposal for the SAA.[75] In 1921, the National Research Council had established the Committee on State Archaeological Surveys, whose original purpose was "to stimulate a greater scientific interest in local archaeology" in the American Midwest, but by the mid-1920s the committee had become "a clearing house and advisory center for North American archaeology." Financially supported since 1929 by the Carnegie Corporation, the committee observed archaeology's increasing popularity among other scholarly disciplines as well as among nonprofessionals, which had led many to relic hunting. With archaeologists selected from different states, the committee had worked to foster a "greater appreciation of scientific standards in archaeology." However, it had three shortcomings. First, it was not a permanent organization. Second, it offered individuals no direct voice in its decisions and policies. And third, it lacked a way of reaching interested Americans who in turn were "becoming self-conscious and organizing societies for collecting relics." Thus, the committee wanted to be permanent, to have a democratic voice for its participants, and to include nonprofessionals in archaeological science.

These ideas were discussed first in 1933, then more seriously at the beginning of 1934, one evening in a smoke-filled room among a small group at an American Anthropological Association meeting.[76] A prospectus was put together and sent out to two hundred people. All but two who responded supported the new endeavor. In the fall, a ballot was sent out to select a committee to work on the organization's constitution and by-laws. "There are several points which should be emphasized," Guthe concluded in his opening remarks at the AAAS dinner. "We are attempting to create a mechanism by which those anthropologists using the archaeological method may be brought into closer contact with the public interest in our work. We are not attempting to isolate ourselves as American archaeologists. We are attempting to create a wider appreciation of the methods and principles of scientific research. We have no intention of lowering the standards of professional archaeological research. Vandalism and destruction, in most cases, are the result of well-intentioned ignorance."

In response to Guthe, Warren King Moorehead, the director of the Department of Archaeology at Phillips Academy in Andover and known to some as the "dean of archaeology," asked, "You refer to non-professionals, and the professionals helping them. It is often difficult to distinguish between these two classes. There are many men who began as non-professionals and who have done excellent scientific work in the field, such as George Will, Dorsey, Parker, Moore, Wilson, and others." Moorehead, perhaps, was not entirely picking on Parker and the others so much as asking about himself: the women and men in the room probably knew that he, like Parker, had not graduated from college, but was a successful archaeologist with Frederic W. Putnam's support and had received an honorary master's degree from Dartmouth College in 1901.[77] Some possibly knew, too, that more than a decade earlier Moorehead had pushed for Parker's nomination to chair the Committee of 100. He had then written kind words about "Dr. Arthur C. Parker of Albany," naming him an Indian "sympathetic and broad-minded."[78] Moorehead anyway seemingly missed Guthe's point that the field had changed since the turn of the century. Guthe was not criticizing those like Moorehead and Parker so much as "serving notice to all coming into the field that some form of certification was necessary for recognition as a professional archaeologist."[79]

Other comments were given at the 1934 meeting, including a long diatribe by Herbert J. Spinden, an ethnologist, about thoughtless destruction and rampant looting done in Central America, including by self-pronounced "archaeologists." Leslie Spier, then a professor at Yale University and the editor of *American Anthropologist*—a man of some influence at the time—retorted that the main issue at hand was quite straightforward. "They hope to induce reasonably serious non-professional archaeologists to join them," he said curtly. "That is the question that has been discussed. Do we here as professional archaeologists wish to affiliate ourselves to further the profession of archaeology?"[80]

After this discussion in the 1934 meeting, a motion was made to accept the constitution and by-laws of the proposed new society. A second was given, and the motion passed. The SAA was officially founded with the express object "to stimulate scientific research in archaeology of the New World by: creating closer professional relations among archaeologists and between them and others interested in American archaeology; guiding, by request, the research work of amateurs; advocating the conservation of archaeological data and furthering the control or elimination of commercialization of archaeological objects; and promoting a more rational public appreciation of the aims and limitations of archaeological research."[81]

The next order of business was to create a council and agree on the SAA's officers. "I took it upon myself to talk this matter over with a number of men in order to eliminate, so far as possible, unnecessary delay," Guthe explained. "The officers and members of the Council must be eligible as Fellows i.e., they must be members who are competent archaeologists, and who have the respect and esteem of the entire personnel. The president must be actively interested in archaeology and in furthering the objectives of the Society." A "nominating group" made up of Fay-Cooper Cole, A. E. Jenks, and Ralph Linton offered a single slate, which included Arthur C. Parker as president. As fate would have it—in a reversal of the roles played in the 1903 expedition—Parker's old friend and then brother-in-law, M. Raymond Harrington, was nominated for vice president. The assembled diners quickly accepted the nominations and "Dr. Guthe was asked to notify the officers of their election." Neither Harrington nor Parker was present at the meeting.

An hour had passed, and it was nearing 11:00 P.M., but Spier got in some final words. He related a concern felt among a handful of scholars that the formation of the SAA was a "separatist movement," an attempt to split archaeology away from anthropology. He explained that he supported the SAA and instead saw the organization as a means to bring together specialists. Thus, the SAA was just one more specialized branch of anthropology, like folklore and linguistics. To be sure, as Guthe would write years later, "the Society was not the expression of a separatist movement, but an attempt to bring anthropologists using the archaeological method into closer contact with the public, and to establish a wider appreciation of the methods and principles of scientific study."[82]

The details of this meeting help explain how it is that Parker could become the first president of a major organization of archaeologists, how he could be chosen to represent a science that dismissed Native American claims to the past and in an age when Indians were still considered second-class citizens.[83] To begin with, the SAA's stated principles closely paralleled Parker's own beliefs and efforts—first, to rail against looters and, second, to change looters to supporters of science through inclusion and public education. Some professionals saw Parker as bridging the worlds of professionals and nonprofessionals, and so he fit another stated aim of the SAA, which would initially depend heavily on amateurs because in 1935 only seven universities were conferring Ph.D.s in archaeology.[84] Furthermore, following from Spier's final comments, there was concern that the SAA represented a splinter organization. Hence, by electing an archaeologist with a strong background in ethnology, concerns about archaeology seceding from anthropology were quelled. Parker, thinking like Spier, wrote that he saw the SAA as the outcome of archaeology's coming to "occupy a highly specialized field."[85] There would be no civil war for anthropology. Politically speaking, Parker was the perfect choice as the first president for the fledgling organization. He was not chosen because he was Indian, but rather in spite of it. In news articles announcing the society's birth, no mention is made of "Dr." Arthur Parker's Seneca heritage.[86] Only years later is his genealogy noted in connection with the SAA, in a 1985 article by James B. Griffin, where he is referred to as "a scion of a prominent Seneca family."[87]

Appointed to the National Research Council in 1929, Parker had only recently been invited to serve on the Committee on State Archaeological Surveys—in August 1934, well after plans for the SAA were under way. But his boosterism had likely caught the committee's attention, and he was a keen and experienced organizer known for being evenhanded and delicately handling difficult matters.[88] The choice of him as SAA's first president was a good one. The SAA's first year went smoothly.[89] Little correspondence about the SAA can be found in Parker's files, indicating that few fires needed putting out. He apparently served with pleasure.[90] Under his watch, an impressive 328 individuals and sixteen institutions joined the nascent organization. Because the society was made up of both professionals and nonprofessionals, it distinguished "affiliates" from "fellows," the latter being professional researchers who had published their work in "recognized scientific media."[91] (Both affiliates and fellows paid three dollars a year to be members, which included a subscription to the newly founded quarterly journal *American Antiquity*.) The nomination form Parker filled out for fellow status was bolstered by his association with Putnam and his 1903 work, mentioned under both "Extent of academic or practical training" ("with Frederic Ward Putnam, 1902–03 [Peabody Museum]; American Museum of Natural History [with M. Raymond Harrington] '03") and "Experience in research" ("Assistant in archaeology, American Museum, '00–02, research work directed by Prof. F. W. Putnam").[92] At the SAA's first annual meeting, thirty-eight men and four women were accepted as fellows, a list that reads like the who's who of twentieth-century American archaeology:[93]

Katherine Bartlett
S. A. Bartett
Earl H. Bell
Glenn A. Black
Henry B. Collins Jr.
Harold S. Colton
Frederica de Laguna
Anna H. Gayton
Harold S. Gladwin
Emerson F. Greenman
Carl E. Guthe
M. R. Harrington
Emil W. Haury
Florence M. Hawley
F. W. Hodge
Edgar B. Howard
Diamond Jenness
A. V. Kidder
A. L. Kroeber
Ralph Linton
Samuel K. Lothrop
Paul S. Martin
J. Alden Mason
W. C. McKern
Warren King Moorehead
Earl H. Morris
N. C. Nelson
Arthur C. Parker
J. E. Pearce
Oliver G. Ricketson Jr.
William A. Ritchie
Frank H. H. Roberts Jr.
Linton Satterthwaite Jr.
Frank M. Setzler
Leslie Spier
Julian Steward

William D. Strong
A. M. Tozzer
George C. Vaillant
William S. Webb
Waldo R. Wedel
William J. Wintemberg

From the start, the SAA was to be the preeminent organization of American archaeologists, as indeed it remains today. Historian of archaeology Thomas C. Patterson argues that this list of powerful scholars was not coincidental, but rather that the SAA was a means for elites ("Eastern Establishment professional archeologists") to control archaeological resources for their own use and to limit the activities of others ("Core Culture nonprofessionals"). He argues that in the first five years the "society's organization minimized the role of the amateurs in decision- and policymaking."[94] Indeed, as Patterson points out, the SAA doubled in size in these years, yet fellows made up barely 13 percent of the membership, even with an upsurge of anthropology Ph.D.s in the 1930s.[95] In 1942, the SAA gave up its controversial two-tiered system, but enshrined in its revised constitution the rule to deny membership to "persons who habitually misuse archaeological objects or sites for commercial purposes."[96] Nevertheless, a decade after its founding, nonprofessionals made up the majority of the SAA membership, and one small study found that between 1955 and 1957, nonprofessionals "had authored 14 percent of the major articles and 21 percent of Facts and Comments" in *American Antiquity*.[97] Despite several attempts to encourage a diversity of authors through the years, by the 1980s the SAA's flagship journal was plainly an outlet for scientific professionals, and "amateurs" were left out in the dark.[98]

From the first issue of *American Antiquity*, the tension between professional and nonprofessional is evident. In the issue's editorial, Parker begins by noting the shift in American archaeology from curio collecting to deductive science. He writes of a hope that the journal will provide a means of standardizing the language of archaeology and that the organization more broadly will help to inspire a spirit of conservation. Bemoaning the loss of archaeological sites, he points the finger solely at uneducated amateurs and commercial excavators. "The fact that anyone with a spade has had the right to excavate ancient sites and hawk relics as a commercial venture has had baneful results," he opines. "It is impossible to guess how many unique sites, key locations and individual objects of surpassing interest have been lost or destroyed by inexpert hands." The SAA therefore is a means to place "facts" in the hands of amateurs so that they will have some guidance in their efforts. If this is not done, Parker warns, nonprofessionals will destroy the field of archaeology.[99]

Although the SAA's desire to share information with the public and include nonprofessionals was not false, Parker's editorial indicates that the society's reasoning was far from altruistic. The tone and implication are condescending. "We real archaeologists will educate you nonprofessionals and allow you to join us" was the message. "But most of you amateurs are apt to wreck our field" was the subtext. Thus, even as the SAA's stated intent was to join professionals and nonprofessionals, the incipient organization contrarily served to exclude large segments of the public. It built a moral community that subscribed to one value: archaeological science. Those who did not subscribe to this value were not just disagreeing, but committing a moral wrong. "You are either with us or against us" was the prevalent attitude among the SAA's founders, as is evident in Parker's condemnation of looters. His argument that archaeological language needed to be standardized similarly reflected a belief that archaeology must be more homogenized. "Through the publication of *American Antiquity*," he explained in the journal's first issue, "it is hoped that literature may be provided for a more uniform nomenclature, for culture classification and for the common facts and methods useful for concerted action." The SAA was to build a community of archaeologists who shared the same language, practices, and beliefs.

The SAA was also attractive to Parker because it allowed him to be further defined as a professional. As Moorehead's comment during the organizational meeting indicated, Parker was known by some to be an amateur turned expert. The SAA presidency confirmed his authority and status as a bona fide archaeologist. The SAA drew the line in the sand, and he knew which side he wanted to be on. Thus, for Parker, his role as SAA president had far less to do with the question of his Indian identity and nearly everything to do with his professional identity. The society enabled him to prove further his commitment to science and his dedication to the preservation of the resources archaeologists needed to conduct their work.

Parker's affiliation with the SAA would continue for some years. In 1939, he was appointed first to the chairmanship of SAA's powerful nominating committee and then in 1945 as a member of that committee.[100] Even after the distinction between fellows and affiliates was no longer made, Parker continued to note proudly that he was a fellow of the SAA.[101]

Errors about Indians

In the space of two years, Parker published three books. The first, published in 1927, was *The Indian How Book*, which combines Parker's knowledge of ethnology and archaeology to focus on Indian material culture, social organization, lifeways, and worldviews. It consists of seventy-four "how" questions, such as how Indians made fire, how Indians bathed, how Indians dressed, how Indians scalped their foes, how Indians came to America, and how civilized Indians are today. Next came two children's books on Iroquois folklore, first *Skunny Wundy and Other Indian Tales*, also in 1927, and then *Rumbling Wings and Other Indian Stories* in 1928.

Unlike in his archaeological work at the time, where he presents himself first and foremost as a professional scholar, in these books geared toward more public audiences he openly projects his Indian identity. *The Indian How Book* begins with a dedication that lets the reader know from the start the author's genealogy: "To My Father, Whose loving hand first gave me guidance to the wonders of the woodland, glen and glade, and whose knowledge of the red race through ancestral inheritance gave me a sympathetic understanding of its history and culture, this book is affectionately dedicated." Indeed, the observant reader likely did not miss the significance of the author's name on the cover, "Arthur C. Parker" and underneath it "Gawaso Wanneh." The dust jackets for *Skunny Wundy* and *Rumbling Wings* similarly announce, "authored by Arthur C. Parker (Gawaso Wanneh)."[102]

Notions of "authenticity" likely motivated Parker to use his two names on these books, a strategy to make the books more legitimate in the eyes of readers. That is, when learning about how Indians made fire, the reader was to understand that a "real" Indian was imparting this information. Or, when wrapped up in the tale of Rumbling Wings, the reader on some level was to imagine he or she was sitting by the campfire, hearing from the lips of a genuine Indian an authentic story passed down through the generations. But, significantly, an emphasis on Parker's Indian heritage would have helped legitimize his archaeological writings as well, especially in his functionalist approach, which often depended on ethnographic analogy where intimate knowledge of Indian affairs was important. The difference with these books was that they were not to be read by scholars, but by nearly the opposite: children. Hence, Parker's professional identity was not in question. He was able to assert his Indian identity not only because it would authenticate the books, but also because it was a venue in which his Indian identity would not undermine his professional identity. Indeed, just writing a nonacademic book was in some measure contrary to a professional persona wholly dedicated to science, so the inscription helped emphasize that this book was by Parker (Gáwasowaneh) the anthropologist-Indian, not Dr. Parker the expert-scholar. Parker used the name "Gáwasowaneh" only in personal correspondence or in publications concerning Indian rights or for a nonacademic audience.[103]

It is difficult not to read into these books and others during this period a certain ambivalence about American Indians. On the one hand, Parker makes great effort to challenge popular notions of Native American culture and history. In one booklet published in 1935, he goes through ten "errors about Indians":

1. Iroquois women were not called squaws and children were not papooses.
2. Indian women did not do all the work.
3. Hunting and fishing were not pleasures as with modern man. (It was work.)
4. Indians were not more cruel than any people of their time and economic condition. (When analyzed the Indians were actually almost as cruel as Europeans! It was a state in human evolution to which even the red man was not exempted.)
5. The Iroquois were not nomads, roaming from place to place.
6. Our eastern forest Indians did not live in tepees or conical tents.
7. Iroquois Indians did not wear the feathered war bonnets characteristic of attested warriors of certain Plains tribes.
8. The Iroquois were not war-like.
9. One of the strangest ideas about Indians is that they had no sense of humor.
10. Some old writers thought the Indians came from the Ten Lost Tribes.[104]

Such statements are indicators of Parker's desire to undermine stereotypes. The list is reminiscent of his talks as far back as 1908, when he presented lectures on Indian humor and the deep origins and historical persistence of the Haudenosaunee.[105] For decades, he had been arguing for a recognition of the humanity of Indian peoples and of their true histories.

And yet in other instances Parker shows a propensity to reinforce popular misconceptions even as he is challenging them. In *The Indian How Book*, the reader learns how Indians smelled. "Every race has its own peculiar scent," Parker lectures.

> The Chinese say they can detect a white man when he comes into the house, and the white man says he can tell the smell of the Oriental. Neither professes to like the smell of the other. It may be that racial smells have a great deal to do with racial likes and dislikes for one another. It may also be that we are scarcely aware that it is the smell that affects us.... The Indian therefore is as scentless and hairless so far as the body is concerned as any race of which we know. This is so far true that some Indians say that they can tell a half-blood by his different smell.... Some persons going to the Indian country were warned to take along perfumes to cover up the Indian smells. Some actually did this but found no use for them for no especial odor was ever evident.[106]

Such passages about race would suggest Parker's own ambivalence about the significance of human biology—the eugenic adherent proud of his Indian ancestry.

As Parker's career blossomed in the 1930s and 1940s, the identity he most often portrayed in the public centered on his professional successes. And, indeed, there were many. In 1935, the *Rochester Times-Union* announced that Parker had obtained an "international reputation" when the Institute of Anthropology and Ethnology of the Academy of Science of Leningrad invited him to contribute two appendices to the Russian edition of Morgan's *Ancient Society*. "Rochester should be proud to have on its municipal pay roll a public servant of the proud capacity and international reputation of Arthur C. Parker, director of the Municipal Museum," the paper proclaimed.[107] The next year, another article announced that Parker had been named the year's "most famous person of Indian descent in the United States."[108] On the heels of the SAA presidency, he was reelected for the fourth time as president of the New York State Archaeological Association. The accolades continued in the next decade, when Keuka College awarded him an honorary doctor of humane letters in 1943 and when near his retirement he would become a fellow of the Royal Society of Arts and the American Association for the Advancement of Science as well as an honorary life fellow of the Rochester Academy of Science. He was also elected president of the New York State Historical Association in 1945, a major organization with members and historical holdings throughout the state.[109]

Although Parker began his career by justifying it with language about his desire to preserve the "memory of my people," toward the end of his career rarely were his successes measured by this youthful goal. Instead, he is seen as a successful professional anthropologist, first and foremost, and hence his academic identity in some measure displaces his Indian identity. For instance, Herbert Gambrell, director of the Dallas Historical Society, wrote in one letter, "I want to say to you today what I have often said behind your back: That to you—your knowledge, your generosity, and your amazing common sense—have been of greater help to me in my work than you could possibly realize. That I have not done better is truly no fault of yours; and I am certain that hundreds of museum people throughout the country are saying precisely the same thing. I have often thought that just as truly as the modern high school is a monument to Horace Mann, so the modern history museum is the creation of Arthur C. Parker."[110] A newspaper article in the *New York Sun* at this same time observed that Parker single-handedly created the Rochester Museum, received numerous awards and honors, and was "a learned geologist, archaeologist, ethnologist, and anthropologist and an authority on Indian cultures and sociological history."[111] These comments are wonderfully laudatory, complimentary of Parker's professional success and winning personality, but neither the letter nor the article mentions Parker's contributions to the cause of Indian betterment. More letters from Rochester's local businessmen (such as Edwin Allen Stebbins, president of the Rochester Savings Bank, and Carey Brown of Eastman Kodak Company) and from professional colleagues (such as A. Wetmore, secretary of the Smithsonian, and Beatrice Winser, director of the Newark Museum) similarly disregard Parker's desire to preserve the memory of his people.[112]

Even when Parker won the Rochester Civic Medal, a local award in which his local connections and Depression-era efforts were certainly factors, almost no mention was made of his Seneca heritage. And letters of support for the medal definitely came from all over—from a New York House representative, a New York State senator, the director of the American Association of Museums, the director of the Hennepin

County Historical Association, the Sons of the American Revolution Empire State Society president, the director of Alabama's state museum, the New York State historian, the director of Columbia University Press, the director of the Southwest Museum, the acting director of the New York State Historical Association, a curator emeritus at the American Museum of Natural History, the director of the Milwaukee Public Museum, and a handful of Parker's masonry brothers.

All of these people wrote about Parker's contributions to museum work and about how much they admired him as a human being, but not how much they admired him as an Indian anthropologist. The absence of the latter is a noticeable shift from Parker's early days as a researcher and museum man, in which nearly every public talk he gave made mention of his Indian heritage. Even in the few exceptions where Parker's Seneca identity is mentioned in these later years, it is not about preserving memories of his ancestors, but rather about presenting evidence of his grand pedigree to give him some advantage in anthropology. For instance, an awards pamphlet started Parker's biography with, "Born in a rural section of Erie County, New York, the descendant of a great chief of the Senecas, the son of a noble New England mother, and the thrice-great grandson of a member of the Committee of Safety and Representative to the Provincial Congress of Massachusetts in 1774." A letter from the vice president of the Allegheny State Park Commission, Charles Congdon, reads, "His unique birthright gave him opportunities which no one else has attained in the study of Indian history and culture." One of Parker's obituaries does not even mention his Seneca genealogy, and another only relates, "His interest in Indians traced partly to his own one-quarter Seneca ancestry."[113] In the end, the later references to Parker's Indian ethnicity remain oblique. The recognition he received for his professional successes came at the price of the recognition of his Seneca identity.

Bertha Parker Cody

In the spring of 2005, an online listserv discussed the possibility of naming a new scholarship in honor of the first female Native American archaeologist. Discussion unfolded about who might hold this honor. One participant in the discussion, Marge Bruchac, made a compelling case that Arthur Parker's daughter, Bertha Parker Cody, was the first woman to pursue archaeology professionally.[114] This designation is

Arthur's daughter, Bertha Parker (*left*), at the field camp of the Gypsum Cave expedition in Nevada, circa 1930. (Courtesy of the Autry National Center, Southwest Museum, Los Angeles, photo no. P.22708)

important because the history of archaeology demonstrates that women as well as Native peoples have long been discriminated against, their historical voices silenced. Although there were a few early pathbreakers, such as Florence Hawley Ellis and Frederica de Laguna, women were long considered unfit for dirt archaeology for decades and even today struggle against prejudice.[115] "The first female Native American archaeologist" is a label that thus indicates a person who overcame not one but two forms of discrimination. The honor is no small thing.

Bertha, affectionately nicknamed "Birdie," grew up in southern California. Although far from her native roots, she must have been acutely aware of her heritage because her mother, Beulah, obtained work as an actress in no small measure because of her ability to play the part of an Indian. In 1927, M. Raymond Harrington became Bertha's stepuncle, and the two must have gotten together at some point after Harrington and his wife, Arthur Parker's sister Edna, moved to California. By that time, Harrington was conducting surveys and excavations in Nevada, and Bertha joined a few of these expeditions.[116]

In 1929, she was on one such expedition when she and her four-year-old daughter, Billie—a third generation of Parkers to grow up amidst archaeology—went for a walk.[117] After a while, Billie sat down and announced that she would walk no farther. Bertha let her sit while she explored the area. "I was about to turn back when my attention was attracted to a lot of broken pottery scattered over the surface of the hill on which I was walking," she recalled. "Looking closely, I spied protruding sandstone slabs. My heart missed a beat. Could this by any chance be an old pueblo ruin?" It was, and she named it "Scorpion Hill" after coming across and killing two of the creatures. Harrington soon examined the things Bertha and Billie brought back with them and said that he thought the artifacts somehow different. Bertha returned to the site repeatedly to excavate it, digging half a room in one day and then the rest the following day. She exposed a large room and then, contrary to a later claim that Bertha "loved to go on field trips but she wouldn't dig in any burial grounds," excavated her first human burial beneath large sandstone slabs.[118] The next day she dug another room, the grave of an infant, and then another room with "only scattered fragments of pottery." She continued in her excitement, uncovering more rooms and graves. Four years later she returned with Beulah and her father-in-law, only to discover the site had been ravaged by looters. But "not wishing to go home empty-handed," the group of excavators began digging again, and while carefully screening the dirt, they recovered more human bones as well as a shell pendent, turquoise fetish, pottery, and lithics. The material was eventually exhibited in its own case at the Southwest Museum.

Although Bertha had participated on previous research projects, this story perhaps relates her true initiation into archaeology, a site of her own to explore. By today's standards, the excavations were not especially scientific, but notes were made, photographs were taken, the materials were exhibited, and the explorations were published: the work shows Bertha's attempt to be a good archaeologist.

While working with Harrington as the Depression took hold, "at everything from telephone operator to caretaker ... to Assistant in Archaeology," Bertha was married to James E. Thurston, a paleontologist.[119] Tragically, Thurston died from kidney or heart failure in February 1932, and then Bertha herself became ill. Her work suffered. "Something must be done about Mrs. Thurston," Southwest Museum director Frederick Webb Hodge instructed Harrington in the spring of

1934. Harrington came to Bertha's defense, arguing that she should be given time to recuperate:

> You may better understand my feelings when you realize that Mrs. Harrington and I regard our niece Bertha Thurston as we would a daughter and have been working for years to give her the chance that we felt was her due. She has had to fight against harrowing odds in every direction since she was a small child; and even since you have been here, she lost the husband who gave her her first taste of happiness.
>
> The illness which culminated in the operation, recently, has been going on for months, dragging her vitality lower and lower, causing her to grow thinner and thinner until she is just a shadow of her former self. No wonder her work is falling off! The pus from septic tonsils is not conducive to work. How she has carried on at all, is a mystery to me.
>
> Bertha Thurston was one of the most useful members of the Gypsum Cave expedition [in Nevada] and her work figured largely in the successful outcome of that project. When in good health her work at the museum was most satisfactory as was her assistance in the preparation of the Gypsum Cave report. It is true that her greatest interest lies along the lines represented in her title, 'Assistant in Archaeology,' rather than in the routine typing and stenography, to which she has been restricted of late.
>
> Therefore, in answer to your dictum that 'Something must be done about Mrs. Thurston,' I offer the following:
>
> Give her two months leave of absence without pay; Mrs. Harrington and I will take care of her at our home during that time. If she has recovered her health by that time, let her come back to work; if not, extend the leave until she does. During her absence employ a substitute on a temporary basis.[120]

Bertha eventually bounced back and no doubt was helped by a new husband. "You will be interested to hear that Bertha is married!" Harrington wrote to Hodge in August 1936. "She married Oscar Cody who has been devoted to her for years. After the event they came out to Ranchito Romulo to tell us but didn't have the nerve! Bertha wrote us afterward. I imagine she will wish to continue her Museum work, but I am not sure of this." Several weeks later, Bertha told Harrington that indeed she'd like to continue her employment, at least for another year.[121]

Bertha continued on at the Southwest Museum for a number of years, even though Cody was horribly unsupportive of her work.[122] She continued to publish short articles, mainly continuing some of her early work in the ethnography of northern California's Native peoples as well as studies in Native American material culture.[123] Her writing style is eminently readable, personal yet unprejudiced. (One of her earlier articles even appeared in the same issue of *Masterkey* as one of her father's articles.)[124] In addition, she was the recording secretary of the Archaeological Survey Association of Southern California, a group of volunteers who surveyed on weekends "to locate and record all aboriginal sites still remaining in southern California."[125]

When Bertha married Oscar Cody, he was an aspiring movie star, having appeared in nearly a dozen films, though only in uncredited roles such as "Cheyenne Rider" in *Fighting with Kit Carson* (1933), "Indian Dancer" in *The Golden West* (1932), and "Indian" in *The Big Trail* (1930).[126] Although born and raised in Louisiana by parents who had emigrated from Italy, Cody invented an Indian persona, saying that "his mother was a Cree Indian who married his Cherokee father and raised the children in Oklahoma."[127] "Iron Eyes Cody," as he named himself, eventually starred in more than 175 movies. In the 1950s, he and Bertha hosted a television show on Native American folklore and history that was broadcast in California; they also together opened the Moosehead Museum of Indian artifacts in their home and published booklets such as *Sign Talk in Pictures* (for which Bertha used her Seneca name "Ye-was") and *Indian Legends*.[128] They became known as "Hollywood's Indian couple." Despite his many appearances and roles, Iron Eyes did not become a nationally recognized persona until he starred in a commercial for the Keep America Beautiful campaign, unveiled on Earth Day in 1971, in which he shed a single, heartrending tear upon seeing a land defiled by waste and smog. The commercial reportedly reached billions of homes.[129] Iron Eyes lived to 1999, and Bertha passed away in 1978.[130] Together they adopted two children, Robert and Arthur, the second no doubt named in honor of his grandfather. Robert married a Nez Perce woman, had two children, and lived on the Umatilla Reservation in Oregon, and Arthur went into the Marines, married a Filipina woman, and had one child. Arthur reportedly died at a young forty-four years old in San Diego, California.[131] Bertha's first daughter, Billie, died during a "hunting accident," more likely a suicide, at the age of seventeen in 1942.[132] She is buried next to her grandmother, Parker's first wife, Beulah.

He Honored His People and Is Honored by Them

Parker retired in 1945, though it would be hard to tell from a list of his publications and activities that he had done so. He continued to publish on anthropology and museology.[133] He gave talks at conferences, such as the Second Conference on Iroquois Research in the fall of 1946, and held a leadership role in various societies and associations.[134]

Several years before his retirement, Parker wrote an article titled "We Can't Get Away from History." The essay is a brief but eloquent plea for Americans to grasp how our past molds our future. "History is the one clue to where we are going and it explains the source of our propulsion," he emphasized. Although Parker was writing about civilization, it's difficult not to think about how he and the friends and family who surrounded him, like society as a whole, could not elude the past. This is not to say that our progress through life is written ahead of us in the cosmos, but rather to suggest that our genealogy, our choices, our youths inescapably shape the eventual courses of our lives. Bertha Parker Cody grew up apart from her father and yet herself became an ethnographer and archaeologist. Her mother, Beulah, who left her life tagging along with Arthur on his expeditions, spent her final years as an anthropologist's assistant for her daughter. M. Raymond Harrington received most of the credit for the 1903 Silverheels expedition, yet ended up Parker's second at the SAA and would marry Arthur's sister and come to nurture both Arthur's daughter and his former wife's anthropological pursuits. Raymond's life would be intertwined with Arthur's to the end.

In the end, Parker couldn't get away from his past either, but as his days dwindled, he noticeably didn't want to escape the past he had inherited. Even as others viewed him first and foremost as a professional by his retirement, evidenced by the accolades and correspondence, Parker asserted for himself a multiplex identity. This choice is perhaps most perfectly illustrated in the stationery he used just a year before he died. The heading read:

Dr. Arthur C. Parker
"Gawaso Waneh"
Archaeologist-Historian
Author-Humanitarian
He Honored His People and Is
Honored by Them
The Six Nations

Arthur C. Parker, circa 1945. Parker had passed formal retirement but remained a vigorous and active contributor to anthropology and museology. (Courtesy of the Rochester Museum & Science Center, Rochester, New York)

Only at the end of his life, then, could he fully embrace an identity that announced he was not just one thing or another, but many things all at once. Arthur could finally see himself, like Nicholson and Ely, as an interpreter between worlds. He could live his life not divided by the buckskin curtain, but with the curtain torn down altogether. He wanted to be Arthur Caswell Parker *and* Gáwasowaneh, a professional archaeologist *and* a Seneca. Even so, perhaps a trace of ambivalence remains. After all, the stationery places his Seneca name in quotes, but not his Anglo name.

We perhaps tend to think of identities as one thing or another. We have trouble imagining how one person can embody at once a diversity of histories and heritages. To simplify our world, perhaps, we want people to live their lives in black or white, without shades of gray. Parker's life in archaeology unmasks how balancing one's past with dreams of one's future is not easy; it was not easy to be an Indian archaeologist in the early twentieth century. But Parker persevered and despite it all lived the life he wanted. He realized the successes he could only dream of as a boy hunting for arrowheads on the banks of Cattaraugus Creek.

When Parker passed away at his desk in 1955, suddenly taken by a heart attack, he did not categorize himself as neatly as some may have liked. As his stationery relates, he wanted to honor his people and be honored by them, to be both archaeologist and historian, both author and humanitarian. In this way, he perhaps imagined himself a bit like a kaleidoscope, a human being made complete from fractured parts. With a slight turn of the hand, he could present one image, and with another turn yet another image. The reflections, though ever changing, are still made by the same parts, still one thing, just rearranged. I believe that by the end of his life, Parker saw that it is the movement of the parts into different configurations that makes the view at the end both beautiful and unique.

Part V
Conclusion

8
THE PROMISE OF INDIGENOUS ARCHAEOLOGIES

The End of Archaeology

In the summer of 1971, four dozen students from a Minneapolis youth program labored to uncover an Indian village nearly five hundred years old.[1] Among the features they uncovered were burials. After five quiet weeks, one evening as dark was quickening over the land, a group of American Indian Movement (AIM) members marched into the camp. Incensed over the excavation of the human burials, they filled in the archaeologists' trenches, set ablaze excavation notes, and spirited away shovels. The AIM members later offered to repay the students for their material losses, but insisted that the study of the graves cease. Resolution to the controversy was elusive. Even after months of heated public debate, Indian activists and their allies insisted archaeologists are no better than grave robbers, but researchers and the broader public failed to grasp why the Indian protestors would go to such lengths to protest the disturbance of the dead.

Now largely forgotten, this protest was just one among many by American Indian activists in the early 1970s. A year before the takeover of the youth camp, an American Indian student group submitted a phony grant application to the National Science Foundation to excavate an Anglo cemetery. In June 1971, New York's Lewis County Historical Society repatriated a skeleton for reburial to Sakokwenonk, a Mohawk leader, after his vocal objection to the scientific appropriation. In this same year, protests led to the occupation of the Southwest Museum in Los Angeles with the aim of getting human remains removed from display and reburied. In Iowa, twenty-seven human bodies were discovered during roadwork around this same time. The twenty-six bodies identified by headstones were immediately reburied in the Glenwood Cemetery, but the one that had no headstone and was accompanied by glass beads and brass rings, presumed to be Indian, was taken to a museum. A Native American woman, Running Moccasins, began a protest for a proper reburial. A year later the Iowa State Historical Society was picketed until the Indian remains were removed by order of the governor. Then, in Illinois, Chicago's Field Museum unearthed nine skeletons dating to the late 1600s. After a protracted public battle, the museum at last gave in to pressure from Indian protestors and returned the bones. In 1976, when an archaeologist did not observe the Canadian Cemeteries Act passed that year, the Canadian Union of Ontario Indians carried out a citizen's arrest. Such demonstrations constituted the start of a broad mobilization aimed at shifting public sentiment as well as archaeological practice. "This movement," according to historian James Riding In, "stands on a paramount footing with the valiant struggles of African Americans for civil rights and women for equality."[2]

These events are important to remember because they illustrate that the debates swirling around NAGPRA, repatriation, and reburial in the 1990s actually stretch back two decades before that. Since at least Vine Deloria Jr.'s 1969 publication of *Custer Died for Your Sins*, the complaints about anthropologists' behavior in Indian country were perfectly well known if not very well addressed.[3]

What Parker's life in part demonstrates is that these predicaments go back even much farther in time. Archaeologists in the 1970s and 1980s may have felt as if their work was being threatened for the first time, but the ethical crises of this period already existed at the very beginning of archaeology's formation as a profession, science, and moral community. The difference was not that earlier Indians failed to protest archaeological practices, but that archaeologists were finally truly forced to listen to these complaints through such powerful voices as Deloria's and through such violent tactics as the invasion of field camps.

When we look closer at the documentary record, we can find a handful of hidden stories about Native peoples resisting archaeological inquiry that date long before AIM ever made an archaeologist tremble. As early as 1632, Gabriel Sagard-Theódat observed among the Huron that "nothing could give them greater offense than to ransack and remove anything in the tombs of their relatives."[4] In the American Northeast at some point before 1854, a Nantucket Wampanoag man named Abram Quary was sent to court for "threatening to shoot some trinket gathers who were digging in a nearby Indian burial ground."[5] When Quary was asked if he truly would shoot raiders if given the chance, he reportedly replied without hesitation, "Yes, I would." On the other end of the continent, in 1897, the Secwepemc of British Columbia, Canada, objected to the removal of human remains excavated by Harlan Smith on behalf of Franz Boas and the American Museum of Natural History.[6] As archaeological expeditions became more common in the American Southwest in the late 1800s, the Native Americans there objected to the work too. When efforts began at the famous site of Mesa Verde in southwestern Colorado, a Ute man opposed the excavations, explaining that the disturbance of ancient Hopi pueblos made the Ute people ill.[7] At Puyé in the 1930s, Pueblo men warned the Anglo researchers that the scientists would die if the work proceeded.[8] After the Hopi Tribal Council was formed, among the council's first acts was to eject a group of Harvard University excavators from the Hopi Reservation; as one Hopi leader wrote in 1939, "What good does it do to dig there? the villagers want to know. If it were on some other mesa, where no one is living we might feel differently. But we are still alive. Our civilization is not dead. They are digging up our ancestors and they are touching things we have said shall not be touched."[9] At a cave site called Wihomki in the 1940s, Arizona's Tohono O'odham tribal government prevented archaeologists from exploring because they believed the cave to be sacred.[10]

In 1927, M. Raymond Harrington himself again ran into trouble with a tribe over the question of excavating burials, although, unlike the Shinnecock and Seneca examples we know about, this time the tribe was more successful.[11] Harrington had received a permit from the U.S. Department of the Interior to conduct excavations in California and Nevada. The scientists arrived in Pyramid Lake and examined some cave sites in the hope of extending the Pueblo culture area. After more than six weeks of excavations of exceptionally rich deposits, however, Harrington received a wire while on his honeymoon with Edna, stating, "Indians making a kick about digging." The caves were located on the Pyramid Lake Indian Reservation, and the tribal council objected to the research on the grounds that Harrington had received permission only from the Interior Department, not from the council, and that the excavations were disturbing burials. Although Harrington had in fact excavated burials, he objected to the council's decision, falsely writing to the secretary of the interior, "we have found no human skeletons." At the Paiute council meeting, all alternative proposals were rebuffed: they did not want the excavations moved to another cave, they did not want to watch the excavations. The Paiutes just "did not want anyone digging around even near where some of their dead may be buried." At a council meeting on December 22, 1927, eight of ten members voted against the excavations, and several weeks later the Department of the Interior revoked Harrington's permit. The superintendent for the Paiute later explained, "I feel convinced that a number of the older Indians conscientiously believe their sacred burial grounds are being desecrated and that it is their duty to their departed ancestors to oppose the disturbance of these grounds in any way."

With just these examples, we see eight disparate Native American communities—Huron, Wampanoag, Secwepemc, Ute, Santa Clara, Hopi, Tohono O'odham, and Paiute—across centuries of time resisting archaeological inquiry in a way not so different from how the Senecas resisted Parker's research. With no major protests until the 1970s, scholars may have believed that Native Americans had acquiesced to archaeological authority,[12] but such an attitude was willful ignorance on their part because Native peoples had continued objecting to archaeology for a long time. These examples illustrate that the resistance Parker experienced was not an anomaly, that in well-documented cases Native communities have long been opposing archaeological research.

The protests in the years just before and since NAGPRA thus do not represent the end of archaeology. Today, archaeology decidedly continues, if not thrives, so we are neither at the end nor at the point of new beginnings. We are instead at one place in the ongoing exchange between those across Indian country and the discipline of archaeology. We must beware of what can be called "moral-historical distancing"— that is, behaving as if our current moral predicaments, like the subitaneous waters of a tsunami, have engulfed our world without warning. Parker's life and legacy make this point perfectly.

Archaeology's moral predicament of *privilege*—the "right" to dig sites and conduct archaeological study—infused Parker's long career. From the first, in the 1903 expedition to the Cattaraugus Reservation, Parker and his Harvard colleagues simply presumed that they, by their accomplishments and aspirations, should have unequaled access to ancient sites. Senecas at the Silverheels Site seriously challenged this assumption, objecting to exploration both in 1903 and some decades earlier when the fort was first uncovered. Parker's Seneca friends even warned him with tales of vampire spirits. In the years immediately following the 1903 fieldwork, Parker initially sought to continue excavations on Indian lands, but soon found that this was no easy task, in part because New York's Indians were so appalled by the notion of digging in graves. He soon resorted to working on private lands outside of reservations. Even on private land, however, his right was challenged. Anglo land owners found that they held a solid economic resource that Parker and New York State would have to pay to mine. Over time, Parker became increasingly militant in his belief that neither tribes nor private landowners should prevent researchers from conducting their work. He wanted the United States, like other countries such as Mexico and Greece, to nationalize heritage so that trained scholars alone would have the right to control archaeological sites.

The predicament of *ownership*—questions of whether the past is a property to be owned and the consequences of commodifying antiquities—similarly was a strong undercurrent in Parker's life in archaeology. On the one hand, Parker consistently said that artifacts belong in the domain of science—that privately benefiting from the sale of antiquities was a "sin against science." On the other hand, for decades he engaged with dealers and collectors who had no interest in the past other than a commercial one. When someone had something good to sell, Parker was willing to compromise his high moral aspirations. And despite pledges to the contrary, he himself occasionally sold artifacts on the side to supplement his meager salary. It was not until his reputation had been gained and he was firmly in place as a museum director that he decided steadfastly not to purchase unprovenienced objects.

Parker also grappled, beginning at least in 1903, with dilemmas arising from issues of *authorship*—how the past is written and who writes it. From the beginning of his career, he had to deal with the implicit question of whether an Indian could write and think as a scientist. After the 1903 expedition, it was Harrington who was given the main task to write up the summer's efforts. However, Parker also wrote a small section, and it was he who would eventually take on the responsibility of publication. Unlike his granduncle Ely Parker, who would be considered only an Indian informant, Arthur demonstrated with time that a man of Native American heritage could write wonderfully and even for both scientific and public audiences. He demonstrated through scores of articles and books that Indians could objectively and scientifically write their own archaeological histories. It was his writing that made him eligible to become an SAA fellow.[13] At first skeptical of the press, Parker grew to depend on it for bolstering his status and disseminating his ideas. His desire to see the common citizen engaged with archaeology, which he put into practice in museums, is also manifest in his writing. Through words the world can change, Parker believed.

And Parker dealt often with dilemmas arising from *participation* as well—which publics and stakeholders should be included in the study, management, and interpretation of the past. A real change can be seen over the course of the two decades from 1903, when he sought to keep the Silverheels expedition a secret from the public, to 1926, when he sought to enlist the public's help to record archaeological sites. In his later excavations with the New York State Museum and the Rochester Museum of Arts and Sciences, he often had volunteer help from locals interested in archaeology. Then, through his popular writings and accessible museum exhibits, he made the fruits of his research accessible and understandable. Parker is often recognized as the creator of a forerunner of the community museum, but he also deserves recognition for his vision of public archaeology. Rather than dismissing those who disagreed with him, such as unrepentant looters, he sought to engage them directly. And so he lectured for and met with collectors, just as through his work with the SAI he sought to convince doubters of the intellectual potential of modern American Indians. Approbation here, however, should perhaps be tempered with the recognition that Parker was not always successful. "I suppose the idea was that if these local enthusiasms could be harnessed, it might be possible, even with a light rein, to furnish some guidance and control," Carl E. Guthe wrote. "The intentions were good, but the policy also encouraged the proliferation of amateur activities."[14]

As archaeologists in the 1970s, 1980s, and 1990s discovered, these moral predicaments are in many ways fundamentally about control and power. When Parker was confronted in 1903 by Senecas who did not want him to dig up burials, the issue was not only about whether he in fact was disturbing spirits or even mainly about his relationship with the community in which he was raised; it was about who had the right to say who can control human remains. The disputes of recent memory, from the 1971 Minnesota protest to the 1996 Kennewick Man discovery, also concern fervently held beliefs about the past, but they are also disputes about power over heritage in the political present. These four moral predicaments do not signal the end of archaeology, but perhaps the increasing recognition of them signals our willingness to confront them boldly at last.

Old Wounds

Long before NAGPRA, Native Americans responded to archaeologists, ethnographers, and even their own community members who overstepped their bounds, demanding that the latter return appropriated objects. In the American Southwest, we see in the late 1800s how when a sacred image in a shrine at Awatovi was taken to a trading post for sale, "the post was at once visited by almost the entire population of Mishongnovi [a Hopi village], descendants of Awatobi clans, begging for the images." The trader, Thomas V. Keams, returned the sacred objects.[15] Years earlier, anthropologist Frank H. Cushing related how some altar materials were once taken from the church at the Pueblo of Zuni. "When this was discovered by the Indians," Cushing later wrote, "consternation seized the whole tribe; council after council was held. . . . [They] entreated [me] to plead with 'Wasintona' [Washington] to have these 'precious saints and sacred masks of their fathers' returned to them."[16] In another Zuni case from around 1890, a young boy stole a mask and sold it to a trader. When the boy eventually confessed, the family went straight to the trader, who agreed to give it back on the condition that, because the family was penniless, the child work off the thirty dollars originally paid.[17] Even in the years before NAGPRA was passed as federal legislation, the return of many cultural objects and human remains was effected: in 1967, the Kwakwaka'wakw began seeking the return of potlatch materials spirited away to the National Museum of Canada; in 1973, the University of Michigan's Museum of Anthropology returned human remains from the Great Lakes for reburial; in 1974, federal lawyers prosecuted a trafficker who had stolen masks taken from a cave on the San Carlos Indian Reservation; in 1978, Zunis began to seek the return of their sacred War Gods; in 1980, three stolen masks were returned to the Hopi; in 1988, the Smithsonian returned a large collection of Blackfoot remains to tribes in Montana; in 1989, the Ohlone received 550 skeletons from Stanford University.[18]

Repatriation is thus a recent term to describe a process that has been ongoing in Indian country for more than a century. Among the Iroquois, express efforts for the return of cultural property reach back to at least the late 1800s. Some of the earliest efforts focused on wampum, the cylindrical purple or white shell beads strung together to mark treaties and histories, decorate objects, convey messages, accompany the dead, and still more. Although some wampum belts are privately owned, many are "tribal property" or "national property," meaning that they are collectively held and cannot be alienated, sold, or traded by any one individual acting alone.[19]

A year after Arthur and his family left the Cattaraugus Reservation for New York City in 1892, the Six Nations Confederacy's Council of

Chiefs tried to retrieve important wampum belts sold by a caretaker's children after he had passed on.[20] Several belts were successfully repatriated, but many had disappeared—purchased by curiosity seekers, collectors, dealers, and museums. In 1899, the Onondaga Nation and New York State filed a lawsuit against a collector for the return of wampum, but the court ruled in the collector's favor. It would be another ten years before an effort was made to have belts returned. In 1909, the Six Nations Council of Chiefs unsuccessfully sought the return of eleven belts from Canada's governor general, and in the United States the New York legislature, with the support of a contingent of Iroquois, declared the state of New York "Wampum Keeper." The controversial belts soon fell into the hands of George Gustav Heye, who purchased them for his museum. For the next five years, anthropologist Leslie Spier and Cameron Scott, deputy superintendent general of Indian Affairs in Ottawa, sought to help the Iroquois gain back their wampum, but the matter was dropped when the tribal leaders did not provide the needed information and affidavits. Scott quit his job, and Spier gave up in frustration. "The chiefs were obviously covering up their own lapse as trustees of a national treasure," Fenton has surmised from historical documents, "and at the same time protecting one or two of their own people."[21] So the belts quietly remained in Heye's Museum of the American Indian until 1977.

Parker apparently advised museums not to purchase the wampum belts at the turn of the century, but a decade later he himself sought to buy them. "No party in this controversy enjoyed a monopoly on virtue," Fenton has pithily observed.[22] Ironically, this statement can be applied to Fenton himself, who, known to some as the "dean" of Iroquois studies, was later embroiled in controversy because he was a voice against repatriation for some years, an anthropologist who came to symbolize "the opposition of academia to native control over the representation of their own culture, history, and identity."[23]

In 1967, Iroquois leaders began a battle to obtain wampum belts held by the New York State Museum.[24] The museum administration maintained that it held the belts with the consent of the Onondaga that "the wampum was to be kept as public records 'forever.'" The leaders responded that their forebears believed they were only lending the wampum to the state. Protests followed in 1970 outside the state capitol building in Albany, with children holding signs such as "Return Our Wampum to Onondaga" and "Indians Have Rights Too!" The next year, Governor Nelson Rockefeller signed the wampum bill that returned the belts on the condition that a museum be built on the Onondaga Reservation to house them.

The Six Nations Council of Chiefs actively sought to reverse the flow of objects from reservations to museums when in 1974 it prohibited the sale of wampum, False Face masks, and other religious paraphernalia.[25] A year later the Buffalo and Erie County Historical Society returned several thousand wampum beads to the Onondaga Nation.[26] In 1977, Paul Williams, with the Union of Ontario Indians, wrote a letter to the Museum of the American Indian requesting information about its belts; controversy was stirred again, and when Williams wrote to the museum in 1985, now as attorney for the Six Nations Confederacy chiefs, negotiations began in earnest. An agreement was reached, and after nearly a century of contention the belts were repatriated with great ceremony in the early summer of 1988. Notably, anthropologist Elizabeth Tooker later argued that these returned wampum were incorrectly attributed and in fact were derived from other proveniences.[27]

In addition to wampum and False Face masks, the return of human remains has also been a significant part of the Iroquois call for repatriation. However, it was not until after the passage of NAGPRA that hundreds of museums were compelled to return the bodies of the ancestors to their descendants. It was through NAGPRA that the human remains and funerary goods excavated at the Silverheels Site in 1903 were returned to the Iroquois people. Through the inventory process, it was found that

> in 1903, human remains representing 122 individuals were recovered from Brant, NY, during a Peabody Museum of Archaeology and Ethnology expedition led by M. R. Harrington and A. C. Parker. No known individuals were identified. The 1,486 associated funerary objects include charred corn and acorns; potter's stones, polishing stones, nutting stones and other worked stones; broken celts; flaked chert and debitage; a piece of chipped quartz or red jasper; ceramic sherds, vessels and pipes; iron knives, scissors, awls, and an axe; pigment; glass, shell, catlinite, copper, and brass beads; bracelets of copper and brass beads; bracelets of iron, brass, and wire; brass jingles, brass earrings, and a brass point; sheet brass; broken and charred wooden objects; shells; animal bones, hide and teeth, including fish teeth; worked turtle shell, fragments that are probably part of a rattle, and small pebbles from a rattle; bone tubes and an awl; antler arrow

flakers; charcoal; bark; an organic concretion; fragments of a brass bracelet; wood fragments; a ceramic pipe elbow; buckskin fragments with glass beads; leather fragments with glass beads; and a brass spoon fragment.[28]

In addition to these human remains and grave goods, 210 cultural items were inventoried. It was determined that the remains and objects belonged to a consortium of Iroquois groups: the Seneca Nation, Cayuga Nation, Oneida Nation, Tuscarora Nation, Tonawanda Band of Seneca Indians of New York, Oneida Tribe of Wisconsin, Onondaga Nation, St. Regis Band of Mohawk Indians of New York, and Seneca-Cayuga Tribe of Oklahoma. These objects were returned to their living descendants without fanfare nearly a century after Parker and Harrington collected them.[29]

Another repatriation included two individuals excavated at Silverheels that Harrington had apparently sold to a private collector in 1907. And as late as 2007, the Peabody Museum repatriated three unassociated funerary objects—two brass sheet fragments and one vial of shell and glass bead fragments—from the Silverheels Site, all found to be affiliated with the Iroquois nations.[30] Repatriation is often not a single event, but a process with an unknown end.[31]

Oversight of NAGPRA for the Haudenosaunee peoples is ensured by the Haudenosaunee Standing Committee on Burial Rules and Regulations, established by the Grand Council of the Haudenosaunee and operating in cooperation with Haudenosaunee governments and the Council of Chiefs and Clan Mothers. The committee has also sought for many years to pass a state burial law in New York, but without success so far. Richard Hill Sr. of the Tuscarora Nation, the committee's chairperson, explains in "Making a Final Resting Place Final" that after much deliberation, the committee decided that all human remains within traditional Haudenosaunee territory should be returned and reburied. "Many of our people were very hurt and angered by the desecration of the graves of our ancestors," Hill writes. "There is a lot of resentment toward archaeologists and museums that look at the dead as objects of study and label our ancestors as if they were specimens."[32]

As seen with Parker's work, many Iroquois have resisted the disturbance of their ancestral graves for more than a century. This resistance is not merely political, though all resistance to colonial practices includes political aspects; it is also thoroughly cultural and spiritual. As Hill explains,

> We have been taught that we bury our dead relatives in the ground so that their bodies can become part of the sacred Earth. We believe that we come from the Mother Earth and that the human remains that rest within the Earth are an important spiritual connection to the spirit of the Earth. The Earth is enriched by the dead as our flesh becomes part of the soil. The souls of the dead have a path of destiny that they must follow. We refer to this as their journey after life. In this way, we feel that the dead are around us and hover over us as we hold our ceremonies or dances. We believe that the dead have power, and it is dangerous to neglect the spiritual needs of the dead. The protection of the human remains and associated graves, sacred burial sites, and related objects from the graves of the Haudenosaunee are the responsibility of each generation of chiefs, clan mothers, and faith keepers. We believe that the remains, the associated burial objects, and the actual soil in which they rest is [sic] sacred. There is no acceptable excuse to justify the desecration of this sacred burial.

Because of these deeply held beliefs, Hill compellingly argues that the intrusion into cemeteries constitutes a violation of Haudenosaunee spiritual rights (unjustly interfering with the spiritual well-being of the living and dead) and human rights (perversely looking at Indians as merely specimens for study). It is also a violation of treaty rights because the Canandaigua Treaty of 1794 was created to ensure that neither the federal government nor the state of New York would disturb "the Haudenosaunee in the free use and enjoyment of their lands." Many Haudenosaunee have been protesting excavations for more than a century, so the continued disturbance of the ancient sites constitutes a breach of the friendship and peace pledged in past treaties.

Despite such idealized statements, the committee members recognize that their ancestors were at times complicit in the thefts of community property and the invasion of sacred burials. As Hill recounts, "We had to ask ourselves some deep questions about the conduct of our ancestors and relatives, those who cooperated with the desecration of the graves or sold sacred objects to curators. We had to face some harsh truths." Parker and those he enjoined indeed add a layer of complexity to these histories that should not be disregarded.

NAGPRA and the repatriation movement have provided new and positive opportunities. Hill explains that "archaeological remains," once the exclusive domain of a small phalanx of scholars, are now open to Native communities as never before. The law and cooperative anthropologists, Hill believes, "have allowed us to rethink our relationship with our ancestors, to reaffirm our shared values, to learn more about the archaeological record, and basically to ask ourselves, What are the most important spiritual traditions that we need to keep alive?" Through NAGPRA, scores of ancestors as well as vital cultural objects have been returned home. As Hill says, the return of objects and ancestors presents a unique opportunity for historical reconciliation and a restorative justice. "Repatriation must heal old wounds," he urges in another article.[33] Nevertheless, the process has been fraught with difficulties—some wounds refuse to heal, it seems—from the attempt to fit traditional and spiritual feelings of affinity into legal frameworks of cultural affiliation to museums' insistence on dealing only with individual tribal governments.[34] And as Hill frankly writes after twenty years on the front lines of the repatriation battle, return is not an easy fix for the many social and political problems that pervade tribes outside of repatriation,[35] including sovereignty issues such as the sale of gasoline and the operation of Indian casinos. Whether and how the repatriation of the ancestors, False Face masks, and wampum can address the Haudenosaunee's livelihood and well-being are yet to be seen.

The Buckskin Curtain

What would Parker have thought if he had been alive in 1969 to read Vine Deloria Jr.'s bombastic *Custer Died for Your Sins*, which opined that "Indians have been cursed above all other people in history. Indians have anthropologists"?[36] Implicit in Deloria's prose is the presumption that there is an unambiguous line between Indians and anthropologists. The researchers, the perpetrators of disrespect and dishonor, are on one side. The Indians, the victims of scholarly cunning, are on the other. As we have seen as we reflect back on Parker's life, however, rather than an effulgent line, we have instead a gray miasma. Parker was both an Indian and an anthropologist who suffered from prejudice even as he at times chose to reinforce the very system of injustice that encumbered his hopes and dreams. (Even Deloria himself, despite his youthful writings, ironically came to be recognized in anthropology. He held an academic post with strong anthropological ties; his books have been used and cited—and argued about—by anthropologists; and he published in anthropological journals.)[37]

Some writers have observed that Parker was "at home on either side of the buckskin curtain," a man who could easily venture between the Anglo and Indian worlds.[38] In many ways, this was true. Along with his Seneca patrilineage, Parker had dark skin, knew the Seneca homeland from his youth, and spoke some of the Seneca language. Along with his Anglo matrilineage, he wore three-piece suits, grew up in part in New York City, and spoke fluent English. Like many "native" anthropologists, Parker mastered a range of linguistic and behavioral strategies to express "communicative competence" and his insider status with different communities.[39] Using language, dress, and kinship to his advantage, he could effectively negotiate both the white academic and the Indian worlds. In one moment, he could speak of growing up on Cattaraugus and recall listening to his granduncle Ely Parker tell stories about fighting the Ogden Land Company, but in the next moment he could speak of his scientific expeditions across New England and his academic guidance under Morgan, Powell, and Putnam.

Yet Parker also often felt uneasy about his mixed identity, never quite at home in either world. He was born neither Seneca nor white American. This unease with himself seeped into his professional identity. For most of his career, he was without a university degree, based in a museum, and he sought to be inclusive with myriad audiences. In turn, from the beginning of the twentieth century, professionals were increasingly recognized as those with a Ph.D., based in universities, and exclusively focused on scientific audiences. Thus, although Parker was in some measure at home in both worlds, it is not surprising that he wanted a world with no curtain at all: a single world in which a man of Indian heritage could freely become a scientist.

In the same way that it is important to recognize how the ethical quandaries we face today stretch back to anthropology's beginning, it is equally important to understand that Native Americans have worked as professional anthropologists for more than a century. Parker, no doubt a pathfinder, was joined by William Jones (Fox), who studied with Putnam at Harvard University and then became the first Native American to receive a Ph.D.—from Columbia University in 1904. He was a successful anthropologist until he was tragically murdered at the age of thirty-eight while conducting fieldwork in the Philippines.[40]

Francis La Flesche was an Omaha who received a law degree in 1893 and like Parker was partly caught between his Native community and the Anglo world that surrounded it; in 1910, La Flesche transferred from the Office of Indian Affairs to the Bureau of American Ethnology, where he worked until 1929.[41] Antonio Apache, a Lipan Apache, was at times a key informant for anthropologists. He also helped create exhibits at the 1893 Columbian Exposition and actively assisted in physical anthropology research in the late 1800s.[42] J. N. B. Hewitt, a Tuscarora from New York, is another important figure who worked for the Bureau of American Ethnology from 1886 until his death in 1937, gathering voluminous data and publishing meticulous reports on linguistics, history, and ceremony.[43] Louis Shotridge, a Tlingit from Alaska, stands as yet another example of an Indigenous man in the early twentieth century who crossed the boundary from informant to anthropological collector and author.[44] Although the story of many of these early Native scholars has yet to be told, Deloria's dichotomy between Indian and anthropologist dismisses more than a century of Native Americans who aspired to broaden the discipline with their presence.

When Joe Watkins read Deloria's words in 1969, he could not help but laugh. As he shares in the essay "Writing Unwritten History," Watkins is a Choctaw who, after finding his way along a winding and rutted path, became a professional archaeologist. At first, he escaped the potential conflict between his Indian heritage and professional aspirations by deciding to work on paleolithic technology in Europe. Nevertheless, he suffered racist whiplash from both a scholarly community that felt an Indian could not be an objective scientist and an Indian community that falsely assumed he was a "bonedigger." Watkins eventually turned to the archaeology of American Indians and has since become a leading figure in North American archaeology, holding academic posts and serving on important committees for the SAA and the American Anthropological Association. Yet even with his success and recognition, he says, "I am still caught in the middle," accepted wholly by neither the archaeological community nor the Native American community.[45]

Watkins's experiences in some ways curiously parallel Parker's life, particularly with regard to how Native American archaeologists have to choose which identity to foreground and which to suppress, depending on the situation. When angry Senecas confronted Parker, there was no theoretical or methodological framework for him to be a scientific archaeologist sympathetic to his community's concerns. With hindsight, we can see that this is what is tragic about Parker's life: he was forced to choose when we now know he didn't have to. What if, in that summer of 1903, Parker had not only stood up to Putnam and said, "I am not an assistant," but also stood with his community and said, "We should not dig this burial ground"?

More than a century after Parker first put shovel to earth, Native American archaeologists are still being forced to choose sides even as they demonstrate the possibility of unifying seemingly disparate worlds.[46] Thus, what is in part tragic about our contemporary context is that the Us versus Them attitude often continues to pervade attitudes and discourses. As Tamara Bray contends, "Binary logic leaves room for no other kind of difference than that determined by an us/them, insider/outsider, colonizer/colonized mentality. Such entrenched binary oppositions are inherently reductionary and hierarchically positioned.... Critiquing the traditional categories of 'Indians' and 'archaeologists' would open up new terrain upon which to theorize and operate."[47] Not long ago, K. Anne Pyburn wrote that the field of archaeology has been beset by a "pernicious dichotomy," a false distinction between science and religion. Science at times is gripped by dogma and belief, just as religion can often be deductive and hypothetical.[48] Although Pyburn was referring to modes of knowing, her phrase also appositely applies to modes of being: Archaeologist versus Indian.

We should think about our professional and personal identities as negotiated—not prescribed positions. Kirin Narayan argues along similar lines "for a reorientation in the ways that we perceive anthropologists as 'outside' or 'inside' a society. The traditional view has been to polarize 'real' anthropologists from 'native' anthropologists, with the underlying assumption that a 'native' anthropologist would forward an authentic insider's view to the profession." She recommends that we instead work toward an "enactment of hybridity," which means in essence embracing the fact that the world is not black and white, and "adopting a narrative voice [that] involves an ethical stance that neither effaces ourselves as hybrid nor defaces the vivid humanity of the people with whom we work."[49] Contemporary Native American archaeologists such as Watkins demonstrate that Parker's ambition was not misplaced, that embracing hybridity not only is possible, but may impel the discipline toward ever more innovative and inclusive approaches. Had scholars of Parker's generation recognized that his multiplex identities were reconcilable, the field of archaeology might have attracted more Native

American students long ago; perhaps it might have long ago transformed the pernicious dichotomy into a creative synthesis.

Expanding the Circle

A moral community can be defined as a group of people drawn together by a common interest in living according to a particular moral philosophy. Anthropologists often write of nation or state as the "moral community," but a profession, in essence, is one as well.[50] Indeed, the English word for "profession" comes from the ancient Greek practice of taking an oath that "professed" an obligation to hold fast to a code of ethics.[51]

Neither natural nor inevitable, moral communities must be creatively made by a collective body. Another dimension of Parker's history demonstrates the complex ways in which archaeology came to be a moral community. In the late 1800s, it was dubious who archaeologists were, what they stood for, and who could belong in the group with them. The confrontations Parker and Harrington faced in 1903 and then in subsequent years are part of the story of archaeology's professional formation. With time, Parker and many of his colleagues increasingly used arguments about looting and science as a way to erect moral boundaries: archaeologists on one side and anti-science advocates and looters on the other. From this perspective, one of the lessons from Parker's experiences is that the moral predicaments archaeologists face are often bound up with questions of professional identity—the construction and maintenance of social boundaries. In 1903, when Parker went *against* the Seneca community's wishes, he argued *for* the rights of science.

Today, the debates over Kennewick Man similarly suggest that arguments about the disposition of this one set of remains was a means for some archaeologists to bond together against Native Americans and vice versa.[52] In parallel, the ferocious arguments over the Taliban's destruction of the Bamiyan Buddhas in 2001 were less about the value of heritage than about distinguishing Western multiculturalism from Islamic fundamentalism.[53]

Although public debates over such topics as the Kennewick Man or the bombing of the Bamiyan Buddhas can serve to *reinforce* the boundaries between archaeologists and others, other debates may ultimately *reconfigure* the margins of archaeology's moral community. Laws such as NAGPRA and the National Museum of the American Indian Act of 1989 have over the past two decades expanded the boundaries of inclusion to allow many publics in archaeological practices more explicitly.[54] Legally mandated consultation compelled archaeologists to work with Native Americans, but now many projects voluntarily and eagerly incorporate collaboration as a key part of their agendas.[55] Many archaeologists are shifting from notions of self-ascribed, narrowly defined scientific stewardship to the notion of "collaborative stewardship," a joint venture among descendant communities and researchers to appreciate and understand the past.[56] Actively addressing Native Americans' concerns and seeking their participation are increasingly perceived to be fundamentally necessary elements of archaeological practice. Including Native Americans and other descendant communities is a categorical means of expanding the circle of archaeology's moral community.

Indigenous Archaeologies

Joe Watkins writes that the troubled relationship between many Native American communities and archaeologists boils down to two key problems: "the perceived threat to the human remains and funerary objects of an indigenous population by a dominant, industrialized society, and the wishes of the indigenous population to gain control over the construction of their culture-history." Overcoming these problems, Watkins indicates, will in part entail a mutual education as non-Native researchers learn about Native worldviews and concerns, and Native nonprofessionals learn about the nature of archaeological inquiry.[57] What is needed, then, is an equitable dialogue among all those who care to meet at the common ground of protecting and understanding heritage sites.

Beyond mutual education is the possibility of forming an "Indigenous archaeology," Watkins suggests, wherein Indigenous peoples control the quantity and quality of research undertaken within their homelands. "Only when indigenous groups are able to control not only the physical manifestations of their culture but also what should be protected and how 'protection' is defined will indigenous archaeology flourish," he argues. Tribally owned or managed archaeology programs may be good, Watkins adds, but the benefits are still limited if the programs are run by non-Indians. "It is more important," he concludes, "that tribal individuals become archaeologists qualified to lead and manage archaeological projects and to influence the development of interpretations about their resources."[58]

Around the time Watkins wrote these words, at the turn of the twenty-first century, a mere fifteen individuals with a Ph.D. and perhaps fifty with a master's degree asserted a Native American identity as their primary identity.[59] Of the thousands of archaeologists in North America with an advanced degree, Native archaeologists make up only a tiny fraction. This basic fact suggests the partial bankruptcy of anthropology's explicit aims. "Native American academics for the most part have pursued other disciplines," Peter Whiteley has observed, "indicating, inter alia, a signal failure of anthropology in its stated goal of serving as a vehicle for genuine, usable intercultural understanding."[60]

Those Native Americans who have pursued advanced degrees in anthropology do so for myriad reasons, but notably because the discipline so obviously focuses on what does and should concern many Native Americans. "Because I am a Navajo, many people ask how I became interested in anthropology," Davina Two Bears has shared. "I majored and became interested in anthropology because it was only anthropology courses in college that allowed me to learn about Native Americans in an academic setting for the first time in my entire education."[61] The natural fit with anthropology, yet the dearth of Native students has led to the development of new pedagogical opportunities, such as the formation of the Applied Indigenous Studies Program at Northern Arizona University, and new support mechanisms, such as the SAA Native American Scholarships Fund. Despite its good intentions, this fund limited. Most awards currently range between fifteen hundred and four thousand dollars—helpful, certainly, but not the kind of substantial material support that will ensure Native students do not face pecuniary hardships.

Another problem, as Roger Echo-Hawk and Larry Zimmerman have written, is the way in which scholarships based on race reify and reinforce the artificial divisions that unjustly separate people. Native scholarships, they write, are a short-term solution for fighting archaeology's "segregationist history of unilateral racism by deploying integrative forms of joint racism."[62] They suggest that in due course race must be dismantled altogether. As Echo-Hawk contends, "Race is fundamentally damaging to our humanity. It distorts the nature of humankind. This is a profound truth about racial identity. It does not reveal to us a mirror-image of ourselves; instead it distorts what can be seen and the stories we tell about what we think we see. We should reject race. If this option does not yet seem a realistic choice for most people, we can at least learn to treat race as culture. Race doesn't dwell in our physical selves; it sits deep inside the more mysterious workings of our minds."[63]

For some, the label *native anthropologist* can be an albatross, an uneasy and unfair categorization that awkwardly situates them in both academic and local communities. It has long implied automatic authenticity, as if merely by growing up in a community, one is a natural authority on it. As Kirin Narayan explains,

> A "native" anthropologist is assumed to be an insider who will forward an authentic point of view to the anthropological community. The fact that the profession remains intrigued by the notion of the "native" anthropologist as carrying a stamp of authenticity is particularly obvious in the ways in which identities are doled out to non-Western, minority, or mixed anthropologists so that exotic difference overshadows commonalities or complexities. That my mother is German-American seems as irrelevant to others' portrayal of me as [an] "Indian" as [are] the American mothers of the "Tewa" Alphonso Ortiz, the "Chicano" Renato Rosaldo, or "Arab" Lila Abu-Lughod. For those of us who are mixed, the darker element in our ancestry serves to define us with or without our own complicity.[64]

Parker certainly fits this categorization, too. Despite his strong Anglo heritage, he was all too often pigeonholed (and indeed at times pigeonholed himself) as an "Indian" anthropologist.

Ergo, merely adding Native Americans to the roster of professional archaeologists will not be enough. Sonya Atalay has observed that many Indigenous people first started receiving training in archaeology "in response to their community's need for a person knowledgeable in archaeological practice who could effectively consult with archaeologists as new legislation required." However, as more Indigenous people received training, they found a number of shared goals between Indigenous communities and archaeological practice, which led to "something that was not only possible but also necessary: an Indigenous archaeology."[65] Indeed, Davina Two Bears argues that "Navajo archaeologist is not an oxymoron," in large part because for generations the Navajo people have been protecting and seeking to understand their material pasts.[66]

Atalay sees Indigenous archaeology as fundamentally a process of decolonization, wherein research is not done just "on Native lands by Native people for Native communities, but rather ... Indigenous archaeology has implications for changes that must take place in the mainstream of archaeological practice if the discipline is to move forward and become a useful tool for the recovery of Indigenous traditions in the twenty-first century and beyond." She thus defines Indigenous archaeology as "research that critiques and deconstructs Western archaeological practice as well as research that works toward recovering and investigating Indigenous experiences, practices, and traditional knowledge systems."[67]

In this sense, Indigenous archaeology moves beyond Watkins's conception as well as that of scholars such as George Nicholas, who once defined the emerging paradigm as "archaeology with, for, and by" Indigenous people, and Desireé Reneé Martinez, who defines it as "methods that protect and conserve traditional cultural sites through stewardship influenced and controlled by Native people and their beliefs."[68] Atalay compellingly argues that Indigenous archaeology can be broader by providing "a model for archaeological practice that can be applied globally as it calls for and provides a methodology for collaboration of descendant communities and stakeholders around the world." It is thus not simply standard archaeology done by Indians, which only serves to "replicate the dominate archaeological paradigm," but instead entails "finding ways to create counter-discourse that speaks back to the power of colonialist and imperialist interpretations of the past."[69] In this way, because Indigenous archaeology is not one idea, process, or product, but rather a broad approach that can be applied in a range of ways, from tribal programs to cultural resource management projects to legal consultations, it is perhaps better presented in the plural: Indigenous *archaeologies*.[70]

In one sense, Arthur C. Parker is a forerunner of Indigenous archaeologies by virtue of his family heritage and his stated desire to pursue archaeology for "the memory of my people." His efforts at inclusiveness, both in the museum and through public archaeology, resonate strongly with the aspirations of Indigenous archaeologies. In another sense, however, he at times replicated colonialist power structures even as his mere presence in the field undermined them. His story is an emblem of both how far the discipline has come and how long the road ahead is. In this sense, his life may recommend Echo-Hawk's argument that decolonizing archaeology means not accepting prevailing views of race, but challenging them. "As I see it," Echo-Hawk writes, "the decolonization movement in Indian country has to do mostly with countering 'white' power with 'Indian' power. Isn't this race at work? Shouldn't 'decolonizing archeology' have something to do with challenging the way race is done in the discipline today? Shouldn't the challenge to colonialism involve a careful rethinking of race?"[71]

The SAA's Arthur C. Parker Scholarship rightly pays tribute to Parker's distinguished career. Given his central efforts in both the SAI and the SAA, Parker would have supported any scholarship that sought to improve opportunities for Native peoples. But what Parker's life—the longer and more conflicted story beneath the simple title "the first Native American archaeologist"—demonstrates is that getting more Indigenous peoples inducted into archaeology will not be enough to transform the discipline. Rather, there is a need to alter radically the field's fundamental political economy—to change its methodological, theoretical, and ethical foundations such that Native American perspectives suffuse archaeological inquiry. Although this is not precisely the path Parker laid out, it nonetheless honors his legacy, his struggles and successes, his life as Arthur C. Parker and Gáwasowaneh.

Wisdom of His Time

Over the course of these pages, I have attempted to say a great deal about one man's life, and in doing so I hope that I have not done a disservice to his experiences. My intent has been to examine Parker's multifaceted life as an anthropological ancestor—to unpack it, unwind it, and uncover what his aspirations and actions meant to him, to those around him, and to those today who now live with the consequences of his choices.

At times, I have judged Parker's actions, but hope that I have not unfairly appraised him. My intent has been to look at his experiences with both accuracy and empathy, to understand him and his times as much as ourselves and our shared future.

As I was completing this book, I began a new position at a museum and within days was overwhelmed by the complexity of negotiating the museum's disparate needs and designs—simultaneously managing a major collection, outmoded exhibits, a demanding public, a rigorous research program, an overcommitment of publications and public talks, and a superfluity of meetings. During these onerous first days, my thoughts often turned to Parker. My respect for his prolific writings, original research, and administrative talents only deepened. Given not only the complexity of a life in museums, but also the racism and prejudice Parker faced, I am profoundly in awe of how much he accomplished in his full life. He was not perfect, but this charge can be leveled at all of us, any of us, by virtue of our humanity. As Henry David Thoreau once wrote, "A man is wise with the wisdom of his time only, and ignorant with its ignorance. Observe how the greatest minds yield in some degree to the superstitions of their age."[72] Parker lived in exhilarating though demanding circumstances. He worked on through difficult days.

Notes

Abbreviations for Archives Used in the Notes

CUL   Cornell University Library, Division of Rare and Manuscript Collections
FHS   Fenton Historical Society
HUA   Harvard University Archives
NAA   National Anthropological Archives, Smithsonian Institution
NMAI   National Museum of the American Indian Archives
NYSL   New York State Library
PMAE   Peabody Museum of Archaeology and Ethnology, Harvard University
RRL   Rush Rhees Library, University of Rochester
SMAI   Southwest Museum of the American Indian, Autry National Center

Preface

1. Hayes, "Published Writings of Arthur Caswell Parker."
2. Fenton, *Parker on the Iroquois*; Hertzberg, "Nationality, Anthropology, and Pan-Indianism"; Porter, "Arthur Caswell Parker" and *To Be Indian*; Zeller, "Arthur C. Parker."

Chapter 1. The Moral Predicaments of Archaeology

1. See Bruning, "Complex Legal Legacies"; Chatters, *Ancient Encounters*; Crawford, "(Re)Constructing Bodies"; Downey, *The Riddle of the Bones*; Kelly, "Kennewick Man Is Native American"; D. Thomas, *Skull Wars*; Watkins, "Becoming American or Becoming Indian?" and "The Politics of American Archaeology"; Zimmerman, "A New and Different Archaeology?" and "Public Heritage."
2. Kyle Carver and Ryan Purcell, directors, *Kennewick Man: An Epic Drama of the West* (Riverside Films, 2001), at http://www.kennewickmanmovie.com.
3. See, for example, Lippert, "In Front of the Mirror"; Nicholas, Welch, and Yellowhorn, "Collaborative Encounters"; Watkins, "Writing Unwritten History."
4. Anyon, Ferguson, and Welch, "Heritage Management by American Indian Tribes."
5. Lippert, "Not the End, Not the Middle," 121.
6. Todorov, *The Conquest of America*.

7. Hemming, *The Conquest of the Incas*; Leon-Portilla, *The Broken Spears*.
8. Casas, *A Short Account of the Destruction of the Indies*, 12–13.
9. Bradford, *A Relation or Journall of the Beginning*, 11–12.
10. Trigger, *A History of Archaeological Thought*, 69.
11. Ibid., 107.
12. Prucha, "American Indian Policy," 6.
13. Deloria, *American Indian Policy*; Wilkens and Lomawaima, *Uneven Ground*.
14. Cornell, *The Return of the Native*.
15. Binford, "Archaeology as Anthropology"; Schiffer, *Behavioral Archaeology*, 68; Trigger, *A History of Archaeological Thought*, 294–303.
16. Bergman and Doershuk, "Cultural Resource Management and the Business of Archaeology"; Cunningham, *Archaeology, Relics, and the Law*; W. Green, "Cultural Resource Management and American Archaeology"; King, *Cultural Resource Laws and Practice*; Richman and Forsyth, *Legal Perspectives on Cultural Resources*.
17. Fenton, "Return of Eleven Wampum Belts"; Ferguson, "The Repatriation of Ahayu:da Zuni War Gods"; E. Green, *Ethics and Values in Archaeology*; Quick, *Proceedings*; Ubelaker and Grant, "Human Skeletal Remains."
18. Earle and Preucel, "Processual Archaeology and the Radical Critique"; Hodder, "Interpretive Archaeology and Its Role"; Patterson, "History and the Post-processual Archaeologies."
19. Ferguson, "Archaeological Values"; Klesert, "A View from Navajoland"; Stapp and Burney, *Tribal Cultural Resource Management*.
20. Dongoske, Aldenderfer, and Doehner, *Working Together*; Ferguson et al., "Working Together"; Swidler et al., *Native Americans and Archaeologists*.
21. Deloria, "Indians, Archaeologists, and the Future"; Goldstein and Kintigh, "Ethics and the Reburial Controversy"; Klesert and Powell, "A Perspective on Ethics and the Reburial Controversy"; Meighan, "Burying American Archaeology" and "Some Scholars' Views on Reburial."
22. Colwell-Chanthaphonh and Ferguson, *Collaboration in Archaeological Practice*; Derry and Malloy, *Archaeologists and Local Communities*; Dowdall and Parrish, "A Meaningful Disturbance of the Earth"; Green, Green, and Góes Neves, "Indigenous Knowledge and Archaeological Science"; Kerber, *Cross-Cultural Collaboration*; Kuwanwisiwma, "Hopi Understanding of the Past"; McDavid, "Archaeologies That Hurt"; Moser et al., "Transforming Archaeology Through Practice"; Shackel and Chambers, *Places in Mind*; Silliman, *Collaborative Indigenous Archaeology at the Trowel's Edge*.
23. Watkins, "Beyond the Margin."
24. Atalay, "Indigenous Archaeology as Decolonizing Practice"; Bray, "The Politics of an Indigenous Archaeology"; Conkey, "Dwelling at the Margins, Action at the Intersection?"; Nicholas and Andrews, "Indigenous Archaeology

in the Post-modern World"; Smith and Wobst, *Indigenous Archaeologies*; Watkins, *Indigenous Archaeology*.

25. Brown, *Who Owns Native Culture*; Handler, "Who Owns the Past?"; McBryde, *Who Owns the Past*; Thornton, "Who Owns Our Past?"

26. Arnold, "The Past as Propaganda" and "Justifying Genocide."

27. Kohl, Kozelsky, and Nachman, *Selective Remembrances*; Meskell, *Archaeology under Fire*.

28. Bender, "Stonehenge—Contested Landscapes"; Chippindale, "Stoned Henge."

29. Hamilakis, "Stories from Exile"; J. Merryman, "Thinking about the Elgin Marbles."

30. Greenfield, *The Return of Cultural Treasures*.

31. Brodie et al., *Archaeology, Cultural Heritage, and the Antiquities Trade*; Messenger, *The Ethics of Collecting Cultural Property*; Renfrew, *Loot, Legitimacy, and Ownership*.

32. Lawler, "Dam Threatens Iraqi Ancient Sites"; Vitelli and Pyburn, "Past Imperfect, Future Tense."

33. Coningham and Lewer, "Paradise Lost"; Meskell, "Sites of Violence."

34. Chapman, "Destruction of a Common Heritage"; Lowenthal, *The Heritage Crusade and the Spoils of War*.

35. Brodie, "Spoils of War"; Garen, "The War within the War."

36. Colwell-Chanthaphonh, "Dismembering/Disremembering the Buddhas"; Meskell, "Negative Heritage and Past Mastering in Archaeology."

37. Watkins, "Beyond the Margin," 275.

38. Appiah, "Whose Culture Is It?"; Cuno, *Who Owns Antiquity*; Lowenthal, "Classical Antiquities as National and Global Heritage"; J. Merryman, "Cultural Property Internationalism" and "Two Ways of Thinking about Cultural Property."

39. Watkins, "Cultural Nationalists, Internationalists, and 'Intra-nationalists'"; Zimmerman, "Public Heritage."

40. Rosen, "The Excavation of American Indian Burial Sites," 8.

41. Brodie and Renfrew, "Looting and the World's Archaeological Heritage"; Ede, "Ethics, the Antiquities Trade, and Archaeology"; Mallouf, "An Unraveling Rope"; S. White, "A Collector's Odyssey."

42. Lippert, "Building a Bridge to Cross a Thousand Years," 432.

43. Nicholas and Bannister, "Copyrighting the Past?"; Riley, *Indigenous Intellectual Property Rights*.

44. Carman, *Against Cultural Property*, 117.

45. Clifford, "On Ethnographic Authority"; Geertz, *Works and Lives*; Marcus and Cushman, "Ethnographies as Texts."

46. Biersack, *Clio in Oceania*; Clifford and Marcus, *Writing Culture*; Lassiter, "From 'Reading over the Shoulders of Natives'"; Marcus, "Ethnography in/of the World System"; Marcus and Fischer, *Anthropology as Culture Critique*.

47. Hodder, "Writing Archaeology"; Joyce, *The Languages of Archaeology*; Sinclair, "This Is an Article about Archaeology as Writing"; Smith, *Archaeological Theory and the Politics of Cultural Heritage*; Watkins, "Communicating Archaeology."

48. Fixico, "Ethics and Responsibilities in Writing American Indian History"; Mihesuah, *Natives and Academics*.

49. For example, Ferguson and Colwell-Chanthaphonh, *History Is in the Land*; Hodder, "Archaeological Reflexivity and the 'Local' Voice"; Pensley, "The Native American Graves Protection and Repatriation Act"; Williams, Wierzbowski, and Preucel, *Objects of Everlasting Esteem*.

50. King, "Professional Responsibility in Public Archaeology"; McGimsey, *Public Archaeology*; Raab et al., "Clients, Contracts, and Profits."

51. Karp, Kreamer, and Lavine, *Museums and Communities*; McManamon, "The Many Publics for Archaeology."

52. Brooks, "Reconstructing the Present with Its Past"; Gadsby and Chidester, "Heritage in Hampden"; Kellett, "Public Archaeology in an Andean Community"; Little, *Public Benefits of Archaeology*; McDavid, "Archaeologies That Hurt; Descendants That Matter"; N. Merryman, *Public Archaeology*; Stanish and Jusimba, "Working Together."

53. D. Thomas, "Afterword," 213.

54. Haslip-Viera, Ortiz de Montellano, and Barbour, "Robbing Native American Cultures"; Martin, "Educating to Combat Racism"; McDavid, "Beyond Strategy and Good Intention"; Orser, "The Challenge of Race to American Historical Archaeology"; Wiwijorra, "German Archaeology and Its Relation to Nationalism and Racism."

55. Echo-Hawk and Zimmerman, "Beyond Racism."

56. Cartmill, "The Status of the Race Concept in Physical Anthropology," 652–53.

57. "AAA Statement on Race," 712.

58. Harrison, "The Persistent Power of 'Race,'" 50–51; Stoler, "Making Empire Respectable."

59. Mukhopadhyay and Moses, "Reestablishing 'Race' in Anthropological Discourse," 518; Stocking, "The Turn-of-the-Century Concept of Race."

60. Pierpont, "The Measure of America"; Stocking, "Franz Boas and the Culture Concept in Historical Perspective"; V. Williams, *The Social Sciences and Theories of Race*, 112.

61. Harrison, "The Persistent Power of 'Race,'" 52–53; see also Mukhopadhyay and Moses, "Reestablishing 'Race' in Anthropological Discourse," 518–21, and Shanklin, "The Profession of the Color Blind," 670–71.

62. Visweswaran, "Race and the Culture of Anthropology," 71.

63. Strong and Van Winkle, "'Indian Blood'"; Tall Bear, "DNA, Blood, and Racializing the Tribe."

64. Keita and Kittles, "The Persistence of Racial Thinking," 534.
65. Echo-Hawk and Zimmerman, "Beyond Racism," 471, 472, emphasis in the original.
66. These morsels of American history come from the American Anthropological Association's excellent exhibit titled RACE: Are We So Different? Information on it is available at http://www.understandingrace.org, consulted June 2008.
67. Stocking, "The Turn-of-the-Century Concept of Race," 6, emphasis in the original.
68. See *Webster's Dictionary, 1913*, at http://machaut.uchicago.edu/cgi-bin/WEBSTER.sh?WORD=race, consulted June 2008.
69. Szasz, *Between Indian and White Worlds*.
70. Kessell, "The Ways and Words of the Other," 26.
71. Narayan, "How Native Is a 'Native' Anthropologist?" 673.
72. Jones, "Anthropology and the Oppressed," 67.
73. See Ferguson, "NHPA," 33–34.
74. Lippert, "Building a Bridge to Cross a Thousand Years," 433–34.
75. Two Bears, "A Navajo Student's Perception," 17.
76. Watkins, "Beyond the Margin," 276.
77. Ibid., 283.
78. Echo-Hawk and Zimmerman, "Beyond Racism," 473, 479–80.
79. Ibid., 473, 482.
80. Mukhopadhyay and Moses, "Reestablishing 'Race' in Anthropological Discourse," 525.
81. Patterson, "The Last Sixty Years," 7; see also Schuyler, "The History of American Archaeology."
82. Handler, *Nationalism and the Politics of Culture*; Parezo, *Hidden Scholars*; Patterson, *Toward a Social History of Archaeology*.
83. See McGuire, "Archaeology and the First Americans"; D. Thomas, *Skull Wars*; Trigger, "Archaeology and the Image of the American Indian."
84. Atalay, "Indigenous Archaeology as Decolonizing Practice," 281–82.
85. Carlson, "Letters from the Field," 135.
86. Lepore, "Historians Who Love Too Much," 131, 132.
87. Barth, *Ethnic Groups and Boundaries*.
88. Geertz, *The Interpretation of Cultures*, 5.

Chapter 2. At Heart I Am

1. Article in scrapbook, "Fiftieth Anniversary of United Mission Church on Reservation," November 7, 1907, SC17396, box 44, vol. 2, NYSL.
2. Fenton, "Editor's Introduction," 5.
3. Abler and Tooker, "Seneca," 510; Fenton, "Toward the Gradual Civilization of the Indian Natives"; Hauptman, *Conspiracy of Interests*, 113.

4. Tooker, "On the Development of the Handsome Lake Religion," 45.
5. Parker, *The Life of General Ely S. Parker*, 191.
6. Hertzberg, "Nationality, Anthropology, and Pan-Indianism," 49.
7. Armstrong, *Warrior in Two Camps*, 14.
8. Ibid., 41; Parker, *The Life of General Ely S. Parker*, 79.
9. Armstrong, *Warrior in Two Camps*, 131.
10. Ibid., 137–65.
11. Parker, *The Life of General Ely S. Parker*, 162–80.
12. Armstrong, *Warrior in Two Camps*, 16.
13. Parker, *The Life of General Ely S. Parker*, 190; quote from W. Thomas, "Arthur Caswell Parker," 2.
14. Fenton, "Editor's Introduction," 2; D. Thomas, "Afterword," 213. Both use this exact phrase.
15. Parker, *The Life of General Ely S. Parker*, 198.
16. Hertzberg, "Nationality, Anthropology, and Pan-Indianism," 52; Porter, *To Be Indian*.
17. Porter, *To Be Indian*, 5.
18. Quoted in "Where Hiawatha's Laws Still Govern," *Albany Argus*, May 29, 1910, SC17396, box 44, vol. 2, NYSL.
19. Quoted in Porter, *To Be Indian*, 95.
20. "Albanian Working for Betterment of Indians," *Albany Argus*, June 14, 1911, SC17396, box 44, vol. 2, NYSL.
21. Snow, *The Iroquois*, 1–51.
22. Abler and Tooker, "Seneca," 505.
23. Mann and Fields, "A Sign in the Sky"; Snow, *The Iroquois*, 60.
24. Snow, *The Iroquois*, 86–87.
25. Abler and Tooker, "Seneca," 506–7.
26. Horsman, "United States Indian Policies," 32.
27. Hauptman, *Conspiracy of Interests*, 92, 107.
28. Abler and Tooker, "Seneca," 509.
29. Hauptman, *Conspiracy of Interests*, 147.
30. Fenton, "Iroquois Studies at the Mid-century," 301; Hauptman, *Conspiracy of Interests*, 155.
31. Snow, *The Iroquois*, 158–59.
32. Hauptman, *The Iroquois Struggle for Survival*, 17, and *Conspiracy of Interests*, 219; Prucha, "United States Indian Policies," 40; Tooker, "Iroquois Since 1820," 450.
33. Hauptman, *Conspiracy of Interests*, 176.
34. Abler and Tooker, "Seneca," 511.
35. Hauptman, *Conspiracy of Interests*, 92–177.
36. Casler, "Report of Agent in New York," 134.
37. Hauptman, *The Iroquois Struggle for Survival*, 18.

38. Peacock, "Report of Agent in New York," 207.
39. Venables, *The Six Nations of New York*, vii.
40. Hagan, "United States Indian Policies," 56.
41. Price, *Annual Reports of the Commissioner of Indian Affairs*, 282–83, 302–3.
42. Cornell, *The Return of the Native*.
43. See Colwell-Chanthaphonh, "The Incorporation of the Native American Past."
44. Leupp, *Annual Report of the Commissioner of Indian Affairs*, 41–42.
45. McLaughlin, "The Antiquities Act of 1906," 69.
46. See also Harmon, McManamon, and Pitcaithley, *The Antiquities Act*; Lee, "The Antiquities Act of 1906."
47. In Hunt, *A Century of Dishonor*, v.
48. Ibid., 3.
49. W. Thomas, "Arthur Caswell Parker," 3.
50. Jack Moranz, "Rochester Portraits," ca. late 1930s, A.P23, box 5, folder 10, RRL.
51. Fenton, "Editor's Introduction," 6.
52. See Parker, *The Life of General Ely S. Parker*, 189–201.
53. Typed obituary for Frederick Ely Parker, 1929, A.P23, box 5, folder 15, RRL.
54. Parker, *The Life of General Ely S. Parker*, 201.
55. Porter, *To Be Indian*, 21.
56. See Snead, *Ruins and Rivals*, 22–23.
57. Thornton, *American Indian Holocaust and Survival*, 32.
58. Kickingbird and Ducheneaux, *One Hundred Million Acres*.
59. Turner, *The Frontier in American History*, 38.

Chapter 3. Then Let Us Spare, at Least, Their Graves

1. Shaw, "Marx and Morgan"; Trautmann, "Morgan, Lewis Henry," 331.
2. Bieder, *Science Encounters the Indian*, 202; Snow, *The Iroquois*, 169.
3. Armstrong, *Warrior in Two Camps*, 6; Bieder, "The Grand Order of the Iroquois"; Tooker, "Lewis H. Morgan and His Contemporaries," 359.
4. Lloyd, "Appendix B," 163; Parker, *The Life of General Ely S. Parker*, 82; Tooker, "Lewis H. Morgan and the Senecas."
5. Quoted in Parker, *The Life of General Ely S. Parker*, 237; see also Tooker, "The Structure of the Iroquois League."
6. Parker, *The Life of General Ely S. Parker*, 86–87.
7. Trautmann and Kabelac, "The Library of Lewis Henry Morgan," 12–13.
8. Lloyd, "Appendix B," 181.
9. Michaelsen, "Ely S. Parker and Amerindian Voices in Ethnography," 617.
10. Mark, "Francis La Flesche," 503.

11. Parker, *The Life of General Ely S. Parker*, 81; Stern, "Lewis Henry Morgan," 348.
12. Armstrong, *Warrior in Two Camps*, 48.
13. Morgan, *League of the Ho-de-no-sau-nee*, ix.
14. See Porter, *To Be Indian*, 26–42.
15. Parker, "Lewis Henry Morgan," 101, and "An Erie Indian Village and Burial Site at Ripley," 460.
16. Quoted in Fenton, "Editor's Introduction," 25.
17. Parker, *The Life of General Ely S. Parker*, 80.
18. Berkhofer, *The White Man's Indian*, 53.
19. Morgan, *League of the Ho-de-no-sau-nee*, 51, 121, 143, 249.
20. Snow, *The Iroquois*, 173.
21. Quoted in Lloyd, "Appendix B," 151.
22. Lurie, "Relations Between Indians and Anthropologists," 549.
23. Parker, "An Erie Indian Village and Burial Site at Ripley," 465–66.
24. Porter, *To Be Indian*, 40.
25. Parker, *The Life of General Ely S. Parker*, 89.
26. Griffin, "The Formation of the Society for American Archaeology," 267.
27. Hertzberg, "Nationality, Anthropology, and Pan-Indianism," 49.
28. Eggan, "Lewis H. Morgan and the Future of the American Indian," 274; cf. Haller, "Race and the Concept of Progress," 712, 719.
29. Morgan, *League of the Ho-de-no-sau-nee*, 121.
30. Lurie, "Relations Between Indians and Anthropologists," 549–50.
31. Harrison, "Introduction," 612.
32. Porter, *To Be Indian*, 32.
33. Ibid., 26, 39.
34. Quoted in ibid., 40, 41.
35. All quoted material in this section is from Nicholson Parker, "The American Red Man," 1851, A.P23, box 5, folder 14, RRL, unless otherwise cited.
36. Parker, *The Life of General Ely S. Parker*, 196.
37. Quoted in F. Ellis, *History of Cattaraugus County*, 11.
38. Ibid., 14.
39. Young, *History of Chautauqua County*, 19, 18.
40. F. Ellis, *History of Cattaraugus County*, 13.
41. Ibid., 14.
42. Silverberg, *Mound Builders of Ancient America*.
43. McGuire, "Archaeology and the First Americans," 818, 821; see also Trigger, "Anglo-American Archaeology," 143.
44. F. Ellis, *History of Cattaraugus County*, 14.
45. Cheney, *Contributions to the Thirteenth Annual Report*; F. Ellis, *History of Cattaraugus County*, 12.
46. Young, *History of Chautauqua County*, 17, 20.

47. Hertzberg, "Nationality, Anthropology, and Pan-Indianism," 51.
48. Report card, June 1892, A.P23, box 5, folder 7, RRL.
49. Letter of recommendation, A. R. Weansley, July 20, 1896, A.P23, box 1, folder 1, RRL.
50. Arthur C. Parker to Harriet Maxwell Converse, January 30, 1900, Joseph Keppler Jr. Iroquois Papers, no. 9184, folder P.2, no. 1, CUL.
51. Geneva H. Parker to Arthur C. Parker, December 10, 1900, A.P23, box 5, folder 15, RRL.
52. Porter, *To Be Indian*, 22.
53. Article in *Dickinson Union* 6 (3), A.P23, box 8, folder 1, RRL.
54. American Museum of Natural History permit, May 18, 1899, A.P23, box 5, folder 6, RRL.
55. W. Thomas, "Arthur Caswell Parker," 3.
56. John W. Powell to Arthur C. Parker, October 24, 1901, A.P23, box 1, folder 1, RRL.
57. Fenton, "Editor's Introduction," 7.
58. Arthur C. Parker's résumé, ca. 1945, A.P23, box 5, folder 4, RRL; Rochester Civic Medal of Achievement program, May 9, 1946, A.P23, box 5, folder 3, RRL. See also Nomination for Fellow in the Society for American Archaeology, Arthur C. Parker, November 15, 1935, Society for American Archaeology, Sec. Tres. Files, Subject Files, box 1, NAA.
59. Sloan, "Science in New York City," 62–63.
60. Parker, "Making a Museologist," 99.
61. Arthur C. Parker to Frank A. Doyle, December 4, 1906, 15513, State Archaeologist Correspondence, box 1, folder 7, NYSL.
62. Parker, "Where Questions Are Answered," 163.
63. Mark, "Francis La Flesche," 507–8.
64. This account of Putnam comes from Browman, "The Peabody Museum."
65. Beck, "Frank G. Speck"; Harrington, "Alanson Skinner."
66. Johansen and Mann, *Encyclopedia of the Haudenosaunee*, 6.
67. Fenton, "Introduction," xiv.
68. Hertzberg, "Nationality, Anthropology, and Pan-Indianism," 52.
69. Fenton, "Editor's Introduction," 10.
70. Arthur C. Parker to Frederic W. Putnam, October 13, 1902, HUG 1717.2.1, box 17, HUA.
71. Parker, "An Erie Indian Village and Burial Site at Ripley," 459.
72. Quoted in Tooker, *Lewis H. Morgan on Iroquois Material Culture*, 44–45.
73. Ibid., 43, 60, 80.
74. Porter, *To Be Indian*, 35.
75. Diary of Marcus B. Sackett, ca. 1890–1904, MS 551, FHS. According to genealogical records in the Haudenosaunee Project, Henry Silverheels was

born in 1811 and died on August 9, 1889, and hence must have discovered the ancient fort prior to 1889. See "The Haudenosaunee Project," RootsWeb, at http://worldconnect.rootsweb.com/cgi-bin/igm.cgi?op=GET&db=erikj&id= I22739#s1, consulted May 2007.

76. Beauchamp, *Aboriginal Occupation of New York*, 65.

77. M. Raymond Harrington, "Exploration of an Iroquoian Stronghold, Erie Co., Western NY, Silverhill [sic] Site, 1903," 1903, Mark Raymond Harrington, New York Records, Accession 04-23, folder 2, PMAE.

Chapter 4. Vast Unexplored Treasure Fields

1. Fenton, "Editor's Introduction," 8–9; M. R. Harrington, "An Ancient Village Site of the Shinnecock Indians"; D. Thomas, "Afterword," 214; obituary of Alanson Skinner, MS.7.MAI.I.620, SMAI; "Skinner, Alanson Buck, 1886–1925," in the National Museum of the American Indian Archives online database, MRC-541, at http://siris-archives.si.edu/ipac20/ipac.jsp?uri=full=3100001~!248794!0&term=, consulted May 2007.

2. "Finds on Long Island," *New York Times*, September 28, 1902.

3. Burtan, "Silences at Silverheels," 43; "M. R. Harrington (1882–1971)," at http://encyclopediaofarkansas.net/encyclopedia/entry-detail.aspx?entryID=576, consulted May 2007.

4. Marie Harrington, *On the Trail of Forgotten People*, 14–20.

5. Ibid., 22; "Mark Raymond Harrington 1882–1971," at http://www.mnsu.edu/emuseum/information/biography/fghij/harrington_mark.html, consulted May 2007; M. Raymond Harrington to Frederic W. Putnam, May 15, 1904, Mark Raymond Harrington, New York Records, Accession 04-23, folder Correspondence, PMAE.

6. Frederic W. Putnam to Ester Putnam, May 26, 1900, HUG 1717.2.1, box 11, HUA.

7. Lyman, O'Brien, and Dunnell, *The Rise and Fall of Culture History*, 25.

8. M. R. Harrington, "Shinnecock Notes."

9. Alanson Skinner to Arthur C. Parker, October 26, 1909, 15513, State Archaeologist Correspondence, box 1, folder 21, NYSL.

10. Parker, "Making a Museologist," 99.

11. Salisbury et al., *First Annual Report of the Trustees of the Peabody Museum*, 5.

12. Browman, "The Peabody Museum," 509.

13. S. Williams, *From the Director's Desk*, 2.

14. Browman, "The Peabody Museum," 510.

15. Jenkins, "Object Lessons and Ethnographic Displays," 242.

16. "Estimate for four month's expedition," Accession 03-32, folder 5, PMAE.

17. Burtan, "Silences at Silverheels," 36; M. Raymond Harrington to Frederic W. Putnam, April 27, 1903, Accession 03-32, folder 5, PMAE.

18. M. Raymond Harrington to Frederic W. Putnam, May 1 and August 31, 1903, Accession 03-32, folder 5, PMAE.

19. M. Raymond Harrington, "Exploration of an Iroquoian Stronghold, Erie Co., Western NY, Silverhill [sic] Site, 1903," 1903, Mark Raymond Harrington, New York Records, Accession 04-23, folder 2, PMAE.

20. W. Thomas, "Arthur Caswell Parker," 4.

21. Quotes in this paragraph come from M. Raymond Harrington to Frederic W. Putnam, May 8, 1903, Accession 03-32, folder 5, PMAE.

22. M. R. Harrington, "A Midcolonial Seneca Site," 212.

23. Field Notebook, 1903, Mark Raymond Harrington, New York Records, Accession 04-23, folder Silverheels Materials, PMAE; Frederic W. Putnam to M. Raymond Harrington, May 26, 1903, and M. Raymond Harrington to Frederic W. Putnam, June 5, 1903, Accession 03-32, folder 5, PMAE.

24. M. Raymond Harrington to Frederic W. Putnam, May 15, 1904, Mark Raymond Harrington, New York Records, Accession 04-23, folder Correspondence, PMAE.

25. "Among the Cottagers of Long Island's Fashionable Colonies," *New York Times*, August 31, 1902.

26. Amato, "Digging Sacred Ground," 7.

27. Engelbrecht, *Iroquoia*, 178. See also Hill and Grinde, "Problems in Prehistory and History of the Iroquois," and Thwaites, *The Jesuit Relations and Allied Documents*.

28. Field Notebook, 1903, PMAE.

29. See Cornell, *The Return of the Native*; D. Thomas, *Skull Wars*.

30. Arthur C. Parker to Department of the Interior, June 15, 1905, and R. B. Weber to Arthur C. Parker, June 17, 1905, 15513, State Archaeologist Correspondence, box 1, folders 30 and 26, NYSL.

31. Arthur C. Parker to Frederic W. Putnam, May 16, 1903, Accession 03-32, folder 5, PMAE.

32. Hill, "Making a Final Resting Place Final," 16.

33. Frederic W. Putnam to M. Raymond Harrington, May 16, 1903, Accession 03-32, folder 5, PMAE.

34. M. Raymond Harrington to Frederic W. Putnam, May 23, 1903, and Arthur C. Parker to Frederic W. Putnam, June 27 and May 30, 1903, both in Accession 03-32, folder 5, PMAE.

35. Quotes in this section are from Arthur C. Parker, "American Anthropology, Its Scope and Its Problems," 1902, A.P23, box 6, folder 6, RRL, emphasis in the original.

36. Harrington, "Exploration of an Iroquoian Stronghold, 1903," PMAE.

37. Field Notebook, 1903, PMAE.

38. Arthur C. Parker to Frederic W. Putnam, May 16, 1903, Accession 03-32, folder 5, PMAE.

39. Harrington, "Exploration of an Iroquoian Stronghold," PMAE.
40. Bieder, "The Representations of Indian Bodies," 20.
41. Ibid., 24, 28.
42. Morenon, "Nagged by NAGPA," 123.
43. Frederic W. Putnam to M. Raymond Harrington, May 26, 1903, Accession 03-32, folder 5, PMAE.
44. Burtan, "Silences at Silverheels," 83.
45. M. Raymond Harrington to Frederic W. Putnam, May 23, 1903, and Frederic W. Putnam to M. Raymond Harrington, May 26, 1903, Accession 03-32, folder 5, PMAE.
46. Arthur C. Parker to Frederic W. Putnam, June 12, 1903, Accession 03-32, folder 5, PMAE.
47. Burtan, "Silences at Silverheels," 46.
48. Peabody, "American Archaeology during the Years 1900–1905," 184.
49. See Bailey, "An Analysis of Iroquoian Ceramic Types," 335; Carpenter, "Iroquoian Figurines," 108; and Zeller, "Arthur C. Parker," 42.
50. Porter, *To Be Indian*, 50.
51. Arthur C. Parker to Frederic W. Putnam, May 30, 1903, Accession 03-32, folder 5, PMAE; "Estimate for four month's expedition," Accession 03-32, folder 5, PMAE.
52. Quotes in this section are from Parker, "Making a Museologist," 99, unless otherwise cited.
53. See also Burtan, "Silences at Silverheels," 39.
54. Arthur C. Parker to Frederic W. Putnam, January 17, 1903, Accession 03-32, folder 5, PMAE.
55. Arthur C. Parker to Frederic W. Putnam, May 30, 1903, Accession 03-32, folder 5, PMAE.
56. M. Raymond Harrington to Frederic W. Putnam, May 30, 1903, Accession 03-32, folder 5, PMAE.
57. M. Raymond Harrington to Frederic W. Putnam, May 10, 1903, Accession 03-32, folder 5, PMAE.
58. Notebook, summer 1903, SC 13604, box 1, folder 32, NYSL.
59. Frederic W. Putnam to M. Raymond Harrington, May 26, 1903, Accession 03-32, folder 5, PMAE.
60. Snead, *Ruins and Rivals*, 17; see also Burtan, "Silences at Silverheels," 85.
61. Arthur C. Parker to Frederic W. Putnam, June 13, 1903, Accession 03-32, folder 5, PMAE.
62. M. Raymond Harrington to Frederic W. Putnam, July 1 and August 15, 1903, Accession 03-32, folder 5, PMAE.
63. Arthur C. Parker to Frederic W. Putnam, August 24, 1903, Accession 03-32, folder 5, PMAE.
64. Field Notebook, 1903, PMAE.

65. Arthur C. Parker to Frederic W. Putnam, May 30, 1903, Accession 03-32, folder 5, PMAE; and Harrington, "A Midcolonial Seneca Site," 222.

66. Arthur C. Parker to George G. Heye, January 4, 1905, and John Kennedy to Arthur C. Parker, March 21, 1905, 15513, State Archaeologist Correspondence, box 1, folders 11 and 14, NYSL.

67. Harrington, "Exploration of an Iroquoian Stronghold," PMAE.

68. M. Raymond Harrington to Arthur C. Parker, November 18, 1907, and Arthur C. Parker to John Kennedy, December 24, 1907, 15513, State Archaeologist Correspondence, box 1, folders 11 and 14, NYSL.

69. M. Raymond Harrington to Arthur C. Parker, December 26, 1907, 15513, State Archaeologist Correspondence, box 1, folder 11, NYSL.

70. Arthur C. Parker to John Kennedy, January 27, 1908, 15513, State Archaeologist Correspondence, box 1, folder 14, NYSL.

71. Arthur C. Parker to J. W. Madison, May 26, 1908, 15513, State Archaeologist Correspondence, box 1, folder 16, NYSL.

72. L. D. Shoemaker to Arthur C. Parker, November 13, 1913, 15513, State Archaeologist Correspondence, box 2, folder 5, NYSL.

73. Correspondence between Burr B. Andrews and Arthur C. Parker, June 1913, 15513, State Archaeologist Correspondence, box 1, folder 32, NYSL.

74. Parker, *Seneca Myths and Folk Tales*, xix–xx.

75. Parker, *An Analytical History of the Seneca Indians*, 13.

76. Quoted in Lloyd, "Appendix B," 169–70; on Seneca burial customs, see Morgan, *League of the Ho-de-no-sau-nee*, 166.

77. Arthur C. Parker to Tom [Gardinier?], summer 1907, 15513, State Archaeologist Correspondence, box 1, folder 23, NYSL.

78. Arthur C. Parker to Frederic W. Putnam, June 13, 1903, Accession 03-32, folder 5, PMAE.

Chapter 5. You Boys Have Dreamed

1. Quotes in this section are from Field Notebook, 1903, Mark Raymond Harrington, New York Records, Accession 04-23, folder Silverheels Materials, PMAE, unless otherwise cited.

2. Arthur C. Parker to Frederic W. Putnam, July 11, 1903, and see also M. Raymond Harrington to Frederic W. Putnam, June 20 and August 31, 1903, Accession 03-32, folder 5, PMAE, emphasis in the original.

3. Arthur C. Parker to Frederic W. Putnam, June 13, 1903, Accession 03-32, folder 5, PMAE.

4. This narrative is based on and loosely quotes from three documents: John Kennedy to Frederic W. Putnam, June 18, 1903, and M. Raymond Harrington to Frederic W. Putnam, June 19, 1903, both in Accession 03-32, folder 5, PMAE; and Field Notebook, 1903, PMAE.

5. John Kennedy to Frederic W. Putnam, June 18, 1903, Accession 03-32, folder 5, PMAE.

6. Parker, *The Life of General Ely S. Parker*, 200.

7. M. Raymond Harrington to Frederic W. Putnam, June 19, 1903, Accession 03-32, folder 5, PMAE.

8. Harriet Maxwell Converse to Joseph Keppler, June 22, 1903, Joseph Keppler Jr. Iroquois Papers, no. 9184, folder C6, no. 16, CUL.

9. Hand-drawn map, n.d., Accession 03-32, folder 5, PMAE.

10. Arthur C. Parker to Frederic W. Putnam, June 27, 1903, Accession 03-32, folder 5, PMAE.

11. Arthur C. Parker to Frederic W. Putnam, August 24, 1903, Accession 03-32, folder 5, PMAE.

12. Johansen and Mann, *Encyclopedia of the Haudenosaunee*, 5. See, for example, Arthur C. Parker to Joseph Keppler, December 1, 1903, Joseph Keppler Jr. Iroquois Papers, no. 9184, folder P.2, no. 2, CUL.

13. Tooker, "Lewis H. Morgan and the Senecas," 52.

14. Parker, "Snow-Snake as Played by the Seneca-Iroquois," and *Seneca Myths and Folk Tales*, 38.

15. Frederic W. Putnam to Arthur C. Parker, September 1, 1903, A.P23, box 1, folder 1, RRL.

16. Notebook, summer 1903, SC 13604, box 1, folder 32, NYSL; Parker, *Seneca Myths and Folk Tales*, xx.

17. Parker, *Seneca Myths and Folk Tales*, 400.

18. Parker, *The Indian How Book*, 61–62. See also Marie Harrington, *On the Trail of Forgotten People*.

19. M. Raymond Harrington to Frederic W. Putnam, June 19, 1903, and Arthur C. Parker to Frederic W. Putnam, June 27 and August 24, 1903, Accession 03-32, folder 5, PMAE.

20. Frederic W. Putnam to Arthur C. Parker, September 1, 1903, A.P23, box 1, folder 1, RRL.

21. See SC17396, box 44, vol. 2, NYSL.

22. M. Raymond Harrington to Frederic W. Putnam, August 1, 1903, Accession 03-32, folder 5, PMAE, emphasis in original.

23. Frances G. Mead to M. Raymond Harrington, August 20, 1903, Accession 03-32, folder 5, PMAE.

24. Arthur C. Parker to Frederic W. Putnam, August 24, 1903, Accession 03-32, folder 5, PMAE.

25. Field Notebook, 1903, PMAE; and M. R. Harrington, "A Midcolonial Seneca Site," 212.

26. M. Raymond Harrington to Frederic W. Putnam, August 31, 1903, Accession 03-32, folder 5, PMAE.

27. Ibid.

28. Putnam, *Thirty-Seventh Report on the Peabody Museum*, 6.
29. "Anthropologic Miscellanea," 580.
30. Silverheels Artifact Catalogue, PMAE.
31. Frederic W. Putnam to Arthur C. Parker, September 1 and November 25, 1903, A.P23, box 1, folder 1, RRL.
32. M. Raymond Harrington to Frederic W. Putnam, November 18 and October 6, 1903, Accession 03-32, folder 5, PMAE.
33. Collier and Tschopik, "The Role of Museums in American Anthropology," 770, 769.
34. Ibid., 771.
35. Ibid.
36. Browman, "The Peabody Museum," 510; Burtan, "Silences at Silverheels," 76; Porter, *To Be Indian*, 49.
37. M. Raymond Harrington to Frederic W. Putnam, October 26, 1904, Mark Raymond Harrington, New York Records, Accession 04-23, folder Correspondence, PMAE; Putnam, *Thirty-Eighth Report on the Peabody Museum*, 6.
38. Exhibit labels, Accession 03-32, folder 3, PMAE.
39. Jacknis, "Exhibition Review," 29.
40. Bean and Krech, "Review," 264.
41. See also Burtan, "Silences at Silverheels," 125.
42. Jacknis, "Exhibition Review," 29.
43. M. Raymond Harrington to Frederic W. Putnam, October 6 and November 18, 1903, Accession 03-32, folder 5, PMAE.
44. M. Raymond Harrington to Frederic W. Putnam, December 9, 1903, Accession 03-32, folder 5, PMAE. On the purchase of the artifacts, see M. Raymond Harrington to Frederic W. Putnam, November 30, 1903, Accession 03-32, folder 5, PMAE.
45. Arthur C. Parker to Frederic W. Putnam, December 20, 1903, HUG 1717.2.1, box 17, HUA; Frederic W. Putnam to Arthur C. Parker, May 12, 1904, A.P23, box 1, folder 1, RRL; loan receipt from Peabody Museum to Arthur C. Parker, November 8, 1909, Mark Raymond Harrington, New York Records, Accession 04-23, PMAE.
46. M. Raymond Harrington to Frederic W. Putnam, May 1, 1904, and Frederic W. Putnam to M. Raymond Harrington, May 12, 1904, Mark Raymond Harrington, New York Records, Accession 04-23, folder Correspondence, PMAE.
47. M. Raymond Harrington to Frederic W. Putnam, October 4, 1904, Mark Raymond Harrington, New York Records, Accession 04-23, PMAE.
48. Frederic W. Putnam to Arthur C. Parker, May 12, 1904, A.P23, box 1, folder 1, RRL.
49. Arthur C. Parker to Frederic W. Putnam, October 26, 1909, and Francis H. Mead to Arthur C. Parker, November 2, 1909, 15513, State Archaeologist Correspondence, box 1, folders 19 and 16, NYSL; loan receipt from Peabody

Museum to Arthur C. Parker, November 8, 1909, Mark Raymond Harrington, New York Records, Accession 04-23, PMAE.

50. C. C. Willoughby to Arthur C. Parker, January 29, 1917, and Arthur C. Parker to C. C. Willoughby, February 8, 1917, UAV677.46, box A 1917, HUA.

51. C. C. Willoughby to Arthur C. Parker, February 12, 1917, UAV677.46, box A 1917, HUA.

52. C. C. Willoughby to Arthur C. Parker, March 15, 1917, UAV677.46, box A 1917, HUA.

53. Skinner, "Review" (1923), 95.

54. Ritchie, "Fifty Years of Archaeology," 412.

55. Harrington, "A Midcolonial Seneca Site," 228, 235, 230, 225.

56. M. Raymond Harrington, "Exploration of an Iroquoian Stronghold, Erie Co., Western NY, Silverhill [sic] Site, 1903," 1903, Mark Raymond Harrington, New York Records, Accession 04-23, folder 2, PMAE.

57. Arthur C. Parker to Frederic W. Putnam, January 7, 1907, 15513, State Archaeologist Correspondence, box 1, folder 19, NYSL.

58. Arthur C. Parker to C. C. Willoughby, February 8, 1917, UAV677.46, box A 1917, HUA.

59. Harrington, "Exploration of an Iroquoian Stronghold," PMAE; see also Harrington, "A Midcolonial Seneca Site," 237.

60. Skinner, "Review" (1923), 97.

Chapter 6. It Is Knowledge, Solely, That We Are Seeking

1. Arthur C. Parker to Frederic W. Putnam, November 19, 1903, HUG 1717.2.1, box 17, HUA.

2. Frederic W. Putnam to Arthur C. Parker, November 25, 1903, A.P23, box 1, folder 1, RRL.

3. Arthur C. Parker's résumé, ca. 1945, A.P23, box 5, folder 4, RRL; Arthur C. Parker to Joseph Keppler, February 25, 1905, Joseph Keppler Jr. Iroquois Papers, no. 9184, folder P.2, no. 6, CUL.

4. John Kenrick [Bange?] to Frederic A. Duneka, June 15, 1904, 15513, State Archaeologist Correspondence, box 1, folder 2, NYSL.

5. Arthur C. Parker to Frances G. Mead, October 28, 1904, A.P23, box 1, folder 1, RRL; Arthur C. Parker's résumé, ca. 1945, RRL.

6. "Seven Million Built This Huge Hotel Pile," *New York Times*, July 10, 1904.

7. Arthur C. Parker to Frederic W. Putnam, April 8, 1904, HUG 1717.2.1, box 17, HUA, emphasis in the original.

8. Frederick J. H. Merrill to Arthur C. Parker, March 1, 1904, 15513, State Archaeologist Correspondence, box 1, folder 14, NYSL.

9. William M. Beauchamp to Arthur C. Parker, June 4, 1904, A.P23, box 1, folder 1, RRL.

10. Arthur C. Parker to Frederic W. Putnam, April 8, 1904, HUG 1717.2.1, box 17, HUA.

11. Fenton, "The Present Status of Anthropology," 505.

12. Frederic W. Putnam to Arthur C. Parker, May 12, 1904, A.P23, box 1, folder 1, RRL.

13. M. Raymond Harrington to Frederic W. Putnam, May 15, 1904, Mark Raymond Harrington, New York Records, Accession 04-23, folder Correspondence, PMAE.

14. Obituary of Alanson Skinner, MS.7.MAI.I.620, SMAI.

15. Arthur C. Parker to Joseph Keppler, February 25, 1905, Joseph Keppler Jr. Iroquois Papers, no. 9184, folder P.2, no. 6, CUL.

16. John M. Clarke to Arthur C. Parker, June 8, 1904, 15513, State Archaeologist Correspondence, box 1, folder 4, NYSL.

17. Arthur C. Parker to Frederic W. Putnam, July 16, 1904, HUG 1717.2.1, box 17, HUA; see also Arthur C. Parker to Joseph Keppler, August 7, 1904, Joseph Keppler Jr. Iroquois Papers, no. 9184, folder P.2, no. 4, CUL.

18. M. R. Harrington, "An Abenaki 'Witch-Story.'"

19. Marie Harrington, *On the Trail of Forgotten People*, 43.

20. "Indians in Public Schools," newspaper unknown, ca. 1900–1901, Joseph Keppler Jr. Iroquois Papers, no. 9184, folder P.2, CUL.

21. "Services Held Here for Former Indian Actress," *Mercury-Register*, January 4, 1946.

22. "A Beautiful Indian Model," *Los Angeles Times*, May 10, 1901; "Art Inventories Catalogue," Smithsonian American Art Museum, at http://siris-artinventories.si.edu/ipac20/ipac.jsp?uri=full=3100001~!338344!0, consulted June 2007.

23. "New York's Indians," *Los Angeles Times*, April 10, 1904.

24. "A Distinguished Abenaki Girl," *Atlanta Constitution*, March 3, 1901.

25. Arthur C. Parker to Frederic W. Putnam, July 16, 1904, HUG 1717.2.1, box 17, HUA.

26. M. Raymond Harrington to Frederic W. Putnam, October 1905, Mark Raymond Harrington, New York Records, Accession 04-23, PMAE; Arthur C. Parker to Joseph Keppler, August 7, 1904, Joseph Keppler Jr. Iroquois Papers, no. 9184, folder P.2, no. 4, CUL.

27. Arthur C. Parker to Howard Rogers, December 30, 1905, 15513, State Archaeologist Correspondence, box 1, folder 20, NYSL.

28. Arthur C. Parker to Joseph Keppler, April 16, 1905, Joseph Keppler Jr. Iroquois Papers, no. 9184, folder P.2, no. 10, CUL.

29. M. Raymond Harrington to Frederick W. Putnam, February 3, 1906, Accession 04-23, folder Correspondence, PMAE.

30. Arthur C. Parker to W. S. Fannell, December 19, 1906, and Arthur C. Parker to Beyer and Williams Co., July 11, 1907, 15513, State Archaeologist

Correspondence, box 1, folders 9 and 2, NYSL; Arthur C. Parker to Frederic W. Putnam, December 27, 1907, HUG 1717.2.1, box 17, HUA.

31. Arthur C. Parker to Edward Cornplanter, December 7, 1908, 15513, State Archaeologist Correspondence, box 1, folder 3, NYSL.

32. Arthur C. Parker to Alanson Skinner, June 20, 1906, and Arthur C. Parker to A. P. Cessman, August 25, 1907, 15513, State Archaeologist Correspondence, box 1, folders 21 and 3, NYSL.

33. Arthur C. Parker to Frederic W. Putnam, July 22, 1909, HUG 1717.2.1, box 17, HUA.

34. Arthur C. Parker to Julia Crouse, October 20, 1909, Alanson Skinner to Arthur C. Parker, March 17, 1910, and Arthur C. Parker to Alanson Skinner, March 18, 1910, all in 15513, State Archaeologist Correspondence, box 1, folders 3 and 22, NYSL.

35. Arthur C. Parker to Joseph Keppler, September 23, 1911, Joseph Keppler Jr. Iroquois Papers, no. 9184, folder C.6, no. 16, CUL; Alanson Skinner to Arthur C. Parker, July 3, 1912, 15513, State Archaeologist Correspondence, box 2, folder 4, NYSL; and Arthur C. Parker to Joseph Keppler, September 23, 1911, Joseph Keppler Jr. Iroquois Papers, no. 9184, folder P.2, no. 36, CUL.

36. Lowe, *An Encyclopedic Dictionary of Women in Early American Films*, 393–94; Truitt, *Who Was Who on Screen*, 111.

37. Bernstein, "First Recipients of Anthropological Doctorates."

38. Ibid., 560.

39. Voegelin, "Anthropology in American Universities," 350.

40. Bernstein, "First Recipients of Anthropological Doctorates," 552.

41. Arthur C. Parker to Frederic W. Putnam, April 30, 1906, HUG 1717.2.1, box 17, HUA.

42. Arthur C. Parker to Frederic W. Putnam, October 22, 1904, A.P23, box 1, folder 1, RRL.

43. Nicholson Parker, "The American Red Man," 1851, A.P23, box 5, folder 14, RRL.

44. A. S. Draper to Arthur C. Parker, October 14, 1904, A.P23, box 1, folder 1, RRL.

45. A. S. Draper to Arthur C. Parker, November 4, 1904, A.P23, box 5, folder 1, RRL.

46. Arthur C. Parker to Joseph Keppler, November 24, 1905, Joseph Keppler Jr. Iroquois Papers, no. 9184, folder P.2, no. 17, CUL.

47. Melvil Dewey to Arthur C. Parker, February 22, 1905, A.P23, box 1, folder 1, RRL.

48. Martha Parker to Arthur C. Parker, March 23, 1905, A.P23, box 1, folder 1, RRL; John Kennedy to Arthur C. Parker, March 21, 1905, 15513, State Archaeologist Correspondence, box 1, folder 14, NYSL; Arthur C. Parker to Joseph

Keppler, March 12, 1905, Joseph Keppler Jr. Iroquois Papers, no. 9184, folder P.2, no. 7, CUL.

49. Arthur C. Parker to Joseph Keppler, March 27 and May 15, 1905, Joseph Keppler Jr. Iroquois Papers, no. 9184, folder P.2, nos. 9 and 12, CUL.

50. Howard Rogers to Arthur C. Parker, April 4 and April 19, 1905, 15513, State Archaeologist Correspondence, box 1, folder 20, NYSL.

51. John M. Clarke to Arthur C. Parker, April 27, 1905, and Howard Rogers to Arthur C. Parker, May 3, 1905, 15513, State Archaeologist Correspondence, box 1, folders 4 and 20, NYSL; Howard Rogers to Arthur C. Parker, May 16, 1905, A.P23, box 5, folder 1, RRL.

52. Howard Rogers to Arthur C. Parker, May 27, 1905, A.P23, box 5, folder 1, RRL.

53. Arthur C. Parker to Howard Rogers, June 11, 1905, and Jacob van Delos to Arthur C. Parker, August 2 and 25, 1905, 15513, State Archaeologist Correspondence, box 1, folders 20 and 25, NYSL; Arthur C. Parker to Joseph Keppler, April 16, 1905, Joseph Keppler Jr. Iroquois Papers, no. 9184, folder P.2, no. 10, CUL.

54. John M. Clarke to Arthur C. Parker, November 16, 1905, 15513, State Archaeologist Correspondence, box 1, folder 4, NYSL.

55. Arthur C. Parker to Howard Rogers, March 20 and April 2, 1906, and Arthur C. Parker to John M. Clarke, April 3 and 14, 1906, 15513, State Archaeologist Correspondence, box 1, folders 20 and 4, NYSL; Arthur C. Parker to Joseph Keppler, March 28, 1906, Joseph Keppler Jr. Iroquois Papers, no. 9184, folder P.2, no. 18, CUL.

56. Arthur C. Parker to William Young, May 1, 1906, 15513, State Archaeologist Correspondence, box 1, folder 27, NYSL.

57. Sullivan, Hunt, and Wilkinson, "History of Excavations," 30; Arthur C. Parker to Alanson Skinner, June 20, 1906, 15513, State Archaeologist Correspondence, box 1, folder 21, NYSL.

58. Parker, "An Erie Indian Village and Burial Site at Ripley"; Wilkinson, "Population Dynamics, Health, and Mortality," 91.

59. Arthur C. Parker to Joseph Keppler, July 27, 1906, Joseph Keppler Jr. Iroquois Papers, no. 9184, folder P.2, no. 20, CUL; and Arthur C. Parker to William Blueskye, August 6, 1906, 15513, State Archaeologist Correspondence, box 1, folder 2, NYSL.

60. The work published is Parker, "An Erie Indian Village and Burial Site at Ripley"; the description of the approach is in Trigger, *A History of Archaeological Thought*, 270.

61. Brose, "The Northeastern United States," 92.

62. Arthur C. Parker to John M. Clarke, September 4, 1906, 15513, State Archaeologist Correspondence, box 1, folder 4, NYSL.

63. John M. Clarke to Arthur C. Parker, September 11, 1906, Arthur C. Parker to John M. Clarke, September 18, 1906, and Arthur C. Parker to William Young, July 8, 1910, all in 15513, State Archaeologist Correspondence, box 1, folders 4 and 27, NYSL.

64. Arthur C. Parker to John M. Clarke, August 15, 1906, 15513, State Archaeologist Correspondence, box 1, folder 4, NYSL.

65. Arthur C. Parker to Frederic W. Putnam, October 25, 1906, HUG 1717.2.1, box 17, HUA.

66. Arthur C. Parker to John M. Clarke, November 18, 1905, 15513, State Archaeologist Correspondence, box 1, folder 4, NYSL.

67. Arthur C. Parker to John M. Clarke, May 7 and May 24, 1906, 15513, State Archaeologist Correspondence, box 1, folder 4, NYSL.

68. Arthur C. Parker to Everett R. Burmaster, July 2, 1907, 15513, State Archaeologist Correspondence, box 1, folder 2, NYSL.

69. Arthur C. Parker to Frederick Bourne, July 25, 1910, 15513, State Archaeologist Correspondence, box 1, folder 2, NYSL.

70. M. Raymond Harrington to Frederic W. Putnam, March 4, 1904, Mark Raymond Harrington, New York Records, Accession 04-23, folder Correspondence, PMAE.

71. M. Raymond Harrington to Arthur C. Parker, October 27 and November 25, 1905, 15513, State Archaeologist Correspondence, box 1, folder 11, NYSL.

72. Arthur C. Parker to John M. Clarke, February 10, 1906, 15513, State Archaeologist Correspondence, box 1, folder 4, NYSL.

73. Arthur C. Parker to Joseph Keppler, March 12, 20, 27, April 16, May 10, October 31, 1905, and October 10, 1908, Joseph Keppler Jr. Iroquois Papers, no. 9184, folder P.2, nos. 7, 8, 9, 10, 11, 16 and 29, respectively, CUL.

74. Parker, "Do Curators Collect?" 67.

75. Sullivan, Hunt, and Wilkinson, "History of Excavations," 31; see also Arthur C. Parker to Joseph Keppler, June 25, 1908, Joseph Keppler Jr. Iroquois Papers, no. 9184, folder P.2, no. 28, CUL.

76. Receipt from Covert & Harrington, November 18, 1907, and M. Raymond Harrington to Arthur C. Parker, November 18, 1907, both in 15513, State Archaeologist Correspondence, box 1, folders 29 and 11, NYSL.

77. Arthur C. Parker to John M. Clarke, July 12, 1906, and John M. Clarke to Arthur C. Parker, July 13, 1906, 15513, State Archaeologist Correspondence, box 1, folder 4, NYSL.

78. Arthur C. Parker to Joseph Keppler, February 25, 1905, Joseph Keppler Jr. Iroquois Papers, no. 9184, folder P.2, no. 6, CUL.

79. J. W. Madison to Arthur C. Parker, April 30, 1908, Arthur C. Parker to J. W. Madison, May 15, 1908, and J. W. Madison to Arthur C. Parker, May 19, 1908, all in 15513, State Archaeologist Correspondence, box 1, folder 16, NYSL.

80. Arthur C. Parker to J. W. Madison, May 26, 1908, 15513, State Archaeologist Correspondence, box 1, folder 16, NYSL.

81. L. D. Shoemaker to Arthur C. Parker, November 13, 1913, 15513, State Archaeologist Correspondence, box 2, folder 5, NYSL; see exchange between Burr B. Andrews and Arthur C. Parker, June 1914, 15513, State Archaeologist Correspondence, box 1, folder 32, NYSL.

82. Herscher, "Scourge of the Forgery Culture"; Whittaker and Stafford, "Replicas, Fakes, and Art."

83. Arthur C. Parker to Simon L. Adler, March 6, 1914, 15513, State Archaeologist Correspondence, box 1, folder 32, NYSL.

84. "Anthropological Notes" (1923), 128; and Parker, "The Perversion of Archaeological Data."

85. Parker, "The Lamoka Report," 34.

86. Parker, "Archaeological Collection" and "Grave Restoration."

87. Parker, "Archaeology Adopts a New Policy," 160.

88. Parker, "Indians versus Pot-Hunters," 268.

89. Osborn, "The State Museum and State Progress," 502.

90. Arthur C. Parker to Howard Rogers, April 2, 1906, 15513, State Archaeologist Correspondence, box 1, folder 20, NYSL.

91. Arthur C. Parker to John M. Clarke, April 3 and 14, 1906, 15513, State Archaeologist Correspondence, box 1, folder 4, NYSL; Arthur C. Parker to Joseph Keppler, July 9, 1906, Joseph Keppler Jr. Iroquois Papers, no. 9184, folder P.2, no. 19, CUL.

92. Parker, "An Erie Indian Village and Burial Site at Ripley."

93. The first three works are republished in Fenton, *Parker on the Iroquois*.

94. Article in scrapbook, "Archaeologist Writes of the Fire," n.d., SC17396, box 44, vol. 2, NYSL; Parker, "Anthropologic Miscellanea"; Arthur C. Parker to Joseph Keppler, March 29, 1911, Joseph Keppler Jr. Iroquois Papers, no. 9184, folder P.2, no. 34, CUL.

95. Arthur C. Parker to S. A. Barrett, May 17, 1911, 15513, State Archaeologist Correspondence, box 1, folder 33, NYSL.

96. Arthur C. Parker to Joseph Keppler, April 11, 1911, Joseph Keppler Jr. Iroquois Papers, no. 9184, folder P.2, no. 35, CUL.

97. Osborn, "The State Museum and State Progress," 494.

98. Porter, "Arthur Caswell Parker," 218.

99. Parker, "Habitat Groups in Wax and Plaster."

100. Porter, *To Be Indian*, 65–66.

101. Zeller, "Arthur C. Parker," 44, emphasis in the original.

102. Tivy, "The Local History Museum in Ontario," 24, 134, 191.

103. Ritchie, "Arthur Caswell Parker," 294; Zeller, "Arthur C. Parker," 46, 50; Arthur C. Parker to Joseph Keppler, January 28, 1938, Joseph Keppler Jr. Iroquois Papers, no. 9184, folder P.2, no. 58, CUL.

104. "Parker's Digging," *Albany Argus*, August 17, 1915, A.P23, box 5, folder 10, RRL.

105. Arthur C. Parker's résumé, ca. 1945, A.P23, box 5, folder 4, RRL; and the New York State Archaeological Association Web site, at http://nysaaweb.bfn.org, consulted June 2007.

106. Parker, "The Origin of the Iroquois."

107. Parker, *The Life of General Ely S. Parker*. See also Parker, *A Contact Period Seneca Site*, *The Great Algonkin Flint Mines*, "The Mound Builder Culture in New York," *The New York Indian Complex and How to Solve It*; and Parker and Skinner, *Outline of the Algonkian Occupation in New York*.

108. "Anthropological Notes" (1919), 345–46; "Anthropological Notes" (1920), 198.

109. Burmaster, "The Chert Pits at Coxsackie, N.Y."

110. "Anthropological Notes" (1922), 394.

111. Arthur C. Parker to Alanson Skinner, September 4, 1924, Alanson Skinner Collection, MS 201.4.5, SMAI.

112. Goldenweiser, "Review"; Hewitt, "Review"; Parker, "The Constitution of the Five Nations"; see also Porter, *To Be Indian*, 84–90.

113. Elmer E. Brown to Frank P. Graves, June 27, 1922, A.P23, box 1, folder 4, RRL.

114. Ritchie, "Fifty Years of Archaeology," 412.

115. Parker, *The Archaeological History of New York*, 13.

116. Ibid., 14, 18–29, 39–46; see also Griffin, "The Pursuit of Archeology in the United States," 383.

117. Dixon, "Some Aspects of North American Archeology," 563, 565; see also Johnson, "A Quarter Century of Growth in American Archaeology," 2.

118. Rush Rhees to Arthur C. Parker, April 25, 1922, A.P23, box 1, folder 4, RRL.

119. Arthur C. Parker to Peter Sundown, March 7, 1906, 15513, State Archaeologist Correspondence, box 1, folder 21, NYSL.

120. Arthur C. Parker to Enoch Schenendoah, September 11, 1907, 15513, State Archaeologist Correspondence, box 1, folder 21, NYSL.

121. Arthur C. Parker to Howard Rogers, April 2, 1906, 15513, State Archaeologist Correspondence, box 1, folder 20, NYSL.

122. Letters from M. Raymond Harrington to Arthur C. Parker, 1905, 15513, State Archaeologist Correspondence, box 1, folder 11, NYSL.

123. Arthur C. Parker to J. L. Appleton, April 26, 1907, 15513, State Archaeologist Correspondence, box 1, folder 1, NYSL.

124. Arthur C. Parker to Frederic W. Putnam, June 20, 1906, HUG 1717.2.1, box 17, HUA.

125. Arthur C. Parker to *Leslie's Weekly*, April 26, 1909, 15513, State Archaeologist Correspondence, box 1, folder 15, NYSL.

126. Quoted in "Where Hiawatha's Laws Still Govern," *Albany Argus*, May 29, 1910, SC17396, box 44, vol. 2, NYSL.

127. Article in scrapbook, "The Indian Nations of New York State," April 26, 1908, SC17396, box 44, vol. 2, NYSL.

128. The quotes are from the following materials in SC17396, box 44, vol. 2, NYSL: "Lecture," *Albany Times Union*, February 1, 1910; article in scrapbook, "The Red Man," n.d.; "Up-State Indians," *Brooklyn Eagle*, November 6, 1910; "Indian to Talk to His People," *Rochester Herald*, January 14, 1910; article in scrapbook, "Work of Ga-Wa-So-Wa-Neh," possibly *Brooklyn Eagle*, n.d.; "Seneca Discusses Indian Lodges," *Albany Knickerbocker Press*, April 12, 1911; and "Great Council of Modern Redskins," *New York Times*, September 12, 1912.

129. Cornell, *The Return of the Native*, 51–67; Prucha, "American Indian Policy in the Twentieth Century," 12.

130. Adams, *Education for Extinction*; Archuleta, Child, and Lomawaima, *Away from Home*.

131. "Parker's Digging," *Albany Argus*, August 17, 1915, A.P23, box 5, folder 10, RRL.

Chapter 7. We Can't Get Away from History

1. Arthur C. Parker to William Sampson, January 20, 1911, 15513, State Archaeologist Correspondence, box 2, folder 3, NYSL.

2. Berg, "Arthur C. Parker and the Society of the American Indian," 239.

3. Bess, "'Kill the Indian and Save the Man!'" 20.

4. Article in scrapbook, "The Indian Nations of New York State," April 26, 1908, SC17396, box 44, vol. 2, NYSL.

5. Parker quoted in Hertzberg, "Nationality, Anthropology, and Pan-Indianism," 59.

6. Parker quoted in Hertzberg, *The Search for an American Indian Identity*, 63.

7. Parker, "Introduction."

8. Barsh, "American Indians in the Great War"; Britten, *American Indians in World War I*, 60; Hanson, "Ethnicity and the Looking Glass," 195–200; Hoxie, *Parading Through History*, 358; Tate, "From Scout to Doughboy," 427–28.

9. Hoxie, *Parading Through History*, 358.

10. Berg, "Arthur C. Parker and the Society of the American Indian"; Hertzberg, *The Search for an American Indian Identity*, 48–64, and "Nationality, Anthropology, and Pan-Indianism"; Porter, *To Be Indian*, 91–142.

11. Hanson, "Ethnicity and the Looking Glass," 196.

12. Quoted in "Albanian Working for Betterment of Indians," *Albany Argus*, June 14, 1911, SC17396, box 44, vol. 2, NYSL; see also Hoxie, *Talking Back to Civilization*, 120–21.

13. Hanson, "Ethnicity and the Looking Glass," 197.

14. Quoted in "Mr. Parker Is Correct," *Albany Argus*, November 12, 1912, SC17396, box 44, vol. 2, NYSL.
15. Porter, *To Be Indian*, 105–6.
16. Skinner, "Review" (1915).
17. Obituary for Frederick Ely Parker (Ha-gonh-sa-do-neh), after March 1929, A.P23, box 5, folder 15, RRL.
18. Warrior, *Tribal Secrets*, 13.
19. Porter, *To Be Indian*, 29–31, 137–38, 215.
20. Hoxie, *Talking Back to Civilization*, 119.
21. Parker, "A Museum Sponsors an Indian Arts Project"; Porter, *To Be Indian*, 139, 199; Warren K. Moorehead to Frederick Webb Hodge, November 23, 1923, MS.7.MAI.I.490, SMAI; "Learning from Indian Policy," *New York Times*, January 10, 1924; "Indian Museum to Open," *New York Times*, June 23, 1935.
22. Parker, *The Archaeological History of New York*, 9.
23. Parker, "The Value of Archaeology to the State," 43.
24. Parker, "Why Archaeology?"
25. Parker, *The Archaeological History of New York*, 7.
26. Quotes in the next few paragraphs are from the pamphlet *Method in Archaeology*, printed by Clarkson W. James by order of the Legislative Assembly of Toronto, 1923, A.P23, box 9, folder 12, RRL, emphases in the original.
27. Parker, "Looking Ahead in Archaeology," 106, excerpted from Parker's longer paper "Anthropology Looks Ahead," which he presented before the National Academy of Science, October 29, 1937, and the Rochester Philosophical Society, March 16, 1942, Call No. 301 qP238 96-19143, NYSL; see also article in scrapbook, "Dr. Parker Calls Science to Stand Guard to Preserve Civilization," October 27, 1937, A.P23, box 5, folder 10, RRL.
28. Parker, *The Great Algonkin Flint Mines*, 105.
29. Quotes in this paragraph are from "Collectors of Aboriginal Traces Gather," *Watertown Standard*, March 5, 1926, A.P23, box 5, folder 10, RRL.
30. Parker, "Archaeological Field Work in North America during 1928," 353.
31. Alanson Skinner, "The Iroquois Indians of New York," *Adventure*, May 20, 1924, MS.201.5.32, SMAI.
32. Arthur C. Parker to Alanson Skinner, November 1924, Alanson Skinner Collection, MS 201.4.5, SMAI; John M. Clarke to Arthur C. Parker, December 24, 1924, and Frank Pierrepont Graves to Arthur C. Parker, December 6, 1924, both in A.P23, box 1, folder 4, RRL.
33. "Scientific Notes and News" (1925), 15; see also Goddard, "Anthropological Notes," 356.
34. Municipal Museum Commission President to the Municipal Civil Service Commission, April 30, 1925, A.P23, box 5, folder 1, RRL.
35. Arthur C. Parker to Alanson Skinner, March 5, 1925, Alanson Skinner Collection, MS 201.4.5, SMAI.

36. Zeller, "Arthur C. Parker," 48.
37. Boas, "Some Principles of Museum Administration," 921.
38. Zeller, "Arthur C. Parker," 48–52.
39. "The Dedication of the Bausch Hall of Science and History"; Porter, *To Be Indian*, 213.
40. Porter, *To Be Indian*, 184.
41. Coleman, "The American Association of Museums."
42. Fay-Cooper Cole to Arthur C. Parker, January 9, 1937, A.P23, box 1, folder 8, RRL.
43. Tivy, "The Local History Museum in Ontario," 179.
44. Zeller, "Arthur C. Parker," 59, 60.
45. "Scientific Notes and News" (1940), 592; Dixon Ryan Fox to Arthur C. Parker, March 7, 1940, A.P23, box 1, folder 8, RRL.
46. "Anthropological Notes" (1926), 583.
47. Kidder, "Archaeological Work by State Agencies in 1925," 689–90.
48. Parker, "Reports" (1928).
49. Parker, "Archaeological Field Work in North America during 1928," 352.
50. "Anthropological Notes and News" (1931), 146; Parker, "Archaeological Field Work in North America during 1929," and "Reports" (1931).
51. Guthe, "Report," 598; Parker, "Archaeological Field Work in North America during 1932."
52. Parker, "Archaeological Field Work in North America during 1934. Part 2," 125.
53. "Notes and News" (1935), 160.
54. "Notes and News" (1938), 280.
55. "Notes and News" (1937), 226.
56. "Scientific Notes and News" (1935), 250.
57. Arthur C. Parker's résumé, ca. 1945, A.P23, box 5, folder 4, RRL; "Dr. Parker Heads Archaeologists," *New York Times*, March 25, 1932.
58. Arthur C. Parker to Howard Rogers, December 26, 1905, 15513, State Archaeologist Correspondence, box 1, folder 20, NYSL.
59. McGimsey, *Public Archaeology*; N. Merryman, *Public Archaeology*; Potter, *Public Archaeology in Annapolis*; Shackel and Chambers, *Places in Mind*.
60. Colwell-Chanthaphonh, "The Quest for Coronado."
61. Porter, *To Be Indian*, 117; and Parker, *The Great Algonkin Flint Mines*, 110.
62. "Seneca Tradition Reaches Out to Give Little Girl Clan Name," *D & C*, July 2, 1931, A.P23, box 5, folder 10, RRL.
63. Except where otherwise cited, this biographical section on Harrington is based on Marie Harrington, *On the Trail of Forgotten People*; "Mark Harrington (1882–1971): Raymond of the Caves," at http://www.1st100.com/part1/harrington.html, consulted June 2007; "M. R. Harrington (1882–1971)," at http://encyclopediaofarkansas.net/encyclopedia/entry-detail.aspx?entryID=576,

consulted May 2007; and "Mark Raymond Harrington 1882–1971," http://www.mnsu.edu/emuseum/information/biography/fghij/ harrington_mark.html, consulted May 2007.

64. Correspondence between Arthur C. Parker and M. Raymond Harrington, 1920–24, 15513, State Archaeologist Correspondence, box 3, folder 12, NYSL.

65. M. Harrington, *On the Trail of Forgotten People*, 173–74.

66. "New Research Chief Named," *Los Angeles Times*, October 2, 1928.

67. Fredrick Parker to Arthur C. Parker, January 30, 1929, A.P23, box 5, folder 15, RRL.

68. "Museum Head Weds Editor in Riverside," *Los Angeles Times*, April 24, 1949.

69. For Beulah's biography, see the following sources: "Beulah Dark Cloud," Internet Movie Database, at http://www.imdb.com/name/nm0201271/, consulted June 2007; Beulah's obituary, "Services Held Here for Former Indian Actress," *Mercury-Register*, January 4, 1946; and Cody and Perry, *Iron Eyes*, 227.

70. Thurston, "A Night in a Maidu Shaman's House."

71. Thurston, "A Rare Treat at a Maidu Medicine-Man's Feast."

72. Cody, "Some Yurok Customs and Beliefs."

73. "Report, Annual Meeting of the Society for American Archaeology," 310.

74. Except where otherwise cited, the re-creation of this meeting is derived from the article "Society for American Archaeology Organization Meeting."

75. Griffin and Jones, "Carl Eugen Guthe."

76. McKern, "Editorial," 449.

77. Byers, "Warren King Moorehead."

78. Warren K. Moorhead to Frederick Webb Hodge, November 23, 1923, MS.7.MAI.I.490, SMAI.

79. Meltzer, "North American Archaeology and Archaeologists," 258.

80. For the quote, see note 74. On Spier, see Basehart and Hill, "Leslie Spier."

81. "Notes and News" (1935), 154.

82. Guthe, "Reflections on the Founding of the Society for American Archaeology," 438.

83. See McLaughlin, "The American Archaeological Record," 354.

84. Griffin, "The Formation of the Society for American Archaeology," 265.

85. Parker, "Archaeology Advances," 27.

86. For example, "For Archaeology a New Society," *Christian Science Monitor*, February 9, 1935.

87. Griffin, "The Formation of the Society for American Archaeology," 267.

88. T. H. Morgan to Arthur C. Parker, June 20, 1929, and Marion Hale Britton to Arthur C. Parker, August 4, 1934, A.P23, box 1, folder 5, RRL; Warren K. Moorhead to Frederick Webb Hodge, November 26, 1923, MS.7.MAI.I.490, SMAI.

89. "Report, Annual Meeting of the Society for American Archaeology," 311.

90. Parker, "Growth in 1935," 6.

91. "Notes and News" (1935), 154.

92. Nomination of Arthur C. Parker for Fellow in the Society for American Archaeology, November 15, 1935, Society for American Archaeology, Sec. Tres. Files, Subject Files, box 1, NAA.

93. "Report, Annual Meeting of the Society for American Archaeology," 315.

94. Patterson, "The Last Sixty Years," 13.

95. Guthe, "Report of the Secretary," 98; Patterson, "The Last Sixty Years," 14; Rogge, "A Look at Academic Anthropology," 833.

96. See McKern, "Editorial," 451; "Society for American Archaeology: Revised Constitution," 206.

97. McKern, "Editorial," 452–53.

98. Sabloff, "American Antiquity's First Fifty Years," 231–32.

99. Parker, "Editorials," 2–3.

100. "Society for American Archaeology Annual Meeting. 1939," 40; "Notes and News" (1945), 319; Carl E. Guthe to Arthur C. Parker, April 5, 1939, and Arthur C. Parker to Carl E. Guthe, April 18, 1939, Society for American Archaeology, Sec. Tres. Files, corr., box 8 (L-R), NAA.

101. Arthur C. Parker's résumé, ca. 1945, A.P23, box 5, folder 4, RRL.

102. Dust jacket for *Rumbling Wings and Other Indian Tales*, 1928, SC 13604, box 1, folder 12, NYSL; *U.S. Catalogue of Copyright Entries (Renewals)*, at http://www.ibiblio.org/ccer/1926a8.htm, consulted June 2007.

103. Hayes, "Published Writings of Arthur Caswell Parker."

104. Arthur C. Parker, *Indian Episodes of New York: A Drama-Story of the Empire State*, 1935, published by Rochester Museum of Arts and Sciences, SC 13604, box 1, folder 13, NYSL.

105. Article in scrapbook, "The Indian Nations of New York State," April 26, 1908, SC17396, box 44, vol. 2, NYSL.

106. Parker, *The Indian How Book*, 117–18.

107. "An International Reputation," *Rochester Times-Union*, February 20, 1935, A.P23, box 5, folder 10, RRL; see also "A. C. Parker Dies; Museum Expert," *New York Times*, January 3, 1955.

108. Article clipping, "Merited Honor," September 26, 1936, A.P23, box 5, folder 10, RRL; "New York Indian Gets Medal," *New York Times*, September 27, 1936.

109. See the following in A.P23, box 5, folders 10 and 4, and box 4, folder 6, RRL: "It's His Work—Day by Day," *Rochester Journal*, March 24, 1936; Arthur C. Parker's résumé, ca. 1945; New York State Historical Association end-of-year report by Arthur C. Parker, December 1945.

110. Herbert Gambrell to Arthur C. Parker, January 1, 1945, A.P23, box 1, folder 8, RRL.

111. "Dr. Parker to Leave Rochester Museum," *New York Sun*, December 7, 1945, A.P23, box 5, folder 1, RRL.

112. See letters in A.P23, box 1, folder 8, RRL.

113. Award pamphlet for Arthur C. Parker, Sons of the American Revolution, October 27, 1947, A.P23, box 5, folder 3, RRL; Charles E. Congdon letter, unknown addressee, 1946, A.P23, box 1, folder 9, RRL; clippings, "Dr. A. C. Parker, Expert on Indians," *New York World-Telegram*, n.d., and "Dr. A. C. Parker's Rites Wednesday," n.d., Joseph Keppler Jr. Iroquois Papers, no. 9184, folder P.2, CUL.

114. Marge Bruchac, "The First Female Native American Archaeologist," April 13, 2005, http://www.umass.edu/anthro/megamemos/mm050413.html#Female, consulted June 2007.

115. Claasen, *Exploring Gender Through Archaeology*; Wright, "Gender Matters."

116. "A Nevada Cave Rolls Back History Ten Thousand Years!" *Los Angeles Times*, August 20, 1933.

117. Quotes in this paragraph are from Thurston, "Scorpion Hill," unless otherwise cited.

118. Cody and Thompson, *Iron Eyes Cody*, 19.

119. Ibid.

120. M. Raymond Harrington to Frederick Webb Hodge, April 18, 1934, MS.7.SWM.I.267, SMAI.

121. M. Raymond Harrington to Frederick Webb Hodge, August 12 and 27, 1936, MS.7.SWM.I.267, SMAI.

122. See Cody and Perry, *Iron Eyes*, 103–10.

123. See the following articles Bertha published as Bertha Parker Cody: "California Indian Baby Cradles"; "Gold Ornaments of Ecuador"; "Kachina Dolls," "A Maidu Myth of the Creation of Woman"; "A Maidu Myth of the First Death"; "A Note on Basket Care"; "Pomo Bear Impersonations"; "Simply Strung on a Single Strand"; "Some Yurok Customs and Beliefs"; "Some Yurok Customs and Beliefs. I."; "A Tale of Witchcraft"; "Yorok Fish-Dam Dance"; and "Yurok Tales." She had published several others earlier as Bertha Parker Thurston: "A Night in a Maidu Shaman's House"; "How He Became a Medicine Man"; and "A Rare Treat at a Maidu Medicine-Man's Feast."

124. Parker, "The History Museum"; Thurston, "How He Became a Medicine Man."

125. "Notes and News" (1948), 268.

126. "Iron Eyes Cody," Internet Movie Database, at http://www.imdb.com/name/nm0002014, consulted June 2007.

127. "Native Son," *Times-Picayune*, May 26, 1996.

128. "Iron Eyes Cody, 94, an Actor and Tearful Anti-littering Icon," *New York Times*, January 5, 1999; Cody and Cody, *Indian Legends*; Cody and Ye-Was, *Sign Talk in Pictures*; Konkle, *Writing Indian Nations*, 285.

129. "Iron Eyes Rides Again," *The Guardian*, February 22, 2000; "Indian Actor Carried Culture to Hollywood," *The Australian*, January 13, 1999; Cody and Thompson, *Iron Eyes Cody*, 68.

130. "Deaths," 5.

131. Cody and Thompson, *Iron Eyes Cody*, 20; "The Haudenosaunee Project," RootsWeb, at http://worldconnect.rootsweb.com/cgi-bin/igm.cgi?op=GET&db=erikj&id=I43011, consulted June 2007.

132. "Pallan Girl's Death Held an Accident," *Oroville Mercury Register*, July 25, 1942; California Death Records, at http://vitals.rootsweb.com/ca/death/search.cgi, consulted November 2007; Cody and Thompson, *Iron Eyes Cody*, 20.

133. See the following works by Parker for this period: "How Shall We Get An Indian Name?"; "Lewis Henry Morgan"; "The Museum Comes of Age"; "The Next Fifty Years"; *Red Jacket*; *Red Streak of the Iroquois*; "The Treaty of Big Tree"; "Where Questions Are Answered"; and "Who Was Hiawatha?"

134. "Notes and News" (1947), 166; and Arthur B. Carr to Arthur C. Parker, January 30, 1946, A.P23, box 1, folder 9, RRL.

Chapter 8. The Promise of Indigenous Archaeologies

1. For discussions of these events and those in the next paragraph, see Cooper, *Spirited Encounters*; Deloria, *God Is Red*, 30–35; Fine-Dare, *Grave Injustice*, 77; Grimes, "Desecration of the Dead," 305; and Watkins, *Indigenous Archaeology*, 11.

2. Riding In, "Repatriation," 110.

3. In addition to Deloria's work, see Whiteley, "The End of Anthropology," and Wylie, "The Promise and Perils of an Ethic of Stewardship," 49–52.

4. Sagard-Theódat, *Sagard's Long Journey to the Country of the Hurons*, 209.

5. Peters, "Consulting with the Bone Keepers," 42–43; Philbrick, *Abram's Eyes*, 3.

6. Carlson, "Letters from the Field," 145–48.

7. Chapin, *Land of the Cliff-Dwellers*, 117.

8. B. Cody, "A Tale of Witchcraft."

9. Quoted in Davis, *Remembering Awatovi*, 147–48; see also Elliott, *Great Excavations*, 180.

10. Hayden, "Wihom-ki."

11. This controversy is described in Marie Harrington, *On the Trail of Forgotten People*, 192–205.

12. See White Deer, "Return of the Sacred," 42.

13. See "Notes and News" (1935), 154.

14. Guthe, "Reflections on the Founding of the Society for American Archaeology," 434.

15. F. H. Ellis, "The Hopi," 217.

16. Cushing, "Outlines of Zuni Creation Myths," 337.

17. Smith and Roberts, *Zuni Law*, 73.

18. Ferguson, "The Repatriation of Ahayu:da Zuni War Gods"; Greenfield, *The Return of Cultural Treasures*, 179; Hill, "Reflections of a Native Repatriator," 86; McLaughlin, "The American Archaeological Record," 354, 372; Merrill, Ladd, and Ferguson, "The Return of the Ahayu:da."

19. Fenton, "Return of Eleven Wampum Belts," 407; Fine-Dare, *Grave Injustice*, 92.

20. These events are recounted in Fenton, "Return of Eleven Wampum Belts"; Fine-Dare, *Grave Injustice*, 91–94; Hill, "Reflections of a Native Repatriator."

21. Fenton, "Return of Eleven Wampum Belts," 407.

22. Ibid., 404–5.

23. Landsman, "Informant as Critic," 167. But see also Becker, "William N. Fenton," 46–47; Campisi, "William Nelson Fenton," 457–58; Fenton, "The New York State Wampum Collection."

24. This controversy is described in "Indians Disputing State on Wampum," *New York Times*, March 25, 1967; "Iroquois Are Seeking Return of Wampum Belts Held by State Museum," *New York Times*, April 17, 1970; and "Rockefeller Signs Bill Allowing Return of Wampum to Indians," *New York Times*, July 2, 1971.

25. Fine-Dare, *Grave Injustice*, 78.

26. Ibid.

27. Fenton, "Return of Eleven Wampum Belts," 398, 401, 408; Tooker, "A Note on the Return of Eleven Wampum Belts."

28. Robbins, "Notice of Inventory Completion for Native American Human Remains," 681.

29. Robbins, "Notice of Intent to Repatriate Cultural Items" and "Notice of Inventory Completion for Native American Human Remains."

30. McManamon, "Notice of Inventory Completion for Native American Human Remains"; and Hutt, "Notice of Intent to Repatriate Cultural Items."

31. Killion, "Opening Archaeology," 7.

32. Quotes in this and subsequent paragraphs in this section are from Hill, "Making a Final Resting Place Final," 6, 14, 16, 7, 4, unless otherwise cited.

33. Hill, "Repatriation Must Heal Old Wounds."

34. See Dongoske et al., "Archaeological Cultures and Cultural Affiliation"; Ferguson, "Anthropological Archaeology Conducted by Tribes"; Versaggi, "Tradition, Sovereignty, Recognition"; Watkins, "Becoming American or Becoming Indian?"; Welch and Ferguson, "Putting Patria Back into Repatriation."

35. Hill, "Reflections of a Native Repatriator," 81.

36. Deloria, *Custer Died for Your Sins*, 78.

37. Biolsi and Zimmerman, *Indians and Anthropologists*; Deloria, "Indians, Archaeologists, and the Future" and "Schlesier, Other Anthropologists, and Wounded Knee."

38. Fenton, *Parker on the Iroquois*; D. Thomas, "Afterword," 213.
39. Jacobs-Huey, "The Natives Are Gazing and Talking Back," 794.
40. Browman, "The Peabody Museum," 515; and Voegelin, "Review," 287.
41. Mark, "Francis La Flesche."
42. Opler, "The Use of Peyote by the Carrizo and Lipan Apache Tribes"; Culin, "Exhibit of Games in the Columbian Exposition," 216; Hrdlička, "Physical and Physiological Observations on the Navaho," 339.
43. Rudes and Crouse, *The Tuscarora Legacy of J. N. B. Hewitt*; Swanton, "John Napoleon Brinton Hewitt."
44. Preucel, Williams, and Wierzbowski, "The Social Lives of Native American Objects," 1–2, 6–7.
45. Watkins, "Writing Unwritten History."
46. For example, Loma'omvaya and Ferguson, "Hisatqatsit Aw Maamatslalwa"; Million, "Developing an Aboriginal Archaeology"; Yellowhorn, "Awakening Internalist Archaeology in the Aboriginal World."
47. Bray, "The Politics of an Indigenous Archaeology," 110–11; see also McGuire, "Why Can't We Be Friends?" 94, and Watkins, "Beyond the Margin," 282.
48. Pyburn, "Native American Religion versus Archaeological Science"; see also Srinivas, "Traditional Knowledge and Intellectual Property Rights," and Clark, "NAGPRA, the Conflict Between Science and Religion, and the Political Consequences," 86.
49. Narayan, "How Native Is a 'Native' Anthropologist?" 682, 681.
50. For example, G. White, "Emotional Remembering," 510.
51. Colwell-Chanthaphonh, Hollowell, and McGill, *Ethics in Action*, 3; cf. Pels, "Professions of Duplexity," 104.
52. Watkins, "The Politics of American Archaeology."
53. Colwell-Chanthaphonh, "Dismembering/Disremembering the Buddhas."
54. For example, McManamon, "The Many Publics for Archaeology"; Potter, *Public Archaeology in Annapolis*; Sandell, "Museums as Agents of Social Inclusion"; Shackel and Chambers, *Places in Mind*.
55. Colwell-Chanthaphonh and Ferguson, *Collaboration in Archaeological Practice*; Dowdall and Parrish, "A Meaningful Disturbance of the Earth"; Green, Green, and Góes Neves, "Indigenous Knowledge and Archaeological Science"; Kerber, *Cross-Cultural Collaboration*.
56. Wylie, "The Promise and Perils of an Ethic of Stewardship," 65–67.
57. Watkins, *Indigenous Archaeology*, 170.
58. Ibid., 178, 177.
59. Watkins, "Beyond the Margin," 279.
60. Whiteley, "The End of Anthropology," 192.
61. Two Bears, "A Navajo Student's Perception," 15.
62. Echo-Hawk and Zimmerman, "Beyond Racism," 480.

63. From an online essay by Echo-Hawk at http://www.echo-hawk.com/roger/closet_chick_chp_07.pdf, consulted July 2008.

64. Narayan, "How Native Is a 'Native' Anthropologist?" 676–77.

65. Atalay, "Guest Editor's Remarks," 271.

66. Two Bears, "Navajo Archaeologist Is Not an Oxymoron."

67. Atalay, "Guest Editor's Remarks," 273, and "Indigenous Archaeology as Decolonizing Practice," 292.

68. Nicholas, "Education and Empowerment," 85; Martinez, "Overcoming Hindrances to Our Enduring Responsibility to the Ancestors," 496.

69. Atalay, "Indigenous Archaeology as Decolonizing Practice," 292, 294.

70. Silliman, "Collaborative Indigenous Archaeology," 2.

71. From http://www.echo-hawk.com/roger/closet_chick_chp_10.pdf, consulted July 2008.

72. Shepard, *The Heart of Thoreau's Journals*, 106.

BIBLIOGRAPHY

"AAA Statement on Race." *American Anthropologist* 100 (3) (1998): 712–13.

Abler, Thomas S., and Elisabeth Tooker. "Seneca." In *Handbook of North American Indians*, vol. 15, edited by B. G. Trigger, 505–17. Washington, D.C.: Smithsonian Institution, 1978.

Adams, David Wallace. *Education for Extinction: American Indians and the Boarding School Experience, 1875–1928*. Lawrence: University Press of Kansas, 1997.

Amato, Christopher A. "Digging Sacred Ground: Burial Site Disturbances and the Loss of New York's Native American Heritage." *Columbia Journal of Environmental Law* 27 (1) (2002): 1–44.

"Anthropological Notes." *American Anthropologist* 21 (3) (1919): 343–46; 22 (2) (1920): 198–201; 24 (3) (1922): 392–96; 25 (1) (1923): 128–33; 28 (3) (1926): 579–83.

"Anthropological Notes and News." *American Anthropologist* 33 (1) (1931): 141–47.

"Anthropologic Miscellanea." *American Anthropologist* 6 (4) (1904): 574–84.

Anyon, Roger, T. J. Ferguson, and John R. Welch. "Heritage Management by American Indian Tribes in the Southwestern United States." In *Cultural Resource Management in Contemporary Society: Perspectives on Managing and Presenting the Past*, edited by F. P. McManamon and A. Hatton, 120–41. London: Routledge, 2000.

Appiah, Kwame Anthony. "Whose Culture Is It?" *New York Review of Books* 53 (2) (2006): 38–41.

Archuleta, Margaret L., Brenda J. Child, and K. Tsianina Lomawaima, eds. *Away from Home: American Indian Boarding School Experiences, 1879–2000*. Phoenix: Heard Museum, 2000.

Armstrong, William H. *Warrior in Two Camps: Ely S. Parker, Union General and Seneca Chief*. Syracuse, N.Y.: Syracuse University Press, 1978.

Arnold, Bettina. "Justifying Genocide: Archaeology and the Construction of Difference." In *Annihilating Difference: The Anthropology of Genocide*, edited by A. Hinton, 95–116. Berkeley and Los Angeles: University of California Press, 2002.

———. "The Past as Propaganda: Totalitarian Archaeology in Nazi Germany." *Antiquity* 64 (244) (1990): 464–78.

Atalay, Sonya. "Guest Editor's Remarks: Decolonizing Archaeology." *American Indian Quarterly* 30 (3–4) (2006): 269–79.
———. "Indigenous Archaeology as Decolonizing Practice." *American Indian Quarterly* 30 (3–4) (2006): 280–310.
Atkinson, John A., Iain Banks, and Jerry O'Sullivan, eds. *Nationalism and Archaeology*. Glasgow: Cruithne Press, 1996.
Bailey, John H. "An Analysis of Iroquoian Ceramic Types." *American Antiquity* 3 (4) (1938): 333–38.
Barsh, Russel Lawrence. "American Indians in the Great War." *Ethnohistory* 38 (3) (1991): 276–303.
Barth, Fredrik. *Ethnic Groups and Boundaries*. Prospect Heights, Ill.: Waveland Press, 1998.
Basehart, Harry W., and W. W. Hill. "Leslie Spier, 1893–1961." *American Anthropologist* 67 (5) (1965): 1258–77.
Bean, Susan S., and Shepard Krech III. "Review: *The Hall of the North American Indian: Change and Continuity*." *American Anthropologist* 93 (1) (1991): 264–65.
Beauchamp, William M. *Aboriginal Occupation of New York*. Bulletin of the New York State Museum no. 32, vol. 7. Albany: University of the State of New York, 1900.
Beck, Horace P. "Frank G. Speck, 1881–1950." *Journal of American Folklore* 64 (254) (1951): 415–18.
Becker, Mary Druke. "William N. Fenton (1908–2005): Relationships, Research, and Museums." *Museum Anthropology* 29 (1) (2006): 44–49.
Bender, Barbara. "Stonehenge—Contested Landscapes (Medieval to Present-Day)." In *Landscape: Politics and Perspectives*, edited by B. Bender, 245–79. Oxford, U.K.: Berg, 1993.
Berg, S. Carol. "Arthur C. Parker and the Society of the American Indian, 1911–1916." *New York History* 81 (2000): 237–46.
Bergman, Christopher A., and John F. Doershuk. "Cultural Resource Management and the Business of Archaeology." In *Ethical Issues in Archaeology*, edited by L. J. Zimmerman, K. D. Vitelli, and J. Hollowell-Zimmer, 85–98. Walnut Creek, Calif.: AltaMira Press, 2003.
Berkhofer, Robert F. *The White Man's Indian: Images of the American Indian from Columbus to the Present*. New York: Vintage Books, 1978.
Bernstein, Jay H. "First Recipients of Anthropological Doctorates in the United States, 1891–1930." *American Anthropologist* 104 (2) (2002): 551–64.
Bess, Jennifer. "'Kill the Indian and Save the Man!' Charles Eastman Surveys His Past." *Wicazo Sa Review* 15 (1) (2000): 7–28.
Bieder, Robert E. "The Grand Order of the Iroquois: Influences on Lewis Henry Morgan's Ethnology." *Ethnohistory* 27 (4) (1980): 349–61.

———. "The Representations of Indian Bodies in Nineteenth-Century American Anthropology." In *Repatriation Reader: Who Owns American Indian Remains?* edited by D. A. Mihesuah, 19–36. Lincoln: University of Nebraska Press, 2000.

———. *Science Encounters the Indian, 1820–1880: The Early Years of American Ethnology.* Norman: University of Oklahoma Press, 1986.

Biersack, Alletta, ed. *Clio in Oceania: Toward a Historical Anthropology.* Washington, D.C: Smithsonian Institution Press, 1991.

Binford, Lewis R. "Archaeology as Anthropology." *American Antiquity* 28 (2) (1962): 217–25.

Biolsi, Thomas, and Larry J. Zimmerman, eds. *Indians and Anthropologists: Vine Deloria Jr. and the Critique of Anthropology.* Tucson: University of Arizona Press, 1997.

Boas, Franz. "Some Principles of Museum Administration." *Science* 25 (650) (1907): 921–33.

Bradford, William. *A Relation or Journall of the Beginning and Proceedings of the English Plantation Setled at Plimoth in New England, by Certaine English Aduenturers Both Merchants and Others.* London: John Bellamie, 1622.

Bray, Tamara L. "The Politics of an Indigenous Archaeology." In *Indigenous People and Archaeology: Proceedings of the 32nd Annual Chacmool Conference*, edited by T. Peck, E. Siegfried, and G. A. Oetelaar, 108–13. Calgary, Canada: Archaeological Association of the University of Calgary, 2003.

Britten, Thomas A. *American Indians in World War I: At War and at Home.* Albuquerque: University of New Mexico Press, 1997.

Brodie, Neil. "Spoils of War." *Archaeology* 56 (4) (2003): 16–19.

Brodie, Neil, Morag M. Kersel, Christina Luke, and Kathryn Walker Tubb, eds. *Archaeology, Cultural Heritage, and the Antiquities Trade.* Gainesville: University Press of Florida, 2006.

Brodie, Neil, and Colin Renfrew. "Looting and the World's Archaeological Heritage: The Inadequate Response. *Annual Review of Anthropology* 34 (2005): 343–61.

Brooks, Meagan. "Reconstructing the Present with Its Past: The Doukhobor Pit House Public Archaeology Project." In *Archaeology as a Tool of Civic Engagement*, edited by B. J. Little and P. A. Shackel, 203–22. Lanham, Md.: AltaMira Press, 2007.

Brose, David S. "The Northeastern United States." In *The Development of North American Archaeology*, edited by J. E. Fitting, 84–115. Garden City, N.Y.: Anchor Books, 1973.

Browman, David L. "The Peabody Museum, Frederic W. Putnam, and the Rise of U.S. Anthropology, 1866–1903." *American Anthropologist* 104 (2) (2002): 508–19.

Brown, Michael F. *Who Owns Native Culture?* Cambridge, Mass.: Harvard University Press, 2003.
Bruning, Susan B. "Complex Legal Legacies: The Native American Graves Protection and Repatriation Act, Scientific Study, and Kennewick Man." *American Antiquity* 71 (3) (2006): 501–21.
Burmaster, Everett R. "The Chert Pits at Coxsackie, N.Y." *Science* 54 (1393) (1921): 221.
Burtan, Isabelle Catherine. "Silences at Silverheels: A Holistic Analysis of the Omission of Seneca Indian Women in One Collection, from Excavation to Museum Display." Honor's thesis, Department of Anthropology, Harvard University, 2006.
Byers, Douglas S. "Warren King Moorehead." *American Anthropologist* 41 (2) (1939): 286–94.
Campisi, Jack. "William Nelson Fenton (1908–2005)." *American Anthropologist* 108 (2) (2006): 456–58.
Carlson, Catherine C. "Letters from the Field: Reflections on the Nineteenth-Century Archaeology of Harlan I. Smith in the Southern Interior of British Columbia, Canada." In *Indigenous Archaeologies: Decolonizing Theory and Practice*, edited by C. Smith and H. M. Wobst, 134–69. London: Routledge, 2005.
Carman, John. *Against Cultural Property: Archaeology, Heritage, and Ownership.* London: Duckworth, 2005.
Carpenter, Edmund. "Iroquoian Figurines." *American Antiquity* 8 (1) (1942): 105–13.
Cartmill, Matt. "The Status of the Race Concept in Physical Anthropology." *American Anthropologist* 100 (3) (1998): 651–60.
Casas, Bartolomé de las. *A Short Account of the Destruction of the Indies.* New York: Penguin, 1992; originally published in 1542.
Casler, Benjamin G. "Report of Agent in New York." In *Annual Report of the Commissioner of Indian Affairs to the Secretary of the Interior for the Year 1882*, 132–34. Washington, D.C.: U.S. Government Printing Office, 1882.
Chapin, Frederick H. *Land of the Cliff-Dwellers.* Tucson: University of Arizona Press, 1988; originally published in 1892.
Chapman, John. "Destruction of a Common Heritage: The Archaeology of War in Croatia, Bosnia, and Hercegovina." *Antiquity* 68 (1994): 120–26.
Chatters, James C. *Ancient Encounters: Kennewick Man and the First Americans.* New York: Simon and Schuster, 2001.
Cheney, T. Apoleon. *Contributions to the Thirteenth Annual Report of the Regents of the University of the State Cabinet of Natural History of the State of New York.* Albany: University of the State of New York, 1860.
Chippindale, Christopher. "Stoned Henge: Events and Issues at the Summer Solstice, 1985." *World Archaeology* 18 (1) (1986): 38–58.

Claasen, Cheryl, ed. *Exploring Gender Through Archaeology: Selected Papers from the 1991 Boone Conference*. Monographs in World Archaeology, vol. 11. Madison, Wisc.: Prehistory Press, 1992.
Clark, G. A. "NAGPRA, the Conflict Between Science and Religion, and the Political Consequences." In *Working Together: Native Americans and Archaeologists*, edited by K. E. Dongoske, M. Aldenderfer, and K. Doehner, 85–90. Washington, D.C.: Society for American Archaeology, 2000.
Clifford, James. "On Ethnographic Authority." *Representations* 1 (2) (1983): 118–46.
Clifford, James, and George E. Marcus, eds. *Writing Culture: The Poetics and Politics of Ethnography*. Berkeley and Los Angeles: University of California Press, 1986.
Cody, Bertha Parker. "California Indian Baby Cradles." *The Masterkey* 14 (3) (1940): 87–96.
———. "Gold Ornaments of Ecuador." *The Masterkey* 15 (3) (1941): 87–95.
———. "Kachina Dolls." *The Masterkey* 13 (1) (1939): 25–30.
———. "A Maidu Myth of the Creation of Woman." *The Masterkey* 13 (2) (1939): 83.
———. "A Maidu Myth of the First Death." *The Masterkey* 13 (4) (1939): 145.
———. "A Note on Basket Care." *The Masterkey* 15 (1) (1941): 23–24.
———. "Pomo Bear Impersonations." *The Masterkey* 14 (4) (1940): 132–37.
———. "Simply Strung on a Single Strand." *The Masterkey* 16 (5) (1942): 175–76.
———. "Some Yurok Customs and Beliefs." *The Masterkey* 17 (3) (1943): 81–87.
———. "Some Yurok Customs and Beliefs. I." *The Masterkey* 16 (5) (1942): 157–62.
———. "A Tale of Witchcraft." *The Masterkey* 13 (5) (1939): 188–89.
———. "Yorok Fish-Dam Dance." *The Masterkey* 16 (3) (1942): 81–86.
———. "Yurok Tales." *The Masterkey* 15 (6) (1941): 228–31.
Cody, Iron Eyes, and Birdie Parker Cody. *Indian Legends*. Amsterdam, N.Y.: Noteworthy, 1980.
Cody, Iron Eyes, and Collin Perry. *Iron Eyes: My Life as a Hollywood Indian*. New York: Everest House, 1982.
Cody, Iron Eyes, and Marietta Thompson. *Iron Eyes Cody, the Proud American*. Madison, N.C.: Empire, 1988.
Cody, Iron Eyes, and Ye-Was. *Sign Talk in Pictures*. La Brea, Calif.: Boelter Classic, 1952.
Coleman, Laurence Vail. "The American Association of Museums." *Science* 66 (1698) (1927): 68.
Collier, Donald, and Harry Tschopik Jr. "The Role of Museums in American Anthropology." *American Anthropologist* 56 (5) (1954): 768–79.

Colwell-Chanthaphonh, Chip. "Dismembering/Disremembering the Buddhas: Renderings on the Internet during the Afghan Purge of the Past." *Journal of Social Archaeology* 3 (1) (2003): 75–98.

———. "The Incorporation of the Native American Past: Cultural Extermination, Archaeological Protection, and the Antiquities Act of 1906." *International Journal of Cultural Property* 12 (3) (2005): 375–91.

———. "The Quest for Coronado." *Archaeology Southwest* 19 (1) (2005): 1.

Colwell-Chanthaphonh, Chip, and T. J. Ferguson, eds. *Collaboration in Archaeological Practice: Engaging Descendant Communities*. Lanham, Md.: AltaMira Press, 2008.

Colwell-Chanthaphonh, Chip, Julie Hollowell, and Dru McGill. *Ethics in Action: Case Studies in Archaeological Dilemmas*. Washington, D.C.: Society for American Archaeology Press, 2008.

Coningham, Robin, and Nick Lewer. "Paradise Lost: The Bombing of the Temple of the Tooth—A UNESCO World Heritage Site in Sri Lanka." *Antiquity* 73 (1999): 857–66.

Conkey, Margaret W. "Dwelling at the Margins, Action at the Intersection? Feminist and Indigenous Archaeologies, 2005." *Archaeologies* 1 (1) (2005): 9–59.

Cooper, Karen Coody. *Spirited Encounters: American Indians Protest Museum Policies and Practices*. Lanham, Md.: AltaMira Press, 2008.

Cornell, Stephen. *The Return of the Native: American Indian Political Resurgence*. New York: Oxford University Press, 1988.

Crawford, Suzanne J. "(Re)Constructing Bodies: Semiotic Sovereignty and the Debate over Kennewick Man." In *Repatriation Reader: Who Owns American Indian Remains?* edited by D. A. Mihesuah, 211–38. Lincoln: University of Nebraska Press, 2000.

Culin, Stewart. "Exhibit of Games in the Columbian Exposition." *Journal of American Folk-Lore* 6 (22) (1893): 205–27.

Cunningham, Richard B. *Archaeology, Relics, and the Law*. Durham, N.C.: Carolina Academic Press, 1999.

Cuno, James. *Who Owns Antiquity? Museums and the Battle over Our Ancient Heritage*. Princeton, N.J.: Princeton University Press, 2008.

Cushing, Frank Hamilton. "Outlines of Zuni Creation Myths." In *Thirteenth Annual Report of the Bureau of Ethnology for the Years 1891–1892*, 321–447. Washington, D.C.: U.S. Government Printing Office, 1896.

Davis, Hester A. *Remembering Awatovi: The Story of an Archaeological Expedition in Northern Arizona, 1935–1939*. Cambridge, Mass.: Peabody Museum Press, 2008.

"Deaths." *Anthropology Newsletter* 20 (6) (1979): 5.

"The Dedication of the Bausch Hall of Science and History." *Science* 95 (2477) (1942): 619.

Deloria, Vine, Jr. *American Indian Policy in the Twentieth Century.* Norman: University of Oklahoma Press, 1985.
———. *Custer Died for Your Sins: An Indian Manifesto.* New York: Macmillan, 1988; originally published in 1969.
———. *God Is Red.* New York: Dell, 1973.
———. "Indians, Archaeologists, and the Future." *American Antiquity* 57 (4) (1992): 595–98.
———. "Schlesier, Other Anthropologists, and Wounded Knee." *American Anthropologist* 82 (3) (1980): 560–61.
Derry, Linda, and Maureen Malloy, eds. *Archaeologists and Local Communities: Partners in Exploring the Past.* Washington, D.C.: Society for American Archaeology, 2003.
Dixon, Roland B. "Some Aspects of North American Archeology." *American Anthropologist* 15 (4) (1913): 549–77.
Dongoske, Kurt E., Mark Aldenderfer, and Karen Doehner, eds. *Working Together: Native Americans and Archaeologists.* Washington, D.C.: Society for American Archaeology, 2000.
Dongoske, Kurt E., Michael Yeatts, Roger Anyon, and T. J. Ferguson. "Archaeological Cultures and Cultural Affiliation: Hopi and Zuni Perspectives in the American Southwest." *American Antiquity* 62 (4) (1997): 600–608.
Dowdall, Katherine M., and Otis O. Parrish. "A Meaningful Disturbance of the Earth." *Journal of Social Archaeology* 3 (1) (2003): 99–133.
Downey, Roger. *The Riddle of the Bones: Politics, Science, Race, and the Story of Kennewick Man.* New York: Springer, 2000.
Earle, Timothy K., and Robert W. Preucel. "Processual Archaeology and the Radical Critique." *Current Anthropology* 28 (4) (1987): 501–38.
Echo-Hawk, Roger C., and Larry J. Zimmerman. "Beyond Racism: Some Opinions about Racialism and American Archaeology." *American Indian Quarterly* 30 (3–4) (2006): 461–85.
Ede, James. "Ethics, the Antiquities Trade, and Archaeology." *International Journal of Cultural Property* 7 (1) (1998): 128–31.
Eggan, Fred. "Lewis H. Morgan and the Future of the American Indian." *Proceedings of the American Philosophical Society* 109 (5) (1965): 272–76.
Elliott, Melinda. *Great Excavations: Tales of Early Southwestern Archaeology, 1888–1939.* Santa Fe: School of American Research Press, 1995.
Ellis, Florence Hawley. "The Hopi: Their History and Use of Lands." In *Hopi Indians,* 25–278. New York: Garland, 1974.
Ellis, Franklin. *History of Cattaraugus County, New York.* Philadelphia: L. H. Everts, 1879.
Engelbrecht, William. *Iroquoia: The Development of a Native World.* Syracuse, N.Y.: Syracuse University Press, 2005.

Fenton, William N. "Editor's Introduction." In *Parker on the Iroquois*, edited by W. N. Fenton, 1–47. Syracuse, N.Y.: Syracuse University Press, 1968.

———. "Introduction." In *Seneca Myths and Folk Tales*, edited by A. C. Parker, xi–xviii. Lincoln: University of Nebraska Press, 1989; originally published in 1923.

———. "Iroquois Studies at the Mid-century." *Proceedings of the American Philosophical Society* 95 (3) (1951): 296–310.

———. "The New York State Wampum Collection: The Case for the Integrity of Cultural Treasures." *Proceedings of the American Philosophical Society* 115 (6) (1971): 437–61.

———, ed. *Parker on the Iroquois*. Syracuse, N.Y.: Syracuse University Press, 1968.

———. "The Present Status of Anthropology in Northeastern North America; a Review Article." *American Anthropologist* 50 (3) (1948): 494–515.

———. "Return of Eleven Wampum Belts to the Six Nations Iroquois Confederacy on Grand River, Canada." *Ethnohistory* 36 (4) (1989): 392–410.

———. "Toward the Gradual Civilization of the Indian Natives: The Missionary and Linguistic Work of Asher Wright (1803–1875) among the Senecas of Western New York." *Proceedings of the American Philosophical Society* 100 (6) (1956): 567–81.

Ferguson, T. J. "Anthropological Archaeology Conducted by Tribes: Traditional Cultural Properties and Cultural Affiliation." In *Archaeology Is Anthropology*, edited by S. D. Gillespie and D. L. Nichols, 137–44. Washington, D.C.: American Anthropological Association, 2003.

———. "Archaeological Values in a Tribal Cultural Resource Management Program at the Pueblo of Zuni." In *Ethics and Values in Archaeology*, edited by E. L. Green, 224–35. New York: Free Press, 1984.

———. "NHPA: Changing the Role of Native Americans in the Archaeological Study of the Past." In *Working Together: Native Americans and Archaeologists*, edited by K. E. Dongoske, M. Aldenderfer, and K. Doehner, 25–36. Washington, D.C.: Society for American Archaeology, 2000.

———. "The Repatriation of Ahayu:da Zuni War Gods: An Interview with the Zuni Tribal Council on April 25, 1990." *Museum Anthropology* 14 (2) (1990): 7–14.

Ferguson, T. J., and Chip Colwell-Chanthaphonh. *History Is in the Land: Multivocal Tribal Traditions in Arizona's San Pedro Valley*. Tucson: University of Arizona Press, 2006.

Ferguson, T. J., Kurt E. Dongoske, Leigh Jenkins, Michael Yeatts, and Eric Polingyouma. "Working Together: The Roles of Archeology and Ethnohistory in Hopi Cultural Preservation." *CRM* 16 (SI) (1993): 27–37.

Fine-Dare, Kathleen S. *Grave Injustice: The American Indian Repatriation Movement and NAGPRA*. Lincoln: University of Nebraska Press, 2002.

Fixico, Donald L. "Ethics and Responsibilities in Writing American Indian History." In *Natives and Academics: Researching and Writing about American Indians*, edited by D. A. Mihesuah, 84–99. Lincoln: University of Nebraska Press, 1998.

Gadsby, David A., and Robert C. Chidester. "Heritage in Hampden: A Participatory Research Design for Public Archaeology in a Working-Class Neighborhood, Baltimore, Maryland." In *Archaeology as a Tool of Civic Engagement*, edited by B. J. Little and P. A. Shackel, 223–42. Lanham, Md.: AltaMira Press, 2007.

Garen, Micah. "The War within the War." In *Archaeological Ethics*, edited by K. D. Vitelli and C. Colwell-Chanthaphonh, 91–95. Walnut Creek, Calif.: AltaMira Press, 2006.

Geertz, Clifford. *The Interpretation of Cultures*. New York: Basic, 1973.

———. *Works and Lives: The Anthropologist as Author*. Stanford, Calif.: Stanford University Press, 1988.

Goddard, P. E. "Anthropological Notes." *American Anthropologist* 27 (2) (1925): 352–56.

Goldenweiser, A. A. "Review: *The Constitution of the Five Nations*." *American Anthropologist* 18 (3) (1916): 431–36.

Goldstein, Lynne, and Keith Kintigh. "Ethics and the Reburial Controversy." *American Antiquity* 55 (3) (1990): 585–91.

Green, Ernestene L., ed. *Ethics and Values in Archaeology*. New York: Free Press, 1984.

Green, Lesley Fordred, David R. Green, and Eduardo Góes Neves. "Indigenous Knowledge and Archaeological Science: The Challenges of Public Archaeology in the Reserva Uaçá." *Journal of Social Archaeology* 3 (3) (2003): 366–98.

Green, William. "Cultural Resource Management and American Archaeology." *Journal of Archaeological Research* 6 (2) (1998): 121–67.

Greenfield, Jeanette. *The Return of Cultural Treasures*. Cambridge, U.K.: Cambridge University Press, 1989.

Griffin, James B. "The Formation of the Society for American Archaeology." *American Antiquity* 50 (2) (1985): 261–71.

———. "The Pursuit of Archeology in the United States." *American Anthropologist* 61 (3) (1959): 379–89.

Griffin, James B., and Volney H. Jones. "Carl Eugen Guthe, 1893–1974." *American Antiquity* 42 (1) (1976): 168–77.

Grimes, Ronald L. "Desecration of the Dead: An Inter-religious Controversy." *American Indian Quarterly* 10 (4) (1986): 305–18.

Guthe, Carl E. "Reflections on the Founding of the Society for American Archaeology." *American Antiquity* 32 (4) (1967): 433–40.

———. "Report." *American Anthropologist* 36 (4) (1934): 595–98.

———. "Report of the Secretary." *American Antiquity* 6 (1) (1940): 97–98.

Hagan, William T. "United States Indian Policies, 1860–1900." In *Handbook of North American Indians*, vol. 4, edited by W. E. Washburn, 51–65. Washington, D.C.: Smithsonian Institution, 1988.

Haller, John S., Jr. "Race and the Concept of Progress in Nineteenth Century American Ethnology." *American Anthropologist* 73 (3) (1971): 710–24.

Hamilakis, Yannis. "Stories from Exile: Fragments from the Cultural Biography of the Parthenon (or 'Elgin') Marbles." *World Archaeology* 31 (2) (1999): 303–20.

Handler, Richard. *Nationalism and the Politics of Culture in Quebec*. Madison: University of Wisconsin Press, 1988.

———. "Who Owns the Past?" In *Politics of Culture*, edited by B. Williams, 63–74. Washington, D.C.: Smithsonian Institution Press, 1991.

Hanson, Jeffery R. "Ethnicity and the Looking Glass: The Dialectics of National Indian Identity." *American Indian Quarterly* 21 (2) (1997): 195–208.

Harmon, David, Francis P. McManamon, and Dwight T. Pitcaithley, eds. *The Antiquities Act: A Century of American Archaeology, Historic Preservation, and Nature Conservation*. Tucson: University of Arizona Press, 2006.

Harrington, Marie. *On the Trail of Forgotten People: A Personal Account of the Life and Career of Mark Raymond Harrington*. Reno, Nev.: Great Basin Press, 1985.

Harrington, M. Raymond. "An Abenaki 'Witch-Story.'" *Journal of American Folk-lore* 14 (54) (1901): 160.

———. "Alanson Skinner." *American Anthropologist* 28 (1) (1926): 275–80.

———. "An Ancient Village Site of the Shinnecock Indians." *Anthropological Papers of the American Museum of Natural History* 22 (5) (1924): 226–83.

———. "A Midcolonial Seneca Site in Erie County. In *The Archaeological History of New York*, edited by A. C. Parker, 207–37. Albany: University of the State of New York, 1922.

———. "Shinnecock Notes." *Journal of American Folk-Lore* 16 (60) (1903): 37–39.

Harrison, Faye V. "Introduction: Expanding the Discourse on 'Race.'" *American Anthropologist* 100 (3) (1998): 609–31.

———. "The Persistent Power of 'Race' in the Cultural and Political Economy of Racism." *Annual Review of Anthropology* 24 (1995): 47–74.

Haslip-Viera, Gabriel, Bernard Ortiz de Montellano, and Warren Barbour. "Robbing Native American Cultures: Van Sertima's Afrocentricity and the Olmecs." *Current Anthropology* 38 (3) (1997): 419–41.

Hauptman, Laurence M. *Conspiracy of Interests: Iroquois Dispossession and the Rise of New York State*. Syracuse, N.Y.: Syracuse University Press, 1999.

———. *The Iroquois Struggle for Survival: World War II to Red Power*. Syracuse, N.Y.: Syracuse University Press, 1986.

Hayden, Julian. "Wihom-ki." *The Kiva* 43 (1) (1977): 31–35.

Hayes, Catherine D. "Published Writings of Arthur Caswell Parker, 1900–1959." Manuscript on file, New York State Library, Albany, 1960.

Hemming, John. *The Conquest of the Incas*. New York: Harcourt, 1970.

Herscher, Ellen. "Scourge of the Forgery Culture." *Archaeology* 54 (1) (2001): 61–66.

Hertzberg, Hazel Whitman. "Nationality, Anthropology, and Pan-Indianism in the Life of Arthur C. Parker (Seneca)." *Proceedings of the American Philosophical Society* 123 (1) (1979): 47–72.

———. *The Search for an American Indian Identity: Modern Pan-Indian Movements*. Syracuse, N.Y.: Syracuse University Press, 1971.

Hewitt, J. N. B. "Review: *The Constitution of the Five Nations, Traditional History of the Confederacy of the Six Nations*, and *Civil, Religious, and Mourning Councils and Ceremonies of Adoption of the New York Indians*." *American Anthropologist* 19 (3) (1917): 429–38.

Hill, Richard, Sr. "Making a Final Resting Place Final: A History of the Repatriation Experience of the Haudenosaunee." In *Cross-Cultural Collaboration: Native Peoples and Archaeology in the Northeastern United States*, edited by J. E. Kerber, 3–17. Lincoln: University of Nebraska Press, 2006.

———. "Reflections of a Native Repatriator." In *Mending the Circle: A Native American Repatriation Guide*, edited by B. Meister, 81–96. New York: American Indian Ritual Object Repatriation Foundation, 1996.

———. "Repatriation Must Heal Old Wounds." In *Reckoning with the Dead: The Larsen Bay Repatriation and the Smithsonian Institute*, edited by T. L. Bray and T. W. Killion, 184–86. Washington, D.C.: Smithsonian Institute Press, 1994.

Hill, Richard, and Donald A. Grinde. "Problems in Prehistory and History of the Iroquois." *Ontario Archaeology* 25 (1975): 57–59.

Hodder, Ian. "Archaeological Reflexivity and the 'Local' Voice." *Anthropological Quarterly* 76 (1) (2003): 55–69.

———. "Interpretive Archaeology and Its Role." *American Antiquity* 56 (1) (1991): 7–18.

———. "Writing Archaeology: Site Reports in Context." *Antiquity* 63 (1989): 268–74.

Horsman, Reginald. "United States Indian Policies, 1776–1815." In *Handbook of North American Indians*, vol. 4, edited by W. E. Washburn, 29–39. Washington, D.C.: Smithsonian Institution, 1988.

Hoxie, Frederick E. *Parading Through History: The Making of the Crow Nation in America 1805–1935*. Cambridge, U.K.: Cambridge University Press, 1997.

———, ed. *Talking Back to Civilization: Indian Voices from the Progressive Era*. Hampshire, U.K.: Palgrave Macmillan, 2001.

Hrdlička, Aleš. "Physical and Physiological Observations on the Navaho." *American Anthropologist* 2 (2) (1900): 339–45.

Hunt, Helen. *A Century of Dishonor*. New York: Harper and Brothers, 1881.
Hutt, Sherry. "Notice of Intent to Repatriate Cultural Items: Peabody Museum of Archaeology and Ethnology, Harvard University, Cambridge, MA." *Federal Register* 72 (164) (2007): 48677–78.
Jacknis, Ira. "Exhibition Review: Heafitz Hall of the North American Indian: Change and Continuity." *Museum Anthropology* 15 (3) (1991): 29–34.
Jacobs-Huey, Lanita. "The Natives Are Gazing and Talking Back: Reviewing the Problematics of Positionality, Voice, and Accountability among 'Native' Anthropologists." *American Anthropologist* 104 (3) (2002): 791–804.
Jenkins, David. "Object Lessons and Ethnographic Displays: Museum Exhibitions and the Making of American Anthropology." *Comparative Studies in Society and History* 36 (2) (1994): 242–70.
Johansen, Bruce Elliott, and Barbara Alice Mann, eds. *Encyclopedia of the Haudenosaunee (Iroquois Confederacy)*. Westport, Conn.: Greenwood Press, 2000.
Johnson, Frederick. "A Quarter Century of Growth in American Archaeology." *American Antiquity* 27 (1) (1961): 1–6.
Jones, Delmos J. "Anthropology and the Oppressed: A Reflection on 'Native' Anthropology." *NAPA Bulletin* 16 (1) (1995): 58–70.
Joyce, Rosemary A. *The Languages of Archaeology: Dialogue, Narrative, and Writing*. Oxford, U.K.: Blackwell, 2002.
Karp, Ivan, Christine M. Kreamer, and Steven D. Lavine, eds. *Museums and Communities: The Politics of Public Culture*. Washington, D.C.: Smithsonian Institution Press, 1992.
Keita, S. O. Y., and Rick A. Kittles. "The Persistence of Racial Thinking and the Myth of Racial Divergence." *American Anthropologist* 99 (3) (1997): 534–44.
Kellett, Lucas C. "Public Archaeology in an Andean Community." *SAA Archaeological Record* 6 (2) (2006): 8–11.
Kelly, Robert L. "Kennewick Man Is Native American." *SAA Archaeological Record* 4 (5) (2004): 33–37.
Kerber, Jordan E., ed. *Cross-Cultural Collaboration: Native Peoples and Archaeology in the Northeastern United States*. Lincoln: University of Nebraska Press, 2006.
Kessell, John L. "The Ways and Words of the Other: Diego de Vargas and Cultural Brokers in Late Seventeenth-Century New Mexico." In *Between Indian and White Worlds: The Cultural Broker*, edited by M. C. Szasz, 25–43. Norman: University of Oklahoma Press, 2001.
Kickingbird, Kirke, and Karen Ducheneaux. *One Hundred Million Acres*. New York: Macmillan, 1973.
Kidder, A. V. "Archaeological Work by State Agencies in 1925." *American Anthropologist* 28 (4) (1926): 679–94.
Killion, Thomas W. "Opening Archaeology: Repatriation's Impact on Contemporary Research and Practice." In *Opening Archaeology: Repatriation's*

Impact on Contemporary Research and Practice, edited by T. W. Killion, 3–26. Santa Fe: SAR Press, 2008.

King, Thomas F. *Cultural Resource Laws and Practice*. Walnut Creek, Calif.: AltaMira Press, 2004.

———. "Professional Responsibility in Public Archaeology." *Annual Review of Anthropology* 12 (1983): 143–64.

Klesert, Anthony L. "A View from Navajoland on the Reconciliation of Anthropologists and Native Americans." *Human Organization* 51 (1) (1992): 17–22.

Klesert, Anthony L., and Shirley Powell. "A Perspective on Ethics and the Reburial Controversy." *American Antiquity* 58 (2) (1993): 348–54.

Kohl, Philip L., Mara Kozelsky, and Ben-Yehuda Nachman, eds. *Selective Remembrances: Archaeology in the Construction, Commemoration, and Consecration of National Pasts*. Chicago: University of Chicago Press, 2007.

Konkle, Maureen. *Writing Indian Nations: Native Intellectuals and the Politics of Historiography, 1827–1863*. Chapel Hill: University of North Carolina Press, 2003.

Kuwanwisiwma, Leigh. "Hopi Understanding of the Past: A Collaborative Approach." In *Public Benefits of Archaeology*, edited by B. J. Little, 46–50. Gainesville: University Press of Florida, 2002.

Landsman, Gail. "Informant as Critic: Conducting Research on a Dispute Between Iroquoianist Scholars and Traditional Iroquois." In *Indians and Anthropologists: Vine Deloria Jr. and the Critique of Anthropology*, edited by T. Biolsi and L. J. Zimmerman, 160–76. Tucson: University of Arizona Press, 1997.

Lassiter, Luke Eric. "From 'Reading over the Shoulders of Natives' to 'Reading Alongside Natives,' Literally: Toward a Collaborative and Reciprocal Ethnography." *Journal of Anthropological Research* 57 (2) (2001): 137–49.

Lawler, Andrew. "Dam Threatens Iraqi Ancient Sites." *Science* 295 (5563) (2002): 2189, 2191.

Lee, Ronald Freeman. "The Antiquities Act of 1906." *Journal of the Southwest* 42 (2) (2000): 197–270.

Leon-Portilla, Miguel, ed. *The Broken Spears: The Aztec Account of the Conquest of Mexico*. Boston: Beacon Press, 1992.

Lepore, Jill. "Historians Who Love Too Much: Reflections on Microhistory and Biography." *Journal of American History* 88 (1) (2001): 129–44.

Leupp, Francis E., ed. *Annual Report of the Commissioner of Indian Affairs to the Secretary of the Interior for the Year 1906*. Washington, D.C.: U.S. Government Printing Office, 1906.

Lippert, Dorothy. "Building a Bridge to Cross a Thousand Years." *American Indian Quarterly* 30 (3–4) (2006): 431–40.

———. "In Front of the Mirror: Native Americans and Academic Archaeology." In *Native Americans and Archaeologists: Stepping Stones to Common*

Ground, edited by N. Swidler, K. E. Dongoske, R. Anyon, and A. S. Downer, 120–27. Walnut Creek, Calif.: AltaMira Press, 1997.

———. "Not the End, Not the Middle, but the Beginning: Repatriation as a Transformative Mechanism for Archaeologists and Indigenous Peoples." In *Collaboration in Archaeological Practice: Engaging Descendant Communities*, edited by C. Colwell-Chanthaphonh and T. J. Ferguson, 119–30. Walnut Creek, Calif.: AltaMira Press, 2008.

Little, Barbara J., ed. *Public Benefits of Archaeology*. Gainesville: University Press of Florida, 2002.

Lloyd, Herbert M. "Appendix B." In *League of the Ho-de-no-sau-nee, or Iroquois*, by L. H. Morgan, 145–310. New York: Dodd, Mead, 1901.

Loma'omvaya, Micah, and T. J. Ferguson. "Hisatqatsit Aw Maamatslalwa—Comprehending Our Past Lifeways: Thoughts about a Hopi Archaeology." In *Indigenous People and Archaeology: Proceedings of the 32nd Annual Chacmool Conference*, edited by T. Peck, E. Siegfried, and G. A. Oetelaar, 43–51. Calgary, Canada: Archaeological Association of the University of Calgary, 2003.

Lowe, Denise. *An Encyclopedic Dictionary of Women in Early American Films: 1895–1930*. Binghamton, U.K.: Haworth Press, 2005.

Lowenthal, David. "Classical Antiquities as National and Global Heritage." *Antiquity* 62 (1988): 726–35.

———. *The Heritage Crusade and the Spoils of War*. Cambridge, U.K.: Cambridge University Press, 1998.

Lurie, Nancy Oestreich. "Relations Between Indians and Anthropologists." In *Handbook of North American Indians*, vol. 4, edited by W. E. Washburn, 548–56. Washington, D.C.: Smithsonian Institution, 1988.

Lyman, R. Lee, Michael J. O'Brien, and Robert C. Dunnell. *The Rise and Fall of Culture History*. New York: Springer, 2006.

Mallouf, Robert J. "An Unraveling Rope: The Looting of America's Past." *American Indian Quarterly* 20 (2) (1996): 197–208.

Mann, Barbara A., and Jerry L. Fields. "A Sign in the Sky: Dating the League of the Haudenosaunee." *American Indian Culture and Research Journal* 21 (2) (1997): 105–63.

Marcus, George E. "Ethnography in/of the World System: The Emergence of Multi-sited Ethnography." *Annual Review of Anthropology* 24 (1995): 95–117.

Marcus, George E., and Dick Cushman. "Ethnographies as Texts." *Annual Review of Anthropology* 11 (1982): 25–69.

Marcus, George E., and Michael Fischer. *Anthropology as Culture Critique: An Experimental Moment in the Human Sciences*. Chicago: University of Chicago Press, 1986.

Mark, Joan. "Francis La Flesche: The American Indian as Anthropologist." *Isis* 73 (4) (1982): 496–510.

Martin, Catherine E. "Educating to Combat Racism: The Civic Role of Anthropology." *Anthropology & Education Quarterly* 27 (2) (1996): 253–69.

Martinez, Desireé Reneé. "Overcoming Hindrances to Our Enduring Responsibility to the Ancestors: Protecting Traditional Cultural Places." *American Indian Quarterly* 30 (3–4) (2006): 486–503.

McBryde, Ian, ed. *Who Owns the Past?* Melbourne: Oxford University Press, 1985.

McDavid, Carol. "Archaeologies That Hurt; Descendants That Matter: A Pragmatic Approach to Collaboration in the Public Interpretation of African-American Archaeology." *World Archaeology* 34 (2) (2002): 303–14.

———. "Beyond Strategy and Good Intention: Archaeology, Race, and White Privilege." In *Archaeology as a Tool of Civic Engagement*, edited by B. J. Little and P. A. Shackel, 67–88. Lanham, Md.: AltaMira Press, 2007.

McGimsey, Charles R., III. *Public Archaeology*. New York: Seminar Press, 1972.

McGuire, Randall H. "Archaeology and the First Americans." *American Anthropologist* 94 (4) (1992): 816–36.

———. "Why Can't We Be Friends?" In *Indigenous People and Archaeology: Proceedings of the 32nd Annual Chacmool Conference*, edited by T. Peck, E. Siegfried, and G. A. Oetelaar, 92–101. Calgary, Canada: Archaeological Association of the University of Calgary, 2003.

McKern, W. C. "Editorial: The First Quarter Century." *American Antiquity* 25 (4) (1960): 449–53.

McLaughlin, Robert H. "The American Archaeological Record: Authority to Dig, Power to Interpret." *International Journal of Cultural Property* 7 (2) (1998): 342–75.

———. "The Antiquities Act of 1906: Politics and the Framing of an American Anthropology and Archaeology." *Oklahoma City University Law Review* 25 (1–2) (1998): 61–91.

McManamon, Francis P. "The Many Publics for Archaeology." *American Antiquity* 56 (1) (1991): 121–30.

———. "Notice of Inventory Completion for Native American Human Remains and Associated Funerary Objects from Chautauqua and Onondaga Counties, NY, in the Possession of the Springfield Science Museum, Springfield, MA." *Federal Register* 62 (46) (1997): 10878.

Meighan, Clement W. "Burying American Archaeology." *Archaeology* 47 (6) (1994): 64, 66, 68.

———. "Some Scholars' Views on Reburial." *American Antiquity* 57 (4) (1992): 704–10.

Meltzer, David J. "North American Archaeology and Archaeologists, 1879–1934." *American Antiquity* 50 (2) (1985): 249–60.

Merrill, William L., Edmund J. Ladd, and T. J. Ferguson. "The Return of the Ahayu:da: Lessons for Repatriation from Zuni Pueblo and the Smithsonian Institution." *Current Anthropology* 34 (5) (1993): 523–67.

Merryman, John H. "Cultural Property Internationalism." *International Journal of Cultural Property* 12 (1) (2005): 11–39.

———. "Thinking about the Elgin Marbles." In *Thinking about the Elgin Marbles: Critical Essays on Cultural Property, Art, and Law*, edited by J. H. Merryman, 21–63. Cambridge, Mass.: Kluwer Law International, 2000.

———. "Two Ways of Thinking about Cultural Property." *American Journal of International Law* 80 (1986): 831–53.

Merryman, Nick, ed. *Public Archaeology*. London: Routledge, 2004.

Meskell, Lynn, ed. *Archaeology under Fire: Nationalism, Politics, and Heritage in the Eastern Mediterranean and Middle East*. London: Routledge Press, 1998.

———. "Negative Heritage and Past Mastering in Archaeology." *Anthropological Quarterly* 75 (3) (2002): 557–74.

———. "Sites of Violence: Terrorism, Tourism, and Heritage in the Archaeological Present." In *Embedding Ethics: Shifting Boundaries of the Anthropological Profession*, edited by L. Meskell and P. Pels, 123–46. Oxford, U.K.: Berg, 2005.

Messenger, Phyllis M., ed. *The Ethics of Collecting Cultural Property: Whose Culture? Whose Property?* 2d. ed. Albuquerque: University of New Mexico Press, 1999.

Michaelsen, Scott. "Ely S. Parker and Amerindian Voices in Ethnography." *American Literary History* 8 (4) (1996): 615–38.

Mihesuah, Devon A., ed. *Natives and Academics: Researching and Writing about American Indians*. Lincoln: University of Nebraska Press, 1998.

Million, Tara. "Developing an Aboriginal Archaeology: Receiving Gifts from White Buffalo Calf Woman." In *Indigenous Archaeologies: Decolonizing Theory and Practice*, edited by C. Smith and H. M. Wobst, 43–55. London: Routledge, 2005.

Morenon, E. Pierre. "Nagged by NAGPA: Is There an Archaeological Ethic?" In *Ethics and the Profession of Anthropology: Dialogue for Ethically Conscious Practice*, edited by C. Fluehr-Lobban, 107–40. Walnut Creek, Calif.: AltaMira Press, 2003.

Morgan, Lewis Henry. *League of the Ho-de-no-sau-nee, or Iroquois*. 2 vols. New York: Dodd, Mead, 1901; originally published in 1851.

Moser, Stephanie, Darren Glazier, James E. Phillips, Lamya Nasser el Nemr, Mohammed Saleh Mousa, Rascha Nasr Aiesh, Susan Richardson, Andrew Conner, and Michael Seymour. "Transforming Archaeology Through Practice: Strategies for Collaborative Archaeology and the Community Archaeology Project at Quseir, Egypt." *World Archaeology* 34 (2) (2002): 220–48.

Mukhopadhyay, Carol C., and Yolanda T. Moses. "Reestablishing 'Race' in Anthropological Discourse." *American Anthropologist* 99 (3) (1997): 517–33.

Narayan, Kirin. "How Native Is a 'Native' Anthropologist?" *American Anthropologist* 95 (3) (1993): 671–86.

Nicholas, George P. "Education and Empowerment: Archaeology with, for, and by the Shuswap Nation, British Columbia." In *At a Crossroads: Archaeology and First Peoples in Canada*, edited by G. P. Nicholas and T. D. Andrews, 85–104. Burnaby, Canada: Archaeology Press, Simon Fraser University, 1997.

Nicholas, George P., and Thomas D. Andrews. "Indigenous Archaeology in the Post-modern World." In *At a Crossroads: Archaeology and First Peoples in Canada*, edited by G. P. Nicholas and T. D. Andrews, 1–18. Burnaby, Canada: Archaeology Press, Simon Fraser University, 1997.

Nicholas, George P., and Kelly P. Bannister. "Copyrighting the Past? Emerging Intellectual Property Rights Issues in Archaeology." *Current Anthropology* 45 (3) (2004): 327–50.

Nicholas, George P., John R. Welch, and Eldon Yellowhorn. "Collaborative Encounters." In *Collaboration in Archaeological Practice: Engaging Descendant Communities*, edited by C. Colwell-Chanthaphonh and T. J. Ferguson, 273–98. Walnut Creek, Calif.: AltaMira Press, 2008.

"Notes and News." *American Anthropologist* 12 (1947): 165–70.

"Notes and News." *American Antiquity* 1 (2) (1935): 154–67; 2 (3) (1937): 217–32; 3 (3) (1938): 271–84; 10 (3) (1945): 319–20; 13 (3) (1948): 267–80.

Opler, Morris Edward. "The Use of Peyote by the Carrizo and Lipan Apache Tribes." *American Anthropologist* 40 (2) (1938): 271–85.

Orser, Charles E., Jr. "The Challenge of Race to American Historical Archaeology." *American Anthropologist* 100 (3) (1998): 661–68.

Osborn, Henry Fairfield. "The State Museum and State Progress." *Science* 36 (929) (1912): 493–504.

Parezo, Nancy J., ed. *Hidden Scholars: Women Anthropologists and the Native American Southwest*. Albuquerque: University of New Mexico Press, 1993.

Parker, Arthur C. *An Analytical History of the Seneca Indians*. Rochester: Researches and Transactions of the New York State Archaeological Association, 1926.

———. "Anthropologic Miscellanea." *American Anthropologist* 13 (1) (1911): 169–71.

———. "Archaeological Collection." *Museum Service* 2 (9) (1927): 55.

———. "Archaeological Field Work in North America during 1928. New York." *American Anthropologist* 31 (2) (1928): 352–53.

———. "Archaeological Field Work in North America during 1929. New York." *American Anthropologist* 32 (2) (1930): 365–66.

———. "Archaeological Field Work in North America during 1932. New York." *American Anthropologist* 35 (3) (1933): 502.

———. "Archaeological Field Work in North America during 1934. Part 2. New York." *American Antiquity* 1 (2) (1935): 125.

———. *The Archaeological History of New York*. Albany: University of the State of New York, 1922.

Parker, Arthur C. "Archaeology Adopts a New Policy." *Museum Service* 10 (7) (1937): 160.

———. "Archaeology Advances." *Museum Service* 8 (5) (1935): 27.

———. "The Constitution of the Five Nations: A Reply." *American Anthropologist* 20 (1) (1918): 120–24.

———. *A Contact Period Seneca Site Situated at Factory Hollow, Ontario Co., N.Y.* Rochester: Researches and Transactions of the New York State Archaeological Association, 1919.

———. "Do Curators Collect?" *Museum Service* 2 (10) (1927): 67.

———. "Editorials." *American Antiquity* 1 (1) (1935): 2–3.

———. "An Erie Indian Village and Burial Site at Ripley, Chautauqua Co., N.Y." *New York State Museum Bulletin* 117 (1907): 459–554.

———. "Grave Restoration." *Museum Service* 2 (6) (1927): 35.

———. *The Great Algonkin Flint Mines.* Rochester: Researches and Transactions of the New York State Archaeological Association, 1924.

———. "Growth in 1935." *Museum Service* 9 (1) (1936): 6–7.

———. "Habitat Groups in Wax and Plaster." *Proceedings of the Association of Museums* (December 1916): 78–81, 84.

———. "The History Museum—An Opportunity." *The Masterkey* 8 (3) (1934): 69–72.

———. "How Shall We Get an Indian Name?" *Museum Service* 26 (2) (1953): 94.

———. *The Indian How Book.* New York: Doubleday, 1946; originally published in 1927.

———. "Indians versus Pot-Hunters." *American Antiquity* 3 (3) (1938): 267–68.

———. "Introduction." In *Tahan: Out of Savagery into Civilization; An Autobiography*, edited by J. K. Griffis, 7–10. New York: George H. Doran, 1915.

———. "The Lamoka Report." *Museum Service* 1 (6) (1926): 34.

———. "Lewis Henry Morgan, 1818–1881." *Museum Service* 25 (9) (1952): 101, 104.

———. *The Life of General Ely S. Parker: Last Grand Sachem of the Iroquois and General Grant's Military Secretary.* Buffalo, N.Y.: Buffalo Historical Society, 1919.

———. "Looking Ahead in Archaeology." *Museum Service* 15 (5) (1942): 105–6.

———. "Making a Museologist." *Museum Service* 12 (5) (1939): 99.

———. "The Mound Builder Culture in New York." *New York State Museum Bulletin* 219–20 (1919): 283–92.

———. "The Museum Comes of Age." *Museum Service* 23 (4) (1950): 41.

———. "A Museum Sponsors an Indian Arts Project." *Social Welfare Bulletin* 7 (1936): 12–14.

———. *The New York Indian Complex and How to Solve It.* Rochester: Researches and Transactions of the New York State Archaeological Association, 1920.

———. "The Next Fifty Years." *Museum Service* 24 (1) (1951): 3.

———. "The Origin of the Iroquois as Suggested by Their Archaeology." *American Anthropologist* 18 (4) (1916): 479–507.
———. "The Perversion of Archaeological Data." *American Antiquity* 5 (1) (1939): 57–58.
———. *Red Jacket, Last of the Seneca*. New York: McGraw-Hill, 1952.
———. *Red Streak of the Iroquois*. Chicago: Children's Press, 1950.
———. "Reports." *American Anthropologist* 30 (3) (1928): 515–16.
———. "Reports." *American Anthropologist* 33 (3) (1931): 477.
———. *Rumbling Wings and Other Indian Tales*. Garden City, N.Y.: Doubleday, 1928.
———. *Seneca Myths and Folk Tales*. Lincoln: University of Nebraska Press, 1989; originally published in 1923.
———. *Skunny Wundy and Other Indian Tales*. New York: George H. Doran, 1927.
———. "Snow-Snake as Played by the Seneca-Iroquois." *American Anthropologist* 11 (2) (1909): 250–56.
———. "The Treaty of Big Tree." *Museum Service* 20 (7) (1947): 77.
———. "The Value of Archaeology to the State." *Museum Service* 4 (6) (1929): 43.
———. "We Can't Get Away from History." *Museum Service* 16 (8) (1943): 66.
———. "Where Questions Are Answered." *Museum Service* 26 (10) (1953): 163.
———. "Who Was Hiawatha?" *Museum Service* 27 (10) (1954): 158.
———. "Why Archaeology?" *Museum Service* 3 (8) (1928): 59.
Parker, Arthur C., and Alanson Buck Skinner. *Outline of the Algonkian Occupation in New York*. Rochester: Researches and Transactions of the New York State Archaeological Association, 1923.
Patterson, Thomas C. "History and the Post-processual Archaeologies." *Man* 24 (4) (1989): 555–66.
———. "The Last Sixty Years: Towards a Social History of Americanist Archaeology in the United States." *American Anthropologist* 88 (1986): 7–26.
———. *Toward a Social History of Archaeology in the United States*. Fort Worth, Tex.: Harcourt Brace College, 1995.
Peabody, Charles. "American Archaeology during the Years 1900–1905: A Summary." *American Journal of Archaeology* 9 (2) (1905): 182–96.
Peacock, W. "Report of Agent in New York." In *Annual Report of the Commissioner of Indian Affairs to the Secretary of the Interior for the Year 1886*, 207. Washington, D.C.: U.S. Government Printing Office, 1886.
Pels, Peter. "Professions of Duplexity: A Prehistory of Ethical Codes in Anthropology." *Current Anthropology* 40 (2) (1999): 101–36.
Pensley, D. S. "The Native American Graves Protection and Repatriation Act (1990): Where the Native Voice Is Missing." *Wicazo Sa Review* 20 (2) (2005): 37–64.
Peters, Ramona L. "Consulting with the Bone Keepers: NAGPRA Consultations and Archaeological Monitoring in the Wampanoag Territory."

In *Cross-Cultural Collaboration: Native Peoples and Archaeology in the Northeastern United States*, edited by J. E. Kerber, 32–43. Lincoln: University of Nebraska Press, 2006.

Philbrick, Nathaniel. *Abram's Eyes: The Native American Legacy of Nantucket Island*. Nantucket, Mass.: Mill Hill Press, 1998.

Pierpont, Claudia Roth. "The Measure of America: How a Rebel Anthropologist Waged War on Racism." *The New Yorker* (March 8, 2004): 48–63.

Porter, Joy. "Arthur Caswell Parker, 1881–1955: Indian American Museum Professional." *New York History* 81 (2000): 211–36.

———. *To Be Indian: The Life of Iroquois-Seneca Arthur Caswell Parker*. Norman: University of Oklahoma Press, 2001.

Potter, Parker B. *Public Archaeology in Annapolis: A Critical Approach to History in Maryland's "Ancient City."* Washington, D.C.: Smithsonian Institution Press, 1994.

Preucel, Robert W., Lucy F. Williams, and William Wierzbowski. "The Social Lives of Native American Objects." In *Objects of Everlasting Esteem: Native American Voices on Identity, Art, and Culture*, edited by L. F. Williams, W. Wierzbowski, and R. W. Preucel, 1–26. Philadelphia: University of Pennsylvania Museum of Archaeology and Anthropology, 2005.

Price, H., ed. *Annual Report of the Commissioner of Indian Affairs to the Secretary of the Interior for the Year 1881*. Washington, D.C.: U.S. Government Printing Office, 1881.

Prucha, Francis Paul. "American Indian Policy in the Twentieth Century." *Western Historical Quarterly* 15 (1) (1984): 4–18.

———. "United States Indian Policies, 1815–1860." In *Handbook of North American Indians*, vol. 4, edited by W. E. Washburn, 40–50. Washington, D.C.: Smithsonian Institution, 1988.

Putnam, Frederic W. *Thirty-Eighth Report on the Peabody Museum of American Archaeology and Ethnology, Harvard University, 1902–03*. Cambridge, Mass.: Harvard University, 1905.

———. *Thirty-Seventh Report on the Peabody Museum of American Archaeology and Ethnology, Harvard University, 1902–03*. Cambridge, Mass.: Harvard University, 1904.

Pyburn, K. Anne. "Native American Religion versus Archaeological Science: A Pernicious Dichotomy Revisited." *Science and Engineering Ethics* 5 (3) (1999): 355–66.

Quick, Polly, ed. *Proceedings: Conference on Reburial Issues*. Washington, D.C.: Society for American Archaeology, 1985.

Raab, L. Mark, Timothy C. Klinger, Michael B. Schiffer, and Albert C. Goodyear. "Clients, Contracts, and Profits: Conflicts in Public Archaeology." *American Anthropologist* 82 (3) (1980): 539–51.

Renfrew, Colin. *Loot, Legitimacy, and Ownership*. London: Duckworth, 2000.

"Report, Annual Meeting of the Society for American Archaeology." *American Antiquity* 1 (4) (1936): 310–16.
Richman, Jennifer R., and Marion P. Forsyth. *Legal Perspectives on Cultural Resources*. Walnut Creek, Calif.: AltaMira Press, 2004.
Riding In, James. "Repatriation: A Pawnee's Perspective." In *Repatriation Reader: Who Owns American Indian Remains?* edited by D. A. Mihesuah, 106–22. Lincoln: University of Nebraska Press, 2000.
Riley, Mary, ed. *Indigenous Intellectual Property Rights*. Walnut Creek, Calif.: AltaMira Press, 2004.
Ritchie, William A. "Arthur Caswell Parker, 1881–1955." *American Antiquity* 21 (3) (1956): 293–95.
———. "Fifty Years of Archaeology in the Northeastern United States: A Retrospect." *American Antiquity* 50 (2) (1985): 412–20.
Robbins, John. "Notice of Intent to Repatriate Cultural Items in the Possession of the Peabody Museum of Archaeology and Ethnology, Harvard University, Cambridge, MA; Correction." *Federal Register* 69 (3) (2004): 682–83.
———. "Notice of Inventory Completion for Native American Human Remains and Associated Funerary Objects in the Possession of the Peabody Museum of Archaeology and Ethnology, Harvard University, Cambridge, MA; Correction." *Federal Register* 69 (3) (2004): 681–82.
Rogge, A. E. "A Look at Academic Anthropology: Through a Graph Darkly." *American Anthropologist* 78 (4) (1976): 829–43.
Rosen, Lawrence. "The Excavation of American Indian Burial Sites: A Problem in Law and Professional Responsibility." *American Anthropologist* 82 (1) (1980): 5–27.
Rudes, Blair A., and Dorothy Crouse. *The Tuscarora Legacy of J. N. B. Hewitt: Materials for the Study of the Tuscarora Language and Culture*. Quebec: Canadian Museum of Civilization, 1989.
Sabloff, Jeremy A. "*American Antiquity*'s First Fifty Years: An Introductory Comment." *American Antiquity* 50 (2) (1985): 228–37.
Sagard-Theódat, Gabriel. *Sagard's Long Journey to the Country of the Hurons (1632)*. New York: Greenwood Press, 1968.
Salisbury, Stephen, Asa Gray, Jeffries Wyman, and George Peabody Russell. *First Annual Report of the Trustees of the Peabody Museum of American Archaeology and Ethnology*. Cambridge, Mass.: John Wilson and Sons, 1868.
Sandell, Richard. "Museums as Agents of Social Inclusion." *Museum Management and Curatorship* 17 (4) (1998): 401–18.
Schiffer, Michael B. *Behavioral Archaeology: First Principles*. Salt Lake City: University of Utah Press, 1995.
Schuyler, Robert L. "The History of American Archaeology: An Examination of Procedure." *American Antiquity* 36 (4) (1971): 383–409.
"Scientific Notes and News." *Science* 61 (1566) (1925): 14–17.

"Scientific Notes and News." *Science* 81 (2097) (1935): 249–52.

———. *Science* 91 (2373) (1940): 591–94.

Shackel, Paul A., and Erve J. Chambers, eds. *Places in Mind: Public Archaeology as Applied Anthropology*. London: Routledge, 2004.

Shanklin, Eugenia. "The Profession of the Color Blind: Sociocultural Anthropology and Racism in the 21st Century." *American Anthropologist* 100 (3) (1998): 669–79.

Shaw, William H. "Marx and Morgan." *History and Theory* 23 (2) (1984): 215–28.

Shepard, Odell, ed. *The Heart of Thoreau's Journals*. New York: Dover, 1961.

Silliman, Stephen W., ed. *Collaborative Indigenous Archaeology at the Trowel's Edge: Exploring Methodology and Education in North American Archaeology*. Tucson: University of Arizona Press, 2008.

———. "Collaborative Indigenous Archaeology: Troweling at the Edges, Eyeing the Center." In *Collaborating at the Trowel's Edge: Teaching and Learning in Indigenous Archaeology*, edited by S. W. Silliman, 1–21. Tucson: University of Arizona Press, 2008.

Silverberg, Robert. *Mound Builders of Ancient America: The Archaeology of a Myth*. Greenwich: New York Graphic Society, 1968.

Sinclair, Anthony. "This Is an Article about Archaeology as Writing." In *Interpretive Archaeology: A Reader*, edited by J. Thomas, 474–88. London: Leicester University Press, 2000.

Skinner, Alanson. "Review: *The Archeological History of New York*." *American Anthropologist* 25 (1) (1923): 94–97.

———. "Review: *The Quarterly Journal of the Society of American Indians*." *American Anthropologist* 17 (3) (1915): 581.

Sloan, Douglas. "Science in New York City, 1867–1907." *Isis* 71 (1) (1980): 35–76.

Smith, Claire, and H. Martin Wobst, eds. *Indigenous Archaeologies: Decolonizing Theory and Practice*. London: Routledge, 2005.

Smith, Laurajane. *Archaeological Theory and the Politics of Cultural Heritage*. New York: Routledge, 2004.

Smith, Watson, and John M. Roberts. *Zuni Law: A Field of Values*. Papers of the Peabody Museum of American Archaeology and Ethnology, vol. 43, no. 1. Cambridge, Mass.: Peabody Museum, 1954.

Snead, James E. *Ruins and Rivals: The Making of Southwest Archaeology*. Tucson: University of Arizona Press, 2001.

Snow, Dean R. *The Iroquois*. Oxford, U.K.: Blackwell, 1994.

"Society for American Archaeology Annual Meeting." *American Antiquity* 5 (1) (1939): 36–41.

"Society for American Archaeology Organization Meeting." *American Antiquity* 1 (2) (1935): 141–46.

"Society for American Archaeology: Revised Constitution." *American Antiquity* 8 (2) (1942): 206–8.

Srinivas, Krishna Ravi. "Traditional Knowledge and Intellectual Property Rights: A Note on Issues, Some Solutions, and Some Suggestions." *Asian Journal of WTO & International Health Law and Policy* 3 (1) (2008): 81–120.

Stanish, Charles, and Chapurukha M. Jusimba. "Working Together—Archaeological Research and Community Participation." In *Working Together: Native Americans and Archaeologists*, edited by K. E. Dongoske, M. Aldenderfer, and K. Doehner, 209–12. Washington, D.C.: Society for American Archaeology, 2000.

Stapp, Darby C., and Michael S. Burney. *Tribal Cultural Resource Management: The Full Circle to Stewardship.* Walnut Creek, Calif.: AltaMira Press, 2002.

Stern, Bernhard J. "Lewis Henry Morgan: American Ethnologist." *Social Forces* 6 (3) (1928): 344–57.

Stocking, George W., Jr. "Franz Boas and the Culture Concept in Historical Perspective." In *Race, Culture, and Evolution: Essays in the History of Anthropology*, edited by G. W. Stocking, 195–233. Chicago: University of Chicago Press, 1982.

———. "The Turn-of-the-Century Concept of Race." *Modernism/Modernity* 1 (1) (1993): 4016.

Stoler, Ann L. "Making Empire Respectable: The Politics of Race and Sexual Morality in 20th-Century Colonial Cultures." *American Ethnologist* 16 (4) (1989): 634–60.

Strong, Pauline Turner, and Barrik Van Winkle. "'Indian Blood': Reflections on the Reckoning and Refiguring of Native North American Identity." *Cultural Anthropology* 11 (4) (1996): 547–76.

Sullivan, Lynne P., Eleazer D. Hunt, and Richard G. Wilkinson. "History of Excavations." In *Reanalyzing the Ripley Site: Earthworks and Late Prehistory on the Lake Erie Plain*, edited by L. P. Sullivan, 28–52. Albany: New York State Museum, 1996.

Swanton, John R. "John Napoleon Brinton Hewitt." *American Anthropologist* 40 (2) (1938): 286–90.

Swidler, Nina, Kurt E. Dongoske, Roger Anyon, and Alan S. Downer, eds. *Native Americans and Archaeologists: Stepping Stones to Common Ground.* Walnut Creek, Calif.: AltaMira Press, 1997.

Szasz, Margaret Connell, ed. *Between Indian and White Worlds: The Cultural Broker.* Norman: University of Oklahoma Press, 2001.

Tall Bear, Kimberly. "DNA, Blood, and Racializing the Tribe." *Wicazo Sa Review* 18 (1) (2003): 81–107.

Tate, Michael L. "From Scout to Doughboy: The National Debate over Integrating American Indians into the Military, 1891–1918." *Western Historical Quarterly* 17 (4) (1986): 417–37.

Thomas, David Hurst. "Afterword: Who Was Arthur C. Parker, Anyway?" In *Working Together: Native Americans and Archaeologists*, edited by

K. E. Dongoske, M. Aldenderfer, and K. Doehner, 213–34. Washington, D.C.: Society for American Archaeology, 2000.

———. *Skull Wars: Kennewick Man, Archaeology, and the Battle for Native American Identity*. New York: Basic Books, 2000.

Thomas, W. Stephen. "Arthur Caswell Parker: 1881–1955." *Rochester History* 17 (3) (1955): 1–20.

Thornton, Russell. *American Indian Holocaust and Survival: A Population History since 1942*. Norman: University of Oklahoma Press, 1987.

———. "Who Owns Our Past? The Repatriation of Native American Human Remains and Cultural Objects." In *Studying Native America: Problems and Prospects*, edited by R. Thornton, 385–415. Madison: University of Wisconsin Press, 1998.

Thurston, Bertha Parker. "How He Became a Medicine Man." *The Masterkey* 8 (3) (1934): 79–81.

———. "A Night in a Maidu Shaman's House." *The Masterkey* 7 (4) (1933): 111–15.

———. "A Rare Treat at a Maidu Medicine-Man's Feast." *The Masterkey* 10 (1) (1936): 16–21.

———. "Scorpion Hill." *The Masterkey* 7 (6) (1933): 171–77.

Thwaites, Rubengold, ed. *The Jesuit Relations and Allied Documents: Travels and Explanations of the Jesuit Missionaries in New France, 1610–1791*. Cleveland: Burrow's Brothers, 1896–1901.

Tivy, Mary Elizabeth. "The Local History Museum in Ontario: An Intellectual History 1851–1985." Ph.D. diss., Department of History, University of Waterloo, 2006.

Todorov, Tzvetan. *The Conquest of America: The Question of the Other*. New York: Harper and Row, 1984.

Tooker, Elisabeth. "Iroquois since 1820." In *Handbook of North American Indians*, vol. 15, edited by B. G. Trigger, 449–65. Washington, D.C.: Smithsonian Institution, 1978.

———. "Lewis H. Morgan and His Contemporaries." *American Anthropologist* 94 (2) (1992): 357–75.

———. "Lewis H. Morgan and the Senecas." In *Strangers to Relatives: The Adoption and Naming of Anthropologists in Native North America*, edited by S. Kan, 29–56. Lincoln: University of Nebraska Press, 2001.

———. *Lewis H. Morgan on Iroquois Material Culture*. Tucson: University of Arizona Press, 1994.

———. "A Note on the Return of Eleven Wampum Belts to the Six Nations Iroquois Confederacy on Grand River, Canada." *Ethnohistory* 45 (2) (1998): 219–36.

———. "On the Development of the Handsome Lake Religion." *Proceedings of the American Philosophical Society* 133 (1) (1989): 35–50.

---. "The Structure of the Iroquois League: Lewis H. Morgan's Research and Observations." *Ethnohistory* 30 (3) (1983): 141–54.
Trautmann, Thomas R. "Morgan, Lewis Henry (1818–81)." In *The Dictionary of Anthropology*, edited by T. Barfield, 330–31. Oxford, U.K.: Blackwell, 1997.
Trautmann, Thomas R., and Karl Sanford Kabelac. "The Library of Lewis Henry Morgan and Mary Elizabeth Morgan." *Transactions of the American Philosophical Society* 84 (6–7) (1944): 1–336.
Trigger, Bruce G. "Anglo-American Archaeology." *World Archaeology* 13 (2) (1981): 138–55.
---. "Archaeology and the Image of the American Indian." *American Antiquity* 45 (4) (1980): 662–76.
---. *A History of Archaeological Thought*. Cambridge, U.K.: Cambridge University Press, 1989.
Truitt, Evelyn Mack. *Who Was Who on Screen*. New York: R. R. Bowker, 1977.
Turner, Frederick Jackson. *The Frontier in American History*. New York: Henry Holt, 1921.
Two Bears, Davina. "Navajo Archaeologist Is Not an Oxymoron: A Tribal Archaeologist's Experience." *American Indian Quarterly* 30 (3–4) (2006): 381–87.
---. "A Navajo Student's Perception: Anthropology and the Navajo Nation Archaeology Department Student Training Program." In *Working Together: Native Americans and Archaeologists*, edited by K. E. Dongoske, M. Aldenderfer, and K. Doehner, 15–22. Washington, D.C.: Society for American Archaeology, 2000.
Ubelaker, Douglas, and Lauryn Guttenplan Grant. "Human Skeletal Remains: Preservation or Reburial?" *Yearbook of Physical Anthropology* 32 (1989): 249–87.
Venables, Robert W., ed. *The Six Nations of New York: The 1892 United States Extra Census Bulletin*. Ithaca, N.Y.: Cornell University Press, 1995.
Versaggi, Nina M. "Tradition, Sovereignty, Recognition: NAGPRA Consultation with the Iroquois Confederacy of Sovereign Nations of New York." In *Cross-Cultural Collaboration: Native Peoples and Archaeology in the Northeastern United States*, edited by J. E. Kerber, 18–31. Lincoln: University of Nebraska Press, 2006.
Visweswaran, Kamala. "Race and the Culture of Anthropology." *American Anthropologist* 100 (1) (1998): 70–83.
Vitelli, Karen D., and K. Anne Pyburn. "Past Imperfect, Future Tense: Archaeology and Development." *Nonrenewable Resources* 6 (2) (1997): 71–84.
Voegelin, Erminie W. "Anthropology in American Universities." *American Anthropologist* 52 (3) (1950): 350–91.
---. "Review: *Ethnography of the Fox Indians* by William Jones, and *War Ceremony and Peace Ceremony of the Osage Indians* by Francis La Flesche." *Journal of American Folklore* 53 (210) (1940): 286–88.

Warrior, Robert Allen. *Tribal Secrets: Recovering American Indian Intellectual Traditions*. Minneapolis: University of Minnesota Press, 1994.

Watkins, Joe. "Becoming American or Becoming Indian? NAGPRA, Kennewick, and Cultural Affiliation." *Journal of Social Archaeology* 4 (1) (2004): 60–80.

———. "Beyond the Margin: American Indians, First Nations, and Archaeology in North America." *American Antiquity* 68 (2) (2003): 273–85.

———. "Communicating Archaeology: Words to the Wise." *Journal of Social Archaeology* 6 (1) (2006): 100–118.

———. "Cultural Nationalists, Internationalists, and 'Intra-nationalists': Who's Right and Whose Right?" *International Journal of Cultural Property* 12 (1) (2005): 78–94.

———. *Indigenous Archaeology: American Indian Values and Scientific Practice*. Walnut Creek, Calif.: AltaMira Press, 2000.

———. "The Politics of American Archaeology: Cultural Resources, Cultural Affiliation, and Kennewick." In *Indigenous Archaeologies: Decolonizing Theory and Practice*, edited by C. Smith and H. M. Wobst, 189–205. London: Routledge, 2005.

———. "Writing Unwritten History." In *Archaeological Ethics*, edited by K. D. Vitelli and C. Colwell-Chanthaphonh, 225–34. Lanham, Md.: AltaMira Press, 2006.

Welch, John R., and T. J. Ferguson. "Putting Patria Back into Repatriation: Cultural Affiliation Assessment of White Mountain Apache Tribal Lands." *Journal of Social Archaeology* 7 (2) (2007): 171–98.

White, Geoffrey M. "Emotional Remembering: The Pragmatics of National Memory." *Ethos* 27 (4) (1999): 505–29.

White, Shelby. "A Collector's Odyssey." *International Journal of Cultural Property* 7 (1) (1998): 170–76.

White Deer, Gary. "Return of the Sacred: Spirituality and the Scientific Imperative." In *Native Americans and Archaeologists: Stepping Stones to Common Ground*, edited by N. Swidler, K. E. Dongoske, R. Anyon, and A. S. Downer, 37–43. Walnut Creek, Calif.: AltaMira Press, 1997.

Whiteley, Peter. "The End of Anthropology (at Hopi)?" In *Indians and Anthropologists: Vine Deloria Jr. and the Critique of Anthropology*, edited by T. Biolsi and L. J. Zimmerman, 177–207. Tucson: University of Arizona Press, 1997.

Whittaker, John C., and Michael Stafford. "Replicas, Fakes, and Art: The Twentieth Century Stone Age and Its Effects on Archaeology. *American Antiquity* 64 (2) (1999): 203–14.

Wilkens, David E., and K. Tsianina Lomawaima. *Uneven Ground: American Indian Sovereignty and Federal Law*. Norman: University of Oklahoma Press, 2002.

Wilkinson, Richard G. "Population Dynamics, Health, and Mortality." In *Reanalyzing the Ripley Site: Earthworks and Late Prehistory on the Lake Erie Plain*, edited by L. P. Sullivan, 90–98. Albany: New York State Museum, 1996.

Williams, Lucy F., William Wierzbowski, and Robert W. Preucel, eds. *Objects of Everlasting Esteem: Native American Voices on Identity, Art, and Culture.* Philadelphia: University of Pennsylvania Museum of Archaeology and Anthropology, 2005.

Williams, Stephen. *From the Director's Desk, 1967–1977.* Cambridge, Mass.: Peabody Museum of Archaeology and Ethnography, 1977.

Williams, Vernon J., Jr. *The Social Sciences and Theories of Race.* Champaign: University of Illinois Press, 2006.

Wiwijorra, Ingo. "German Archaeology and Its Relation to Nationalism and Racism." In *Nationalism and Archaeology in Europe,* edited by M. Diaz-Andreu and T. Champion, 164–88. London: University College of London Press, 1996.

Wright, Rita P. "Gender Matters—A Question of Ethics." In *Ethical Issues in Archaeology,* edited by L. J. Zimmerman, K. D. Vitelli, and J. Hollowell-Zimmer, 225–38. Walnut Creek, Calif.: AltaMira Press, 2003.

Wylie, Alison. "The Promise and Perils of an Ethic of Stewardship." In *Embedding Ethics: Shifting Boundaries of the Anthropological Profession,* edited by L. Meskell and P. Pels, 47–68. Oxford, U.K.: Berg, 2005.

Yellowhorn, Eldon. "Awakening Internalist Archaeology in the Aboriginal World." Ph.D. diss., Department of Anthropology, McGill University, Montreal, 2002.

Young, Andrew W., ed. *History of Chautauqua County, New York.* Buffalo, N.Y.: Matthews & Warren, 1875.

Zeller, Terry. "Arthur C. Parker: A Pioneer in American Museums." *Curator* 30 (1) (1987): 41–62.

Zimmerman, Larry J. "A New and Different Archaeology? With a Postscript on the Impact of the Kennewick Dispute." In *Repatriation Reader: Who Owns American Indian Remains?* edited by D. A. Mihesuah, 294–306. Lincoln: University of Nebraska Press, 2000.

———. "Public Heritage, a Desire for a 'White' History of America, and Some Impacts of the Kennewick Man/Ancient One Decision." *International Journal of Cultural Property* 12 (2) (2005): 261–70.

Index

"Aboriginal Occupants of the Silverheels Site, The" (Parker), 108
Alima, 154
American Anthropological Association, 13, 59, 135, 157–58
American Anthropologist, 102, 133–34
"American Anthropology, Its Scope and Its Problems" (Parker), 75–77
American Antiquity, 163–64
American Association for the Advancement of Science, 158, 168
American Association of Museums, 5, 151, 168
American Indian Day, 141, 143
American Indian Movement (AIM), 179
American Indian Religious Freedom Act, 7
American Museum of Natural History, 57, 58, 59, 65–66, 103, 181
"American Red Man, The" (N. Parker), 51–53
American Revolution, 34
Amidon, Dr., 128–29
Ancient Mounds of the Mississippi Valley, 7
Ancient One, xiii, xv, 3–4, 194
Ancient Society (Morgan), 48, 167
anthropologists, 142, 191–93, 196
anthropology, 14–15, 18–19, 76–77, 83, 196
anti-looting, 145–47
antiquities. *See* artifacts

Antiquities Act (1906), 39–40
Apache, Antonio, 59, 192
Archaeological History of New York, The (Parker), 109–10, 134–35, 144; review of, 111–121
Archaeological Institute of America, 59
archaeological resources, 7–8, 39, 147, 171
Archaeological Resources Protection Act, 8
Archaeological Survey Association of Southern California, 173
archaeologists, 9, 24, 25; Native American, 4–5, 19–20, 195–96
archaeology, 20, 39, 125; amateur, 148–49; burial mound, 6–7; on Cattaraugus Reservation, 60, 61–62, 69–75; vs. collection, 129–30; histories of, 21–22; Indigenous, 18, 195–99; law and, 194–95; mentorship, 58–59; moral issues of, 10–12; in New York, 53–56; for New York State Museum, 122–24, 133–35; Peabody Museum, 65–68; politics and, 9–10; professionalism in, 145–46; righteousness of, 126–27; Rochester Museum, 152–53; Silverheels Site, 77–80, 91–93, 97(fig.), 100–102; state support of, 144–45
artifacts: museum, 85–86, 105, 107, 116–17, 122, 131–32; in private collection, 87–88, 96, 127–29, 130, 146–48, 188

assimilation, 18, 37, 41, 48–49, 50–51, 143
Atalay, Sonya, 22, 197–98
authorship, xiv, 11, 13, 22, 183
Awatovi, 185

Bainbridge, 153
Bear Clan: adoption into, 96–97
Beauchamp, William M., 62, 116, 130
blood quantum, 14, 142
Blueskye, William, 123
Boas, Franz, 14, 42, 49, 50, 150, 181
Boughton Hill, 134
British Columbia, 180–81
burial mounds, 6–7, 54–55
burials, 8, 18, 19, 83, 123, 153, 155; on Cattaraugus Reservation, 62, 71, 73, 78–79, 86, 128; excavation of, 6–7, 91–94, 101, 134, 188–89; protection of, 10, 125; respect for, 88–90; treatment of, 179–82; in western New York, 54–56
Burmaster, Everett R., 123, 126, 128, 134
Burning Spring Site, 123, 125

Cabinet of Natural History, 60–61
Canada, 146, 180–81, 186
Canadian Cemeteries Act, 180
Canadian Union of Ontario Indians, 180
Canandaigua, 153, 154
Canandaigua Lake, 134
Canandaigua Treaty, 35, 189
Carnegie Corporation, 158
Casas, Bartolomé de las, 6
Cassadaga Lakes, 54
Caswell, Harriet S., 42
Cattaraugus Indian Reservation, 23, 24, 29, 35, 36, 41, 128, 140, 144; archaeology, 60, 61–62, 66, 68, 69–75, 77–80; community, 38–39; ethnological collections, 102, 122

Cattaraugus Valley, 123–24, 126
Cayuga Lake, 134
cemeteries, 86, 134, 153, 188–89. See also burial mounds; burials
Centenary Collegiate Institute, 56
Century of Dishonor, A (Hunt), 40–41
Chautauqua County, 68
Civilian Conservation Corps, 156
Clarke, John Mason, 116, 122–23, 127, 149–50
Code of Handsome Lake, the Seneca Prophet, The (Parker), 131
Cody, Arthur, 173
Cody, Bertha Parker, 24, 118, 119, 157, 174; as archaeologist, 169–70; at Southwest Museum, 171–73
Cody, Oscar "Iron Eyes," 172, 173
Cody, Robert, 173
Cole, Fay-Cooper, 160
collections. See artifacts; ethnographic collections
collectors: commercial, 86–88, 122; private, 12, 84–86, 96, 127–29, 130, 146–48, 186, 188
colonial era, 34
colonialism, 22, 35, 52, 199
Columbia University, 59, 102, 155–56, 191
Commissioner of Indian Affairs, 31, 37
Committee of One Hundred, 144, 149
Committee on State Archaeological Surveys, 158, 161
Constitution of the Five Nations, The (Parker), 131
Converse, Harriet Maxwell, 19, 32, 59, 95, 115, 117, 122, 130, 137
Converse Collection, Harriet M., 131
Cooke Anne Theresa. See Parker, Anne Theresa Cooke
Covert, Frank, 156
Covert & Harrington, 87

Coxsackie, 134
Crania americana (Morton), 79
cultural broker: Parker as, 17–18
Cushing, Frank Hamilton, 112, 185
Custer Died for Your Sins (Deloria), 180, 190

Dartmouth College, 159
Dawes Act, 7, 18, 36–37, 43
decolonization, 198–99
Deloria, Vine, Jr., 180, 190
Depression, 144, 151, 156, 171
descendant communities, xiv, 9, 10, 20, 195, 198
Dewey, Melvil, 122
Dickinson Seminary, 56
Dixon, Roland B., 135
documentation, 147
Double Walled Site, 73(fig.)
Draper, Andrew S., 121, 122

earthworks: western New York, 69–71
Eastern States Archaeological Association, 154
Echo-Hawk, Roger, 196–97; on decolonization, 198–99
education, 132–33
Erie County Historical Society, 187
ethnicity: Parker's, 137–39
ethnographic collections, 86, 87, 101, 102; exhibition of, 103, 104–5; hotel decor, 115–16; in New York State Museum, 123, 131–32, 136; private, 127–28
ethnography, 121–22, 131, 136
eugenics, 5, 15, 143, 167
excavations: amateur, 148–49; by collectors, 86, 87–88, 96; New York State Museum, 123–24; resistance to, 188–89; Rochester Museum, 153–54; Silverheels Site, 77–80, 91–93, 97(fig.), 100–102

exhibits, 103–4, 144–45
"Exploration of an Iroquoian Stronghold, . . ." (Harrington), 108

False Face Society, 86, 98, 101, 107, 123, 187
Fenton Historical Society, 62
Field Museum, 103, 180
films, 119, 156–57, 173
Filson, Beulah T., 157
Finger Lakes region, 153
Fletcher, Alice, 46–47
forgeries/fakes, 129
forts/fortifications, 62
functionalism, 123–24

Gahweh Seneca, 97
Gambrell, Herbert, 168
General Allotment Act. *See* Dawes Act
Genesee County Historical Federation, 154
Genesee Valley, 153
Grand Council of the Haudenosaunee, 188
Grand Order of the Iroquois, 44
Grant, Ulysses S., 30–31
graves. *See* burials
Graves, Frank Pierrepont, 150
Griffin, James B., 161
Griffiths, D. W., 119
Guthe, Carl E., 158, 159, 160, 162, 184

Handsome Lake, 32
Harrington, Edna L. Parker, 29, 156, 170, 181
Harrington, Mark Raymond, 59, 65–66, 67(fig.), 98, 117, 136, 155, 160, 170, 174, 181; archaeology, 68, 69–75, 77–80, 91–95, 99–100, 101–2, 104, 107–8, 110–11, 188; as collector, 85–86, 87, 127; and Putnam, 80–81; Southwest Museum, 156, 171–72

Harrington & Co., M. R., 127
Harvard University, 59, 181
Haudenosaunee. *See* Iroquois
Haudenosaunee Standing Committee on Burial Rules and Regulations, 188–89
Hewitt, J.N.B., 141, 142, 192
Heye, George G., 87, 128, 186
Hill, Richard, Sr., 74, 188
histories: of archaeology, 21–22
history, 11, 39, 75–76; archaeology as, 145–46; Iroquois, 166–67
Hodge, Frederick Webb, 171
Holland Land Company, 35
Hopi Reservation, 181, 185
Hotel Astor, 115–16
Hoyt, Martha. *See* Parker, Martha Hoyt
human remains. *See* burials
Hunt, Helen, 40–41

identity: multiple, 193–94; pan-Indian, 16, 140–43; Parker's, 33, 136–39, 165–66, 169, 176, 191; Seneca, 48–49
Indian How Book, The (Parker), 165, 167
"Indian problem," 39, 40–41, 49
Indian Reorganization Act, 7
informants, 30, 46–47
Institute of Anthropology and Ethnology of the Academy of Science (USSR), 167
Iowa: burials in, 179–80
Iroquois, 153, 166–67; dispossession, 53–54; origin myth, 33–34; resistance by, 188–89; wampum belts, 186–87
Iroquois Uses of Maize and Other Food Plants (Parker), 47, 131

Jefferson, Thomas, 6
Jefferson County (NY), 128–29

Jelderks, John, 3–4
Jenks, A. E., 160
Jimerson, George D., 85, 88, 98
Jones, William, 59, 191
Journal of American Folk-lore, 117

Keams, Thomas V., 185
Kennedy, John, 78; as collector, 86–88, 122, 128; and Silverheels Site, 93–96
Kennewick Man. *See* Ancient One
Keppler, Joseph, 96, 116, 128, 129
Keuka College, 167
kinship, 49, 137
Knox, Henry, 34, 36
Kwakwaka'wakw, 185

La Flesche, Francis, 46–47, 141, 142, 192
Lamoka Site, 153
land: Seneca, 34–37, 88
Landing of the Pilgrim Fathers, The, 157
League of the Haudenosaunee (Iroquois), 32, 34, 35–36
League of the Ho-de-no-sau-nee, or Iroquois (Morgan), 30, 45, 47–48
Leupp, Francis E., 39–40
Levanna Site, 153
Lewis County Historical Society, 179
Linton, Ralph, 160
Lippert, Dorothy, 4, 11, 19
Lost City, 156

Manual of History Museums, A (Parker), 152
marriages, 24, 118, 119, 155
Martinez, Desireé Reneé, 198
Massachusetts: land claims in, 34–35
matrilineality: Seneca, 29, 33, 35, 96
Mental Elevator, The (newspaper), 30
Merrill, Frederick J. H., 116

Mesa Verde, 181
Method in Archaeology (Parker), 145
microhistory, 22–23
Mishongnovi, 185
missionaries, 29–30
Moorehead, Warren King, 159
moral community, xx, 12, 13, 24, 164, 180, 194, 195
moral values, 10–12, 83, 84, 182–83
Morgan, Lewis H., 14, 23, 42, 49, 50, 60–61, 130, 131; Parker and, 44–46, 82; publications by, 30, 45, 47–48, 167
Morton, Samuel G., 79
Mountpleasant, Caroline Parker, 46(fig.), 56
M. R. Harrington & Co., 127
Mulkins, Jesse, 123
Murie, James, 142
museums, 103–4, 120, 128, 147, 187
Museum Service, 151
Myrtle, Minnie, 42

Nantucket Wampanoag, 180
National Historic Preservation Act, 8
nationalism: American, 55
National Museum of Canada, 185
National Museum of the American Indian, 8, 156, 194–95
National Register of Historic Places, 8
National Research Council, 158, 161
National Science Foundation, 179
Native American Graves Protection and Repatriation Act (NAGPRA), xv, 3–4, 187–88, 190, 194–95
Native Americans, 7; protests, 179–80
Nevada: Bertha Parker in, 170–71
newspapers, 100
New York (state), 129, 153, 179, 186; archaeological collections, 60–61; archaeology, 53–56, 183; ethnography, 121–22; Seneca land, 34–35;
state archaeologist, 24, 124–25, 149–50
New York City, 58, 83, 117, 118
New York Indian Commission, 140
New York State Archaeological Association, 133, 154, 167
New York State Education Department, 124–25
New York State Historical Association, 154, 168
New York State Museum, 61, 108, 116–17, 184; archaeology, 122–24, 133–35; collections, 87, 88, 128–29, 130; ethnology, 121–22; fire, 131–32; Parker's resignation from, 149–50; publications, 109–10; reopening, 132–33; wampum belts, 186–87
New York Sun (newspaper), 100, 115
Northern Arizona University, 196

objects of cultural patrimony, 8, 183; repatriation of, 185–87
Occidental College, 156
Office of Indian Affairs, 39–40
Ogden, David A., 35
Ogden Land Company, 36, 47
Oil Spring Reservation, 36
Onandaga Nation, 186–87
Onandoga Castle, 136–37
Oneida Lake, 153
Ontario, 138
origin myth: Iroquois, 33–34
Osborn, Henry Fairfield, 132–33
ownership, 10–11, 183
Oyster Bay, 65

pageants: by Beulah Parker, 156–57
Pallan, Billie (Wilma Mae), 171, 173
pan-Indian issues, 7, 16; SAI, 140–44
Parker, Anne Theresa Cooke, 155
Parker, Bertha A. *See* Cody, Bertha Parker

Parker, Beulah Tahamont, 117–18, 119, 123, 156–57, 171, 173
Parker, Carrie, 47
Parker, Dorothy, 29
Parker, Edna. *See* Harrington, Edna Parker
Parker, Elizabeth Johnson, 30, 32, 44, 98
Parker, Ely S., 23, 41–42, 48, 50–51, 98, 134, 183, 191; career of, 30–32; and Lewis H. Morgan, 44–46, 47, 82
Parker, Frederick Ely, 29, 33, 143
Parker, Geneva Hortense Griswold, 29, 57
Parker, Levi, 46(fig.)
Parker, Martha Anne, 155
Parker, Martha Hoyt, 29, 30, 41–42
Parker, Melville A., 118, 119, 123
Parker, Minnie C., 69
Parker, Minnie Sackett, 30
Parker, Newton, 47
Parker, Nicholson Henry, 23, 30, 31(fig.), 32, 41–42, 56, 98; "The American Red Man," 51–53
Parker, Samuel, 30
Parker, Sherman, 69
Parker, Spencer, 44–45
Parker, William, 30, 32, 44, 97–98
Parker family: dual worlds of, 32–33
Parker Scholarship, Arthur C., 5, 199
participation, 11–12
Peabody Museum of Archaeology and Ethnology, 59, 80, 116; collections, 66–68, 85–86, 105–7, 188; public exhibits, 103–5; Silverheels Site, 68–75, 82, 107–8, 109
Pennsylvania, 152–53
Pilgrims, 6
Pleasantville (NY), 57
politics: archaeology and, 9–10; pan-Indian, 140–43
Powell, John Wesley, 19, 42, 48, 57

press: public archaeology, 154
privilege, xiv, 10, 13, 22, 182–83
public archaeology, 12, 154, 184, 198
publics, 12, 195; New York State Museum, 132–33
Putnam, Fredric Ward, 23, 42, 58, 59, 60, 77, 82, 115, 116, 120, 121; and Harrington, 65–66, 72, 80–81; museum collections, 66–68, 85–86; public exhibits, 103–4; Silverheels Site, 79–80, 100–101, 102, 107–8
Puyé, 181
Pyramid Lake Reservation, 181–82

Quakers, 36
Quary, Abram, 180

race, xiv–xv, xvii, 13–14, 20–21, 82–83; defining, 15–16. *See also* identity
racialism, 14–15, 20, 21, 196–97
racism, xv, 13, 14, 15, 19–21, 143
Red Jacket, 32, 53
relic hunting, 129, 145, 146–47
repatriation, xiii, xv, 180; of human remains and cultural objects, 8, 107, 185–88, 190
Ripley Site, 123–24
Ritchie, William A., 153, 155
Rochester Academy of Science, 168
Rochester City Museum; Rochester Museum of Arts and Sciences, 150–51, 168, 184; archaeology, 152–54
Rochester Civic Medal, 168–69
Rockefeller, Nelson, 186
Royal Society of Arts, 168
Rumbling Wings and Other Indian Stories (Parker), 165
Running Moccasins, 179–80

Sackett, Marcus B., 62, 88
Sackett, Minnie. *See* Parker, Minnie Sackett

SAI. *See* Society of American Indians
Schenendoah, Enoch, 136–37
scholarships, 196–97, 199
Schoolcraft, Henry, 42
science, 4, 76–77, 83, 84, 125–27
Scorpion Hill, 171
Scott, Cameron, 186
Secwepemc, 180–81
Seelye, Julius H., 41
Seneca Arts Project, 151
Seneca Myths and Folktales (Parker), 88, 131
Seneca Nation, 16, 23, 29, 30, 33, 125, 130, 134, 140; adoptions into, 96, 119, 155; on burials, 88–90; cultural objects, 85–86; culture loss, 48–49; Dawes Act and, 36–37; ethnography, 122–23; land base, 34–36; Morgan and, 44–48; Silverheels Site, 92–93. *See also* Cattaraugus Indian Reservation
Shotridge, Louis, 192
Silverheels, Henry, 61–62, 78, 209–10n75
Silverheels Site, 24, 70(fig.), 71, 104, 134, 154; collections, 82, 105; excavations, 77–80, 91–93, 97(fig.), 100–102; J. Kennedy and, 93–95; NAGPRA, 187–88; publicity, 99–100; reports, 107–8, 109, 110–11
Six Nations Confederacy: Council of Chiefs, 185–86, 187
Skinner, Alanson, 59, 111–12, 116, 142, 149
Skull Wars (Thomas), 21–22
Skunny Wundy and Other Indian Tales (Parker), 165
Smith, Harlan, 181
social evolution, 125–26
Society for American Archaeology, 5, 165; annual meeting, 161–63; organization of, 158–59; Parker as president, xvii, 24, 157, 160–61

Society of American Indians (SAI), 140, 144, 184; organization and goals of, 141–43
Southwest Museum, 130, 157, 179; Bertha Cody at, 172–73; Harrington at, 156, 171–72
Soviet Union, 167
Speck, Frank G., 59, 142
Spier, Leslie, 159, 186
Spinden, Herbert J., 159
St. Lawrence Valley, 154
states: and site protection, 144–45
stereotypes: addressing, 166–67
Stó:lo Nation, 22
Sundown, Peter, 136
Supplementary Treaty of 1842, 36
surveys: Rochester Museum, 152–54

Tahamont, Bessie, 118
Tahamont, Beulah. *See* Parker, Beulah Tahamont
Tahamont, Elijah, 117–18
Thomas, David Hurst, 21–22
Thurston, James E., 171
Tohono O'odham, 181
Tonawanda Band: adoption by, 96–98
Tonawanda Reservation, 32, 36, 44–45, 136
traditional cultural properties, 8
Treaty of Big Tree, 35
Treaty of Buffalo, 35–36
Treaty of Paris, 34
Tribal Historic Preservation Offices (THPOs), 8, 9
"Triumph of Woman's Wit, The" (Parker), 57
Turner, Frederick Jackson, 43
Tuscarora, 188, 192
Two Bears, Davina, 196, 197

Union College, 152
Union of Ontario Indians, 187

U.S. Army Corps of Engineers, 3
U.S. Court of Appeals, Ninth Circuit, xv, 4
U.S. Department of the Interior, 3–4
University of California, Berkeley, 59
University of Michigan, 185
University of Rochester, 135–36
"Use of the Bannerstone" (Parker), 108
Utes, 181

Walker, Bishop, 90
wampum belts: repatriation of, 186–87
Watkins, Joe, 4, 10, 20, 192–93, 195
Weber, R. B., 72
Wenonah, Princess, 118
Whiteley, Peter, 196
White Plains: Parkers in, 42, 56, 115

Wihomki, 181
Williams, Paul, 187
Williamson, Charles, 54
Willoughby, C. C., 109
Willow Point Site, 153
Wolf Clan, 155
World's Columbian Exposition, 42–43, 59, 103, 192
World War I, 140, 141
Wright, Laura Sheldon, 29–30
Wyoming Historical and Geological Society, 152

Young, John, 60
Young, William, 123, 124, 125

Zimmerman, Larry, 196–97
Zuni, 8, 157, 185